Public Crisis Management

How and Why Organizations Work Together to Solve Society's Most Threatening Problems

Michael J. Hillyard

Writers Club Press
San Jose New York Lincoln Shanghai

Public Crisis Management
How and Why Organizations Work Together to
Solve Society's Most Threatening Problems

Published by Writers Club Press
an imprint of iUniverse.com, Inc.

For information address:
iUniverse.com, Inc.
620 North 48th Street
Suite 201
Lincoln, NE 68504-3467
www.iuniverse.com

ISBN: 0-595-00717-1

Printed in the United States of America

To the crisis responders:
Men and women who toe the line—the fireline, frontline,
stormline, crimeline.
You bring stability to a dangerous world.

Table of Contents

List of Abbreviations

CAAFA   Columbus African-American Firefighter's Association

CIFC   Canadian Interagency Fire Center

CMOC   Civil-Military Operations Center

DELMARVA   Delaware/Maryland/Virginia

DEMA   Delaware Emergency Management Agency

DEOP   Delaware Emergency Operations Plan

EDI   Electronic Data Interchange

EOC   Emergency Operations Center

EEO   Equal Employment Opportunity

EIS   Emergency Information System

EMS   Emergency Medical Services

EPCRA   Emergency Planning and Community Right-to-Know Act

ESF   Emergency Support Function

FEMA   Federal Emergency Management Agency

GACC   Geographic Area Coordination Center

GIS   Global Information System

GPS   Global Positioning System

ICS   Incident Command System

LEADS   Law Enforcement Automatic Data System

MAC   Multi-Agency Coordinating Group

NGO   Non-Governmental Organization

NICC   National Interagency Coordination Center

NIFC   National Interagency Fire Center

NIIMS   National Interagency Incident Management System

NIRC   National Incident Radio Cache

NWCG   National Wildfire Coordinating Group

UCM   Unified Command Model

WMD   Weapons of Mass Destruction

Introduction

Today's complex and uncertain world periodically causes major disruptions in most every facet of life. Crises seem to emerge somewhere, in some way, every day. The rapid rate of change across industries, trends of rampant destabilization in many economies, and the rise of unforecasted complexities around the world force collaboration among peoples, groups, and nations. These relationships are the result of man's attempt to match the environment's increased complexity with the comprehensives of new human structure—structure that pulls together the whole from an assemblage of parts, the complex from the previously simple, the body from its individual limbs. Some of these relationships meet the world's challenges particularly well, while others have not managed well at all.

The nature and characteristics of crises set these disturbing events apart from the functionings of life's everyday activities, yet they range across the spectrum of life's activities. Answering the call of a crisis, be it environmental, economic, military, criminal, or political in nature, is a unique and daunting challenge for those who seek it. That special, adventuresome membership to an elite cast, which includes those who handle human conflict, natural disaster, and domestic disturbance, generally warrants high esteem from society in return for the perilous efforts to preserve well-being.

While special recognition may accompany some communities that perform crisis response, special consideration of the unique nature and characteristics of crises sometimes escapes the academic community. One area where consideration is sorely needed, but has been insufficiently provided, is in interorganizational networks. Theories that may apply under the "normal" operations of life, may in fact be inconceivable for explanation or implementation in crisis networks. However, the complexities of the environment that encouraged the formation of interorganizational business, volunteer, or government networks are often the same forces that create and act upon crisis response networks.

This book identifies the interorganizational principles that apply to crisis responses and provides organizations involved in the very heat of the modern complexity battle—the crisis responders—with examples, checklists, questionnaires, practices, vignettes, and tools to help them link with like-minded organizations to bring certainty out of chaos, hope in the face of despair, and relief out of painful adversity. For it is the crisis responders whose job it is to plan for, respond to, and resolve the oftentimes ugly manifestations of turbulence. Many of the crisis responders operate in very specific narrow niches unmindful of how fellow members—public, private, non-profit, and volunteer—assemble in interorganizational networks at international, national, regional, state, and local levels.

The primary purpose of this work is to provide crisis response communities with common understandings of their daunting tasks, which are to operate among many crisis response organizations to deal effectively with public problems. Both theoretical and "on-the-ground" empirical evidence that surrounds interorganizational networks are integrated with the unique nature and demands of crises. A secondary purpose is to provide an intellectual foundation from which policy makers may consider the concept of a national, or even international, crisis response task force network. Such a network is envisioned to provide a comprehensive "on-the-ground," institutionalized response to national and international security threats by incorporating international, transnational, federal, state, and local government agencies, private organizations, and Non-Governmental Organizations (NGOs).

The study accomplishes its purposes by focusing on the identification and description of common characteristics that underlie effective responses to crises from several different interorganizational crisis response networks.

These characteristics, or underlying principles, emerge after an extensive review of interorganizational and crisis response literature and a detailed analysis of three very different crisis response networks—a federal wildland firefighting network, state emergency management agency, and metropolitan public safety system.

In eight chapters, crises are defined, a crisis response model is described and analyzed, and five crisis response principles are exhaustively detailed for general application. Chapter One defines both crises and crisis management. Chapter Two describes the unique characteristics of the fire, emergency management, and public safety networks. Chapters Three through Seven each detail one of the interorganizational principles— common purpose, authority, incentives, macroculture, and structure. Chapter Eight models the types of public crises and analyzes their corresponding organizational and interorganizational responses. The appendices provide further information through which crisis responders can evaluate existing networks in hopes that objective recognition of a network's character and structure might identify strengths and weaknesses as a foundation for more effective crisis resolution.

Chapter 1

Defining Crises and Crisis Management

An environment described as being "in crisis" is one that defies the usual, orderly, linear processes of human or natural systems. Whereas stable systems dependably exhibit trends or expectations and evolve based on their pasts, crises offer no such certainly and cannot be depended upon to display familiarity, stability, or predictability.

Crises are more accurately grouped in the relatively new sub-field of systems theory, called nonlinear dynamics, or what some academicians refer to as "chaos theory." As nonlinear events, crises produce instability and "behave in very erratic and unpredictable ways."[1] As a result of the new systems thinking, crises are no longer viewed as bizarre, unexplainable phenomena but rather as quite "normal" aspects of reality which are not unusual or exceptional when viewed as manifestations of human or natural systems' innate ability to create increasingly higher orders of complexity over time.[2]

Public crises occur in varied degrees and in diverse aspects of life. They are commonly identified by titles such as natural disaster, human conflict, or political upheaval (see Table 1–1 for examples of public crises). Typically,

---

[1] L. Douglas Kiel, *Managing Chaos and Complexity in Government* (San Francisco: Jossey-Bass Publishers, 1994), 5.

[2] W. Mitchell Waldrop, *Complexity: The Emerging Science at the Edge of Chaos* (New York: Bantam Books, 1992).

an environment in crisis influences related (as well as seemingly unrelated) environments in ways that have repercussions of different dimensions. The crises of the twentieth century included war, genocide, hurricanes, revolutions, and riots (to name just a few), and they crossed environmental, civic, psychological, media, health and safety, and political dimensions regardless of their original natures.

Table 1–1: Examples of Public Crises

Natural
- Hurricane
- Tornado
- Tidal Wave
- Blizzard
- Meteor

Technological
- Nuclear meltdown
- Water supply contamination
- Electrical power outage
- Widespread computer virus

Political
- Economic Recession
- Genocide
- Revolution
- Riot

Human Conflict
- War
- Crime
- Terrorism
- Weapons of Mass Destruction

Since crises disrupt the certainty and stability of everyday routines, they demand levels of preparation and treatment quite different from environments experienced in the stable processes of life, in the conduct of daily business, or in the maintenance of orderly systems. Unlike the remarkably similar characteristics and simplistic assumptions shared by smoothly functioning linear systems, crises are viewed as unique situations based on the culmination of many specific events (although crises do exhibit many similarities, hence the need for experienced, organized networks to respond to them), and the characteristics of one crisis are usually vastly different than those faced in even similar categories of the crisis from the past.

What sets crises apart in systems theory is their mathematical functional properties. In chaotic systems, functions are composed of variable components that fluctuate in much greater proportions than do the variables that comprise stable, orderly functions of linear systems. When plotted mathematically, linear systems, show clearly definable input/output equations based on fairly predictable mathematical functions. In such systems, inputs provide readily expected outputs based on the functional relationships between the parts of the system.[3] In nonlinear or chaotic systems of which crises are a part, inputs into the system can have unexpected outputs; sometimes seemingly small inputs can have astoundingly large output effects, while at other times, huge inputs can have relatively minuscule results in output.[4]

While mathematical functions accurately depict the functional properties of a system in crisis, and systems theory explains why a system could experience a crisis, it is difficult to describe exactly what a crisis looks or feels like, unless the crisis can be explained in an abstract manner. For it is

---

[3]Keith Warren, Cynthia Franklin, and Calvin Streeter, "New Directions in Systems Theory: Chaos and Complexity," *Social Work: Journal of the National Association of Social Workers* 43 (July 1998): 362.

[4]Kiel, 5.

only in "knowing" a crisis that individuals and society can ever expect to adequately prepare for, resolve, and recover from one. A way to enhance understanding of the chaotic environment is to look at one type of crisis in its environment through the eyes of a master theorist.

The eighteenth century military philosopher, Carl von Clausewitz, provides modern day academicians, military enthusiasts, and practicing military leaders with a way of thinking about war that clearly describes the characteristics of a system in crisis. Clausewitz found war to be a complex process comprised of political, civic, moral, and technical (i.e.: warfighting) dimensions, with no single dimension worthy of solitary consideration apart from the others.[5] He was quite clear to distinguish that no sole actor in the system could independently exert control over all aspects of the system. In war, Clausewitz said that precedent was no guide, for in the conduct of war, each conflict was shaped by interconnected forces in a unique way; therefore, only the most basic generalities could ever apply to specific situations.

War was viewed by Clausewitz as a system in crisis because it operated on a completely different set of assumptions from everyday life. He was particularly interested in the idea of "friction" in a crisis, where the easy was made difficult, the routine a continuous struggle. He said:

> ...everything in war is very simple, but the simplest thing is very difficult...countless minor incidents—the kind you can never really foresee—combine to lower the general level of performance, so that one always falls short of the intended goal...the machine is

---

[5]Michael Howard, *Clausewitz* (Oxford: Oxford University Press, 1983).

> composed of individuals, every one of whom retains his
> potential of friction...the least important of whom
> may chance to delay things and sometimes make them
> go wrong.[6]

Clausewitz found that in times of crisis, the inevitable friction encountered through uncertainty, danger, unpredictability, and fear was countered with moral forces, which consist of attributes such as courage and self-confidence. Inherent in successful crisis response systems are the moral forces of teamwork, pride, esprit, and sense of duty. If these forces are absent, then problems can endure throughout the crisis and overwhelm attempts to resolve it.

Clausewitz's descriptions of war and the unique characteristics of its human response justify the special attention that crises demand in human systems. With an ability to simultaneously impact a society across a range of dimensions, as well as being inherently unpredictable by nature, crises are rarely handled by one organization. The complexity of a crisis is important to understand its human response, because organizations rarely operate well across a range of different functional expertise or capabilities. Organizations that attempt to grow in breadth and depth of expertise typically take on the characteristics of what University of Southern California Professor Gerald Caiden terms "bureaupathologies." Such clearly unhealthy organizations attempt to do many things well in response to their changing environments, but in reality they perform little, if nothing, well at all. Management experts have rightly advised organizations to pare themselves down to a set of interrelated core capabilities,

---

[6]Carl von Clausewitz, *On War*, trans. Michael Howard and Peter Paret (Princeton: Princeton University Press, 1976), 119-121.

train hard to provide those capabilities, and then implement those capabilities relentlessly in their environments.[7]

Whether a crisis is environmental, political, human, or technological in nature, it demands preparation, response, and resolution at a level of organizational complexity that matches the needs of the situation. We must remember that crises are nonlinear; their inputs and outputs are not proportional; the situation is not equal to the sum of its constituent components; it is difficult to see the boundaries of their scope.[8] Therefore, the response to a crisis must possess capacities to deal with nonlinear, chaotic, muti-dimentional realities through intense collaboration and coordination with reasonable potential to draw on all available resources to respond effectively.

How do human systems achieve the capacities to deal with complexities found in the sometimes chaotic environments that they face? Whereas everyday recurring activities can be planned, coordinated, and implemented in relatively bounded organizational forms or through lengthy negotiations and compromises between and among organizations, crises demand a relatively different order of human organization called an institutional crisis response network. Management specialist Rupert Chisholm describes this form of human organization necessary to resolve the complexities of the most confounding crises:

> Many important problems are "messes" or "wicked problems." Examples of these problems include unemployment, public education quality, and community development. These types of broad, complex problems

---

[7]James Q. Wilson, *Bureaucracy: What Government Agencies Do and Why They Do It* (New York: Basic Books, 1989).

[8]David Alberts and Thomas Czerwinski, *Complexity, Global Politics, and National Security* (Washington: National Defense University, 1997), xiii.

defy definition and have no simple solutions. Work toward apparent solutions by one organization that fails to account for impacts on other interconnected constituents usually fails. Dealing with these complex, interrelated problems requires development and use of equally complex networks. Often, these networks require involvement of organizations from different sectors (e.g.: public, private, labor, and education) and from different levels (e.g.: local, state, federal; basic education and higher education).[9]

Chisholm's observation that complex human structures are needed to match the complexities of a crisis are borne out in the United States' successful attempts to resolve the crises that have enveloped many of its inner cities. Early attempts to solve the "urban ghetto problem" emphasized unilateral "sting" or "crackdown" measures directed and controlled by police organizations. Today, comprehensive models of organization involve varied aspects of the urban crisis, from education, to policing, to neighborhood watches, to day care, to work from welfare, to home ownership, and so on.

One example of an effective network response to a devastating urban crisis is described in Melody Ermachild Chavis's award winning book, *Altars in the Street: A Neighborhood Fights to Survive.*[10] Chavis's account of the south side of Berkeley, California describes one urban community's transition from a police-centric control model to a comprehensive, multidimensional response to the urban dilemma. Chavis and other area residents began efforts to "take back" their neighborhoods from the forces

---

[9]Rupert Chisholm, "On the Meaning of Networks," *Group and Organization Management* 21 (June 1997): 217.

[10]Melody Ermachild Chavis, *Altars in the Street: A Neighborhood Fights to Survive* (New York: Bell Tower, 1997).

of drug traffic, failed schools, murder, rape, and urban decay by enlisting support from neighbors, youngsters, the elderly, the unemployed, drug addicts, police, and even drug dealers. The fight was eventually waged by schools, businesses, environmental groups, and volunteers. These disparate groups, operating in their respective areas, pulled together and resolved the crisis, which effectively restored public order from decadence. The forces involved were similar to those described by Clausewitz: intestinal fortitude, moral courage, self-reliance, love of the cause, and a willingness to die in the struggle.

This brief introduction to the multi-dimensional properties of crises identifies the fundamental issue for their corresponding human responses. The human struggle is to mirror the dynamics of a crisis with an assemblage of organizations that collectively possesses the requisite core competencies do resolve each of the major dimensions posed by a crisis. The resolution of a crisis is called *crisis management*, and although single organizations can and have resolved certain crises through individual efforts, the purpose of this book is to identify the effective interorganizational principles behind multi-organizational crisis resolution efforts.

Crisis Management

Objectives

Crisis management is defined as helping avert crises or more effectively manage those that do occur.[11] The fundamental driving factor preceding

---

[11]Christine Pearson, Sarah Misra, Judith Clair, and Ian Mitroff, "Managing the Unthinkable," *Organizational Dynamics* 26 (Autumn 1997): 51-64.

effective crisis management is awareness and vigilance to the possibility and repercussions that a crisis, or several different types of crises, can in fact occur. Identification of the potential, endorsement of proactive preparation, and active participation among senior management prior to signals of an impending crisis are critical precursors to any crisis management effort.[12] So, in an interorganizational sense, effective crisis management is preceded by recognition among senior executives that collective preparation and response measures be taken.

Unfortunately, reality oftentimes reveals crisis consideration as a crisis unfolds or only after its damages have been done. With organizational vigilance as a key to averting many crises, manage others more effectively, and learn more fully from crises that occur,[13] it is essential to identify the general objectives of any interorganizational crisis response network. The objectives are:

(1) *Anticipation*—a commitment to analyzing, attempting to predict, forewarn, and steer clear of emerging crises,

(2) *Preparation*—providing the planning, training, and collective responsibilities prior to a crisis,

(3) *Response*—actually implementing the collective resolution arm when a crisis occurs, and

(4) *Wisdom*—learning together from the event in order to prevent, lesson the severity of, or improve upon responses to future crises.

---

[12]Pearson, et al.

[13]See Pearson et al. and Mitroff et al., 1996.

There are several ways in which crisis objectives are achieved. The section below describes four different methods that, if properly implemented, achieve the crisis management objectives; each method possesses some commonalties with its peers, but peculiar characteristics based on the types of crises faced through the different methods provide slightly different means to similar ends.

Method #1: Five-Phase Sequence

A group of crisis management scholars recommends a five-phase sequence to achieve the interorganizational objectives.[14] Underlying the sequence is a belief in organizational cultures guided by values as a network's top priority. In crisis response, the culture triggers the needs of important stakeholders and the responsibilities of all members. The values are demonstrated by pursuing quality in disaster processes and procedures, applying first rate resources and personnel to crisis management planning, and clearly promoting the "crisis values" through written, verbal, and electronic communications. The cultural expectations in crisis response must become a mindset, not a catch phrase or lip-serviced experience.

The five-phase sequence describes how crises are handled among "best case" organizations or networks. Phase one is the *signal detection phase*, where crisis warning signals flash. Best-case scenarios provide environmental probes to look for signals that could indicate disasters; unfortunately, many organizations and networks either (1)have little or no signal detection capability or (2)do not monitor the signals that come through.[15] The United States' intelligence community's failure to collate and analyze

---

[14]Pearson et al.

[15]Pearson et al.

Japanese warning signals prior to the 1947 attack on Pearl Harbor illustrates one example of a network design poorly structured for signal detection analysis.

Phase two is *preparation*. It is in this phase where time, effort, and other resources are spent to avoid crises wherever possible and effectively manage those that occur. Preparation includes senior executive planning, the establishment of cross-functional crisis management teams, the dissemination of values and strategies throughout the network, and the simulation of hypothetical disaster incidents.[16] The preparatory phase of the Year 2000 (Y2K) computer crisis was a brilliant example of crisis foresight and planning by a small U.S. government team. That team pulled together a network of businesses and nations to stave off a near-miss technological disaster.[17]

Phase three is *damage containment*. It is in this phase that the bulk of the organization's resources are applied, mainly due to the fact that damage containment is the first stage where the crisis cannot be escaped. The crisis is literally upon an organization or community at this point. Damage containment includes stifling the intensity of the crisis, keeping it from spreading, and mustering additional resources to combat it.[18] Most crisis response networks handle this phase quite well *for those crises they repeatedly face*. For example, the U.S. military uses expeditionary forces such as the U.S. Marine Corps and the U.S. Army's 82nd Airborne Division, and public safety departments use SWATs, for quick hitting responses aimed at holding down the effects of planned crises if and when they occur.

---

[16]Pearson et al.

[17]M.J. Zuckerman, "He 'Snookered' the World into Beating Y2K," *USA Today*, 3 January 2000, A-1.

[18]Pearson et al.

Phase four is *recovery*. It is in this phase that "business as usual" is sought, and, if that goal is unattainable, key functions are identified and restored to working order.[19] Delays are kept to a minimum, and the psychological factor of operating some services provides a boost in morale to affected workers or citizens.

Phase five is *learning*. This phase includes raising the awareness of, assessing, and reflecting on, the issues facing the entity as a result of the crisis and the response in steps one through four. This phase should be seen as an opportunity to identify successes, improve on previous situations, learn what facilitated and what hindered crisis management performance, and improve on weaknesses and build on strengths for better crisis management in the future.

Method #2: Self-Assessment Questioning

Many organizations and networks use a self-assessment questionnaire to determine the level of crisis preparedness among key members of a network.[20] The phases and their corresponding questions are provided at the back of this chapter in Table 1–2. The questionnaire focuses on the *what, where, when,* and *who* of crisis management. Key questions identify *what* kinds of crises are prepared (and not prepared) for; *what* current management capabilities exist; *what* is missing; and *what* is senior management doing to eliminate the gap. These questions are followed by: *when* stakeholders recognize potential warning signals of a crisis: do they know what to do, have the time and resources to act, receive support from management, and know useful ways to share their

---

[19]Pearson et al.

[20]Pearson et al.

experiences? *Where* a crisis occurs is important in the recognition of physical liabilities, determination of the organization's ability to respond, and identification of the cultural incentives (and impediments) to act. Finally, *who* is focused on identification and recognition of key internal crisis management personnel, as well as key external personnel who participate in internal crisis resolution.

This question framework allows communities, networks, and organizations to assess their planning, preparedness, and response mechanisms for the disasters that they can count on and those that might not be anticipated. The questionnaire can be distributed at all levels of an organization, and, in a network, it can be distributed to all members of all of the organizations to see how well crisis management is understood across the interorganizational structure.

Method #3: The Corporate Way

Another useful framework for crisis management is provided by business crisis expert Ian Mitroff and business writers L. Harrington and Eric Gai. The corporate planning model seeks to eliminate crises where possible and minimize damages when they do occur. Its five action issues include:

1.   *Form and train crisis management teams.* These teams provide planning, protocols, meetings, and drills for a wide variety of disaster scenarios.

2.   *Create a crisis portfolio.* A portfolio analyzes possible scenarios and their likelihood, formulates plans to counteract each of them, and provides a risk assessment for each issue in the portfolio. Contributions to such a portfolio should come from cross-functional sources in one organization and cross-organizational sources in a network situation.

3.   *Work at signal detection.* Signal detection has been proven best in organizations where active, well-developed programs supported by top management are in place to allow for the warning of emerging issues.

4.   *Audit continuously.* The best organizations regularly audit their external environment, technologies, and organizational culture to identify vulnerabilities and take corrective action.

5.   *Integrate lessons learned.* Solid disaster response organizations practice continual improvement and get better and better with each disaster identification or experience.[21]

Action issue four—audit continuously—is a critical component in disaster planning.[22] Auditor Christy Chapman states that knowledgeable audit specialists, armed with a broad vantage point, should provide (1)simple, understandable disaster plans, (2)flexible, adaptable procedures, (3)lower-level and top-level involvement in disaster planning (as opposed to "expert" planning and member implementation), and (4)training.[23] The key to these four points is that the auditor cannot prepare every member organization or every employee for the exact nature and components of a crisis, but the audit specialist can contribute to a cultural atmosphere of thinking, doing, and acting during a crisis to cope with even the most insurmountable disasters. Effective auditor planning and participation in this manner led to impressive crisis resolution of two highly publicized cases:

---

[21]Ian Mitroff, L. Harrington, and Eric Gai, "Thinking about the Unthinkable," *Across the Board*, 33, no. 8 (1996): 44-48.

[22]Christy Chapman, "Before Disaster Strikes," *Internal Auditor* 53, no. 6 (1996): 22-28

[23]Christy Chapman, "Before Disaster Strikes," *Internal Auditor* 53, no. 6 (1996): 22-28.

Event	Planning
1992 IRA Bombings	Several recovery sites provided computer systems and help desk facilities; liaison with neighboring boroughs to provide needed social services such as housing, post-traumatic stress management, counseling, health services, engineering services, and other public services.
1994 Northridge Quake	Emergency center containing tents, food storage area, generators, phones, fax machine, radios, personal computers, database containing vendor, employee, and other resource lists.[24]

Method #4: Mandate It

Not all crisis planning is voluntary, and much planning must be conducted in accordance with public law in the form of federal, state, or local regulations. In one effective example of such a mandate, the *Emergency Planning and Community Right-to-Know Act* (EPCRA) spells out the structure of emergency plans that focus efforts to bring organizations together in planning and preparation. EPCRA includes the following mandates:

---

[24]Ibid.

(1)   identification of facilities and transportation routes that contain hazardous materials;

(2)   emergency response procedures to be used at the disaster site and in surrounding areas;

(3)   identification of personnel designated as community andfacility coordinators responsible for the plan's implementation;

(4)   procedures for notifying authorities and potentially affected parties;

(5)   methods for determining when a disaster has occurred and the areas at risk;

(6)   descriptions of the emergency equipment and facilities available in a community; and

(7)   plans for evacuating facilities and potentially affected areas.[25]

Inherent within the seven objectives is training. Training for such dire circumstances includes two key components: (1)response manuals and outlined procedures are clearly understood; and (2)on-site, in-the-field personnel are trained to control emergency situations. Lessons must be easy to read and procedures easy to understand, because they will be applied under periods of intense duress. On-site personnel must be trained in at least a minimum of emergency responses so that they can hold or cope with a situation until follow-on help arrives. EPCRA makes a solid step toward crisis awareness by legislating broad reporting

---

[25]Gaylord Bridegan, Dan Chilcutt, B.H. Basehart, and Marvin Dickerson, "Contained Response: Environmental Emergency Planning," *Risk Management* 44, no. 5 (1997): 40-42.

requirements for community involvement in potential disasters, as well as providing communal knowledge of what to do if disaster does strike.

Communications is a critical component of several public laws, because disruptions in communications, or the inability of communications systems to work across organizations, often lead to many other problems in a chaotic situation. Integrated crisis management information systems usually function well in the military, but a history of some poorly coordinated domestic activities shows that defects are relatively more common in civilian emergency response systems.[26] Interoperability of systems is lacking *among* federal, state, and local jurisdictions and *between* functional systems (such as fire, police, and airborne emergency units).[27]

Communications expert Gary Anthes describes several problems that limit communications during a crisis response, and he also provides workable solutions. The problems: inadequate voice service; congested wireline and wireless services; unknown radio frequencies in use by relief organizations; limited access to remote situations and limited information among organizations; lack of E-mail capability between local users and regional offices; and slow setup of telecommunications facilities at crisis scenes.[28] These problems can stem from resource deficiencies or a failure to identify and coordinate about the need for information interoperability during times of crisis.

Anthes's solutions include self-configuring wireless data networks, adaptive networks that discover and react to damage and changes in use, "judgment support" tools drawing on data from diverse and unanticipated sources, remotely accessible metacomputer systems for modeling and

---

[26]Gary Anthes, "Red Alert," *Computerworld* 31, no. 27 (1997): 83.
[27]Ibid.
[28]Ibid.

simulation, multimedia fusion of data from varied and unexpected sources, distributed virtual crisis management anchor desks, adaptive interfaces that analyze use and signal when crisis managers make errors, and more flexible and powerful geographic information systems. These solutions help get varying levels of government to work with one another to solve problems, and they also provide shared communications networks for functional organizations (e.g.: police, fire, and so on) to coordinate their responsibilities in dealing with common disaster scenarios.

Table 1–2: Aligning Crisis Response Methods to Interorganizational Practices

Interorganizational Objectives	5 Phase Sequence (Pearson et al., 1997)	Questionnaire (Pearson et al., 1997)	Public Mandate: Emergency Planning and Right to Know Act	Corporate (Mitroff et. al, 1996)
1) Anticipation	Signal Phase • Analyze • Monitor • Probe	What kind of crises will be faced, what capabilities exist, what is missing, what is being done about the gaps?	• Must have method for determining when event has occurred (EPRKA) • Identify common resources needed	Signal Detection • Active warning mechanism in place
(2) Preparation	Preparation • Senior executive planning • Cross-functional teams • Dissemination of values/strategies • Simulation of hypothetical incidents	When stakeholders identify a problem, do they know what to do? Do they have time and resources to act?	• Description of community resources available • Plans for facility evacuation and affected areas • Authority notification • Identification of key response personnel • Develop response procedures • Coordinate information interoperability between systems	Crisis Portfolio • Analyzes scenarios and associated risks • Scenario counteraction plans • Developed across competencies
(3) Resolution	Damage Containment • Muster resources • React • Stifle crisis intensity Recovery • Working back to normal	*Where a crisis occurs is important.*	• Use response procedures • Redundant communications systems • Radio • Email • Diverse sources • Adaptive networks	*Formed and Trained Crisis Management Teams*

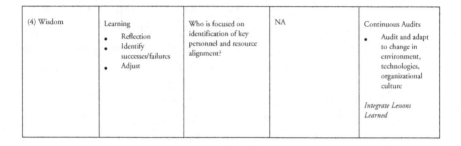

(4) Wisdom	Learning • Reflection • Identify successes/failures • Adjust	Who is focused on identification of key personnel and resource alignment?	NA	Continuous Audits • Audit and adapt to change in environment, technologies, organizational culture *Integrate Lessons Learned*

Crisis Management Summary

Because public crisis management spans so many contexts—government, business, volunteer, organizational, interorganizational—it incorporates lessons from many disciplines and walks of life. These lessons must coalesce into a cultural mindset that results in a set of objectives that are followed regardless of the particular scenario or environment. How each network achieves its objectives will vary, but the successful ones work together in (1)anticipation, (2)preparation, (3)resolution, and (4)wisdom. They effectively answer the following questions:

(1) *Anticipation:* Have we visualized what potential crises exist in our environment and the likelihood that a crisis might occur? Do we actively monitor the environment for warning signs of potential crises? Do we know what our network's capabilities and shortfalls are, and are we working to close the gaps between the two?

(2) *Preparation:* Are senior executives involved in the crisis management process? Do they coordinate their efforts with interorganizational counterparts? Does the network plan,

train, and simulate crises and our corresponding resolutions? Do we have the appropriate resources identified and stockpiled? Do key personnel, general personnel, and outside stakeholders know what to do should a crisis occur?

(3)   *Resolution*: Do we have backup communications systems to keep the organizations of the network connected to each other in the event of primary system failure? Do we have response procedures for organizations to follow?

(4)   *Wisdom*: Do we make adjustments based on our training? Do we periodically audit our procedures and make changes based on those audits? Do we incorporate new technologies to enhance our response capabilities? After a crisis has occurred in our network or elsewhere, do we study it for ways to improve upon our own efforts?

With the identification of general objectives and methods, it is critical to reveal exactly *how* networks can achieve such difficult objectives. For anyone who has worked in and between organizations as a liaison or conduit knows that coordination towards effective collective action is very difficult to sustain. The objectives are reached by following fundamental interorganizational principles that can be broadly applied regardless of the specific type of crisis being studied. First, three different crisis response networks will be described and analyzed, and then their general applicability based on fundamental principles will be discussed.

Chapter 2

Three Crisis Management Networks

This chapter focuses on institutionalized crisis response networks that handle three different types of crises at three different levels of public service. In analyzing different networks, it is possible to identify common network characteristics based on how groups of organizations are consistently able to work together and resolve public crises. Wildland fire, emergency management, and metropolitan public safety environments are the environments and the National Interagency Fire Center (NIFC), Delaware Emergency Management Agency (DEMA), and Columbus, Ohio Public Safety Department are the cases.

Wildland Fire and the National Interagency Fire Center

Originally called the Boise Interagency Fire Center, the National Interagency Fire Center was established in 1965 from separate efforts by the U.S. Bureau of Land Management and the U.S. Forest Service to improve fire and aviation support in the Great Basin and Intermountain West.[29] Later, the Weather Service added its forecasting capability to the

---

[29]National Interagency Fire Center, *Lifeline to the Fireline: National Interagency Fire Center* (Boise: National Interagency Fire Center, 1994), 1-12.

project, and over time, three more natural resource agencies joined the center to round out the interagency team. In 1993, the center replaced "Boise" with "National" in its title to reflect the truly national scope of the network.

The NIFC now functions as the nation's logistical and coordination support center for wildfire suppression. A network affiliation of the United States Bureau of Land Management, Forest Service, Bureau of Indian Affairs, National Park Service, and Fish and Wildlife Service (along with the National Weather Service as a quasi-member),[30] the NIFC provides national interagency facilitation for wildfire and tangentially related responses. Its mission is accomplished through a network of the federal agencies, 50 state wildfire organizations, and several other groups. These organizations are represented at the NIFC through the Forest Service's Cooperative State and Private Forestry authorities. Agreements are also held with Canada, several other foreign nations, and the Office of Foreign Disaster Assistance.

The member organizations belong to the National Wildfire Coordinating Group. This group was created in 1976 to assure development of common standards, practices, and training throughout the wildfire community. As a result of such close-knit coordination, firefighting supplies, equipment, and personnel are shared to make the daunting firefighting task easier, more effective, and less expensive to American taxpayers.

A description of each of the functions of the NIFC conveys the truly coordinated, comprehensive efforts in the wildfire suppression:

---

[30]National Interagency *Fire Center, Lifeline to the Fireline: National Interagency Fire Center* (Boise: National Interagency Fire Center, 1994), 1-12.

(1) *The Multi-Agency Coordinating Group (MAC)*. The MAC Group is activated when national fire situations reach severity. It is composed of the individual NIFC member organization directors, a General Services Administration representative, a military liaison, and a state forester. The group's roles are to identify national or interagency issues and set priorities for scarce resources.

(2) *The National Interagency Coordination Center (NICC)*. This center provides all logistical and intelligence information to the NIFC member organizations. As local and regional resources are depleted during a crisis, the NICC coordinates resource reallocation to priority missions. Resources are allocated according to the closest available supply, regardless of agency or affiliation. The NICC sends analysis teams to foreign countries to assist with disasters there as well.

(3) *The National Incident Radio Support Cache (NIRSC)*. This interagency (Interior/Forest Service) operation provides communications for wildfire resolution efforts. The NIRSC also trains federal, state, and local emergency employees to set up and operate communication centers in a crisis. Its radio cache includes 5,000 hand-held radios, thousands of telephones, satellites, repeaters, and microwave stations. This equipment is configured into kits for specific situations, and each kit is used approximately five to ten times per year by network member organizations.

(4) *Other Functions*. A supply and equipment warehouse is available as the regional stockpile for key fire states: Utah, Nevada, Idaho, and Wyoming. This warehouse also acts as a reserve stockpile for other regional warehouses. It is filled with all necessary fire fighting gear and tools to be sent out at a moment's notice. During the fire season, these items are shipped, trucked, and flown all over the country. The NIFC also coordinates technical training and support, fire and aviation training, "smokejumper" (i.e.: first responder) team movements between geographic regions, air tanker base operations, equipment development laboratory projects,

infrared mapping, aerial imagery, and several wildland fire detection communications systems.[31]

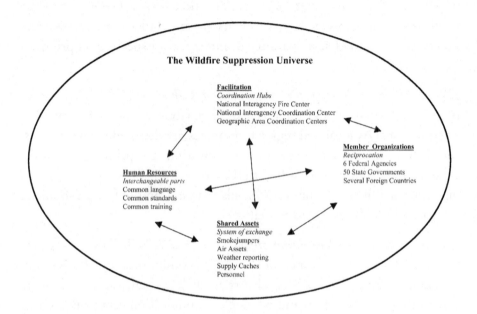

Emergency Management and the Delaware Emergency Management Agency

State governments maintain emergency management agencies. These agencies provide emergency relief planning, operations, and recovery for

[31]National Interagency Fire Center, *Lifeline to the Fireline: National Interagency Fire Center* (Boise: National Interagency Fire Center, 1994), 1-12.

the 50 states through coordination with federal government agencies, such as the Federal Emergency Management Agency (FEMA), other state departments and agencies, and local jurisdictions. They also establish partnerships with private businesses and nonprofit organizations. Some states limit their emergency management responsibilities to planning and coordination, but other states, such as Delaware provide a completely independent emergency function, called an emergency management operations center, to centrally manage the state's response to environmental or man-made disasters.

The Delaware Emergency Management Agency (DEMA) is responsible for the development and maintenance of the Delaware Emergency Operations Plan, coordination with FEMA for recovery and mitigation grants following a disaster, and planning, training, and responding to radiological, chemical, and natural hazards.[32] The agency headquarters facility also acts as the State Emergency Operations Center, which provides a "central point of coordination for pre, during, and post disaster activity through a combined staff of 30–120 personnel depending on the crisis."[33] Organizations coordinated at the operations center include Delaware government departments and agencies, local and county agencies, private organizations, and federal liaison personnel.

DEMA is organized according to the nature of the threats it is designed to handle. It is composed of natural hazards, radiological emergency preparedness, training, chemical hazard, and headquarters sections. [34] This form of organization is quite different from most state emergency management agencies. For example, the Massachusetts Emergency Management Agency is more traditionally aligned into planning,

---

[32]State of Delaware, *Delaware Emergency Management Agency Online [Internet]*, State of Delaware Webmaster, WWW: http://www.state.de.us/govern/agencies/pubsafe/ dema/indxdema.htm., August 1998.

[33]Ibid.

[34]Ibid.

operations, communications, recovery, and training divisions.[35] Delaware's threat-based organization provides advantages over functionally organized state agencies.

DEMA's Natural Hazards Section is responsible for ice and snow storms, lightning, hurricanes, tornadoes, extra-tropical systems, and coastal and inland flooding.[36] It is also responsible for upkeep of the Delaware Emergency Operations Plan (which incorporates both natural and technological disaster plans) and the State Relief and Recovery Plan (which is the long term community recovery plan). The Natural Hazards Section also assists local and county representatives with their individual emergency operations plans. Finally, this section is used as DEMA's outreach coordinator for outside technical hazard experts, public and private property damage assessments, and hazard mitigation programs (through FEMA).[37]

The Radiological Emergency Preparedness (REP) Section is responsible for preventing, reducing damages, and recovering from nuclear power plant disasters. This section's planning arm develops policies and procedures for assessments of accidents, responses to emergencies, and recovery from nuclear problems.[38] As part of its training function, the REP Section provides courses, workshops, tabletops, drills, seminars, and exercises related to nuclear disasters.[39] In the area of public relations, the section

[35]State of Massachusetts, Massachusetts Emergency Management Agency, *Massachusetts Emergency Management Agency Online [Internet]*, State of Massachusetts Webmaster, WWW: www.http://www.magnet.state.ma.us/mema/ deptdes.html, August 1998.

[36]State of Delaware, *Delaware Emergency Management Agency Online [Internet]*, *Natural Hazards Section*, State of Delaware Webmaster, WWW: http://www.state.de.us/govern/agencies/pub-safe/dema/nathaz.htm., August 1998.

[37]Ibid.

[38]State of Delaware, *Delaware Emergency Management Agency Online [Internet]*, *Radiological Programs Section*, State of Delaware Webmaster, WWW: http://www.state.de.us/govern/agen-cies/pubsafe/dema/rep.htm., August 1998.

[39]Ibid.

maintains a public outreach program through power plant tours, annual mailings, a Joint Information Center, a rumor control program, press releases, advertisements, and school programs.[40] The REP Section also coordinates nuclear issues with other issue-related bodies such as the Northeast High-Level Radioactive Waste Transportation Task Force and the REP National Steering Committee.[41]

The Chemical Hazard Section is mainly responsible to provide staff support to the State Emergency Response Commission (SERC), whose mission is to "protect public health, safety, and the environment by ensuring effective use of resources to plan for the response to incidents involving hazardous and other toxic substances."[42] The SERC is also responsible for ensuring that citizens are provided information surrounding chemical substances. The Chemical Hazard Section works with the SERC in these functions and also provides ancillary support to other DEMA sections.

The Training Section provides courses and information to the public in all areas of emergency management. Its information offerings include courses based on FEMA's Emergency Management Institute training; state and regional emergency management issues; and specific courses for local policy makers. This section also assists in exercise development to test local counties and agencies preparedness, lines of communication, planning, and cooperation for disaster contingencies. A final Training Section function is to conduct large and small outreach presentations across the state.

---

[40]Ibid.

[41]Ibid.

[42]State of Delaware, *Delaware Emergency Management Agency Online [Internet], Chemical Hazards Section*, State of Delaware Webmaster, WWW: http://www.state.de.us/govern/agencies/pub-safe/dema/chemhaz.htm., August 1998.

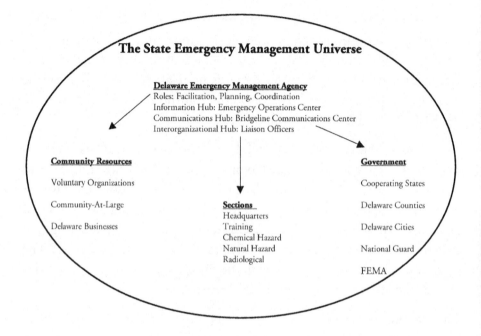

The State Emergency Management Universe

Delaware Emergency Management Agency
Roles: Facilitation, Planning, Coordination
Information Hub: Emergency Operations Center
Communications Hub: Bridgeline Communications Center
Interorganizational Hub: Liaison Officers

Community Resources

Voluntary Organizations

Community-At-Large

Delaware Businesses

Sections
Headquarters
Training
Chemical Hazard
Natural Hazard
Radiological

Government

Cooperating States

Delaware Counties

Delaware Cities

National Guard

FEMA

Metropolitan Public Safety and the Columbus Public Safety Department

While explanations of wildfire and emergency management are necessary for all but the professionals who work in those communities, public safety is generally understood by every schoolchild who grew up watching fire, police, and emergency medical personnel respond to emergencies in their neighborhoods. The Columbus system is organized along traditional lines of fire, police, and emergency medical services, with special functions such as SWAT and bomb squads embedded in its structure. The great changes in public safety are broader than any one city's system, and they are influencing events in Columbus, just as they are in every major metropolitan city in the United States.

Public safety, whether it be at the metropolitan, town, village, or county levels, is changing dramatically due to increases in the number and types of crises in the operating environment, the heightened expectations of the public, and the dramatic evolution of technology. The specific challenges facing local response systems are sometimes similar, but they can also be peculiar to the government being studied. Both the commonalties and disparities of the different areas and levels of government show where problems and solutions for public safety may be found for the future.

Some of the common problems being faced in public safety include:

(1)   traditional crises, such as health, fire, and police emergencies;

(2)   nontraditional crises, such as terrorism, chemical/biological threat, information attack, or radiological hazard;

(3)   increased budget constraints and heightened citizen expectation/scrutiny;

(4)   operations under tentative political leadership; and incorporation of advanced technologies into operating systems.[43]

While traditional problems were adequately managed in the past, such "routine" responses now face two difficult trends: (1)they must be handled as the nontraditional scenarios have drawn away public resources; and (2)what was previously considered adequate might now be unacceptable to the public because sunshine laws, technology, media scrutiny, and other changes provide public access to historically inaccessible information.[44]

---

[43]Robert Thomas, President of 9–1–1 Mapping Systems, interview by author, 22 June 1998, Erlanger, Kentucky, notes with author.

[44]Michael Cretien, President of The Avatar Group, interview by author, 24 June 1998, Columbus, Ohio, notes with author.

To deal with increases in number, type, and effectiveness of responses that public safety systems must provide, many communities have turned to innovative solutions that involve radical departures from tradition and incorporate geographic economies of scale and scope, technology, and public/private cooperation. The goal in most of these systems is to address the needs and demands of the citizenry more adequately. The clear trends to incorporate the new methods and achieve the ultimate goal of citizen service are: fundamental changes in the focal point of the public safety system—the 9–1–1 emergency call system; incorporation of new technologies at all levels of public safety networks; and regional consolidation of services among city, county, state, and other levels of government.

The 9–1–1 emergency response system changes constitute a major trend in the local-level public safety community. The traditional organization for public safety encompassed interorganizational arrangements to solve public problems through the centralization of emergency communications in the 9–1–1 emergency response system. In such systems, fire, police, and public health services all revolved around the focal point of crisis response: the 9–1–1 emergency call. The 9–1–1 system was modeled after the 9–9–9 system in Great Britain, and it has existed close to current form since its 1968 inception in America.[45] Table 2–1 details the four major movements in the 9–1–1 system over its three decade history.

---

[45]John Eller, "9–1–1 Has Become a Real 'Life-Saver,'" *9–1–1 Magazine*, May/June 1998: 72.

Table 2–1: The Evolution of the 9–1–1 Emergency Response System

(1) *Basic 9-1-1* provided a knowledgeable dispatcher (usually a policeman or fireman on convalescent leave) to offer advice to citizens during an emergency;

(2) *Enhanced 9–1–1* provided dispatch services as well as automated name, address, and phone number via phone company computer database linkages;

(3) *Digital 9–1–1* provides database information to the dispatcher in approximately one second. That information can range from ten digit map coordinates, to third party identification information, to special medical and health records, and other features;

(4) Future 9–1–1 could provide even further specialized services such as disaster recovery information, business continuity procedures, and on-line emergency surgery consultation for patients who must be treated on-site.

Unfortunately, many communities have no 9–1–1 system, others operate under the archaic constraints of *Basic 9–1–1*, while still others, such as the City of Los Angeles, sign multi-million dollar contracts to provide early *Future 9–1–1* capabilities. This disparity coexists even in neighboring jurisdictions because funding formulas are typically local[46] and rural areas

---

[46]The state of Texas is one exception in that it pools funds from taxpayers and then redistributes budgets among all of its public safety jurisdictions based on a number of indices to include population and crime rates.

do not possess tax bases broad and deep enough to support special features in their emergency systems.[47] It is a common joke in the 9–1–1 profession to wish that loved ones, if they must suffer severe injury, do so in a major metropolitan area.[48]

The jurisdictional disparity is compounded by the fact that 9–1–1 service levels now vary within jurisdictions as well. In many areas of the country, citizens can purchase additional database information about themselves for a monthly surcharge, much like a cable subscriber who orders extra movie channels for television. The jurisdictional and pay-for-service disparities have pushed the 9–1–1 system from its origins as a common-service national asset to a local "have" versus "have-not" system which could have severe implications for the future.

The 9–1–1 services differ, not only in the operating systems themselves, but also in the people that run the systems. Dramatic disparities exist in the qualifications, education, and training of the personnel operating at the heart of the public safety system—the emergency call dispatchers. Depending on the locale, personnel range from grade school education levels, to college graduates, to retired or active duty policemen with graduate degrees.[49] There are currently no national level standards for the education or training required of emergency call dispatchers, and each state or local government system has a different set of requirements.[50] The National Emergency Number Association is attempting to incorporate common minimum standards across emergency systems that will include dispatchers, as well as technologies, equipment, and infrastructure requirements.[51]

---

[47]Robert Thomas, President of 9–1–1 Mapping Systems, interview by author, 22 June 1998, Erlanger, Kentucky, notes with author.

[48]Ibid.

[49]Ibid.

[50]Ibid.

[51]Advisory Commission on State Emergency Communications, *TDD/TTY Accessibility: Checklist for PSAP's in Texas* (Austin, Texas: 1998), 2.

The incorporation of new technology is a second major trend witnessed across public safety systems, and, while it was just described as one driver in 9–1–1 operating system change, new technologies are also extending into every other area of the broader public safety response system. One example of the impact of technology has been in the organization of public criminal and health records for government, corporate, and citizen uses. A major burden of local governments used to be the provision of clerks and managers to write, copy, file, and serve the public in all areas of public safety records administration. Many governments have discovered computerized databases to be a more efficient and cost effective way to maintain and provide public safety documents to those who need them; and these new systems enable personnel reassignment for field duties to meet other priorities.

Columbus typifies one type of change in the public safety database management field. Local governments are provided with computerized warehouse information databases of significant storage capacity, varying levels of database access for government, insurance company, and public users, security from illegal access, cross-software linkages between dispersed storage media, and remote access capability for users in the field or on the road.[52] Across Ohio, the following innovative information management features appear:

(1) *Auditor of State*: personnel and payroll information on-line for access to up to 250,000 documents in three second retrieval time;

(2) *Ohio State Highway Patrol*: on-line central records unit converts 300 daily traffic crash reports, case investigations,

---

[52]*Intellinetics Online [Internet]*, Intellinetics, Inc., WWW: http://www.intellinetics.com, July 1998

background and polygraph information, and other important information to CD-ROM media. The initial configura-
tion provides access to one million documents in three
seconds and five million documents in eight seconds.

(3)   *City of Whitehall:* the police department links documents
through virtual files; shares digital mug shots with other
departments in central Ohio; and scans and stores police
sketches and drawings for on-line access.[53]

Satellite use is also on the rise to pinpoint crime locations. With the
proliferation of cellular phone usage, public safety systems lost capacities
to track distressed citizens through land-line phone calls, so global
positioning receivers (GPS) are embedded in some cellular phones for
immediate location identification.[54] An alternative way of tracking
cellular phone calls for emergency service is through cellular system
antennas located on community towers.[55] These antennae function
together to "triangulate" a distressed citizen's ten-digit grid location to
help authorities respond to a dilemma. Regardless of whether the GPS or
tower system is selected by local governments, the Federal
Communications Commission has mandated that all systems will identify
the location of a crisis within 125 meters by 2001.[56] Along with database
and cellular phone technologies, new technological advances are being
realized in identification, information retrieval, communications,
geographical location, and other areas every day across the United States.

---

[53]Michael Cretien, President of *The Avatar Group*, interview by author, 24 June 1998, Columbus,
Ohio, notes with author.

[54]Kenneth Terrell, "Help, 911! Where Am I?" *U.S. News and World Report* 124, no. 24 (22 June
1998): 73.

[55]Ibid.

[56]Phillip Pina, "911 Soon Could Track Cell Calls," *The Cincinnati Enquirer* (24 June 1998), B1.

Regionalization, the third major trend in local public safety administration, grew out of the historical model for public safety, which was composed of the following characteristics:

(1)   isolated agencies (i.e.: fire, police, emergency medical services) within the same department;

(2)   stand alone communication and database systems within the same functional areas (e.g.: federal, state, county, municipal law enforcement); and

(3)   little or no coordination between jurisdictions or levels of government.[57]

The isolation, "turf" protection, and independence that were fostered and maintained in the historical model have fallen as interstate, cross-jurisdictional, public/private solutions respond to decreased budgets, aging infrastructure, costly new technologies, and increased public scrutiny.[58]

The concept of regionalization creates a new paradigm in public safety that incorporates resource sharing among different levels and agencies of government. It can include three degrees of sharing that go from as little as common infrastructure (e.g.: radio towers), to combined dispatch services, to total integration of all public safety operations.[59] Since the historical model is still prevalent in the public safety community, pitfalls to successful regionalization exist, and they include: poor track records of interagency participation, inadequate planning, ignorance of future needs, and single agency dominance.[60]

---

[57]Michael Thayer, presentation at the National Emergency Number Association National Convention, 23 June 1998, notes with author.

[58]Ibid.

[59]Ibid.

[60]Ibid.

Transforming Public Safety: Three Major Trends

(1) The evolution of 9-1-1 into a fully capable *information network hub* for medical, crime, and fire information;

(2) The influence of new technologies that bring *real-time information* to the scene, between functions, and among regions;

(3) Breaking the turf barrier to coordinate *integrated regional approaches* between county/city, city/city, city/state, and city/state/federal systems.

Effective regionalization systems exhibit strong political support across the jurisdictions involved, cost sharing, and technical compatibility.[61] Politically, successful regional arrangements arise out of a solid public relations campaign to sell senior decision makers, ownership stakes for every participating organization or jurisdiction, equitable distributions of authority in decision making, avoidance of single agency dominance, clearly stated objectives, agreements, and expectations, long-term commitments, and clear distinctions between political and operational responsibilities.[62]

Cost sharing is a second feature of effective regional efforts. Cost sharing creates incentives for participation of member organizations. A quality cost sharing arrangement includes realistic budgets, identification of funding

---

[61]Ibid.
[62]Ibid.

sources, balance and compromise among member organizations, entry and exit mechanisms (i.e.: how to get new members in and how to allow old members to leave contracts), and equitable cost sharing formulas.[63]

The technical aspects of a regional public safety network are the final characteristic of effective systems. These aspects include both the operating system requirements and the organizational and staffing needs. The system requirements include understanding the requirements of the system as a whole (as well as needs of the member groups or governments); use of the appropriate technology; identification of long-term vendor relations; and modularity. The important feature of the technical side of the relationship is understanding that it is not equipment or service that is bought; instead, it is a relationship that is purchased.[64]

---

[63]Ibid.
[64]Ibid.

Organization and staffing considerations include well defined policies and procedures, consideration of career paths, common training, quality personnel, open communications between organizations, and empowerment of the regional management.[65]

As public safety systems move from traditional organization to a regional orientation, they are attempting to retain traditional functional advantages of having separate police and fire specialties and local dispatchers who know the local areas, while expanding their networks to include federal and state linkages, neighboring communities, towns, and cities, and other networks such as the National Guard to respond more comprehensively to the complexities of modern-day crises.

Analyzing Three Different Crisis Environments and Their Networks

This brief familiarization with wildfire, emergency management, and public safety unveils early "do and don't" lessons of crisis response. Key factors, such as resource sharing and information technology integration emerge as precursors to successful response efforts. These factors and others will be analyzed in the next five chapters under the prism of key interorganizational crisis response principles.

---

[65]Ibid.

Chapter 3

Principle #1—
Common Purposes

"There was a common purpose; we set aside the competition and worked as an industry."[66]

—Dick Brown,
Electronic Data Systems,
in describing how the Y2K computer crisis was avoided

Solving shared problems is the reason why interorganizational network relationships form. Without an anticipated common crisis or set of crises that exhibit dynamics spanning beyond individual organizational management competencies, there would be no need for organizations to collectivize their efforts. This section provides the "why" behind effective network arrangements. To put it simply, organizations come together when all member organizations see an opportunity to solve a problem together that none can deal with alone; and their coming together serves the self-interest motivations of each of the individual organizations of the network.

In interorganizational relationships, the following elements are present:

---

[66]http://www.usatoday.com/news/acoumon.htm, January 3, 2000, 3.

(1)   behavior among members is aimed at achieving both collective and member organization self-interest goals;

(2)   interdependent processes emerge through the division of tasks and functions among member organizations; and

(3)   an interorganizational relationship acts as a unit and possesses a unique identity separate from its member organizations.[67]

These three elements, being common among interorganizational relationships, clearly show organizations in a network relationship pulling together to achieve shared purposes useful for the whole as well as for the individual parts. The elements also display divisions of labor and other features that can only take place within the context of the interorganizational relationship. In short, the individual parts become one collective body.

For a number of reasons, organizations join together instead of pursuing paths of individual organizational behavior:

(1)   to promote areas of common interest;

(2)   to obtain and allocate a greater amount of resources than would be possible in an independent arrangement; and

(3)   to adjudicate areas of dispute or competition.[68]

Empirical studies prove shared purposes as an essential aspect of intergroup relations. In a study of hotel populations around the Niagara Falls tourist

[67]Andrew Van de Ven and Diane Ferry, *Measuring and Assessing Organizations* (New York, John Wiley and Sons, 1980): 299.

[68]Eugene Litwak and Lydia Hylton, "Interorganizational Analysis: A Hypothesis on Coordinating Agencies," *Administrative Science Quarterly* 6 (1997): 395-420.

area, two interorganizational factors ensured well maintained, attractive, affordable lodging and tourism in the cultural mecca.[69] The first factor was a common, similar interest in a resource. In the case of the hotel populations, the similar interest was in attracting tourism. A second factor was an opportunity for relative advantage. The opportunity for relative advantage at Niagara Falls was evident in the two groups of hotel/restaurants that formed on separate sides of the Canadian/U.S. border.

The Niagara Falls research indicated that common interest and relative advantage could be extrapolated to a more general application of situations in which organizations pull together based on perceived individual organizational and collective gains. It is clear in this study that interorganizational relationships form, at least in part, due to two or more organizations' perceptions of a common purpose for coming together.

What Interorganizational Relationships Possess:
(a) Distinct collective behavior from individual organizational behaviors
(b) Divisions of Labor among the individual organizations to support the whole
(c) A separate identity as an organizational entity

Why Organizations Join:
- Promote areas of common interest
- Gain access to more resources than those available alone
- Clear up competition or areas of dispute
- Gain relative advantage over another organization or group of organizations
- Promote shared interests

---

[69]Paul Ingram and Crist Inman, "Institutions, Intergroup Competition, and the Evolution of Hotel Populations around Niagara Falls," *Administrative Science Quarterly* 41, no. 4 (December 1996): 629-658.

A common network purpose is critical for effective collective action, but common agreement on each individual organization's role in the network is also essential. In the *resource dependence* model of interorganizational relations, one organization seeks out partners for an interorganizational relationship because it cannot attain necessary resources on its own. Two key factors govern the member organizations of such a relationship:

(1)　each organization must be *aware* of the self-interest benefits to be gained from each of the other organizations in the network; and

(2)　a *consensus* among all organizations must be achieved concerning the roles and responsibilities that each organization will contribute in the network.[70]

The resource dependence model may or may not be predominant in interorganizational relations (because conflicting models may explain the relations as well), but the two factors do indicate that organizations act out of perceived needs to secure resources. It is the common pursuit of scarce resources that leads organizations to each other into collective arrangements.

Sometimes, arrangements can be found where the common network purpose is clear but individual organizational responsibilities are unclear or lack consensus. The United States military system contains many overlapping functions, where each military service (and service subcomponents) views certain issues or areas as its own, while another service also lays claim to the same issue or area. This problem of role agreement is evident, for example, in the debate over maritime prepositioning assets between the Army and the Marine Corps.

---

[70]Van de Ven and Ferry, 299-304.

An alternative justification for interorganizational network relations is the *system change* model, and it arrives at the same conclusion as the *resource dependence* model (i.e.: common network purpose and consensus on organizational roles). The difference in the two models is not in the end state, but in the logic used to arrive at the end state. This model states that external criteria (e.g.: new budgetary outlays, regulatory changes, revenue sharing) drive organizations with divergent motivations and objectives to merge based on negotiation and bargaining for joint collaboration in the new environment.[71] Regardless of their origins, both the internally driven resource dependence model and the externally driven *system change* model arrive at common purposes for member organizations of a network.

Two approaches to common purposes: System Change versus Resource Dependence

System Change
- External influence
- Environment changes and forces or encourages collaboration
- Examples include: new threat; legislation; classic disaster case study reveals shortfalls and shifts response paradigm.

Resource Dependence
- Internal influence
- Organizations seek resources so they pull together
- Self-interest motivations
- Examples include: access to pooled information, assets, resources, property; mutual aid in responses; and access to new or expensive technologies.

---

[71]Warren, 44.

The questions in Table 3–1 identify a network's common purposes and the external, internal, or combination of factors that drive those purposes.

Table 3-1: Questioning a Network's Purpose: The Foundation of Interorganizational Relationships

1. **Why?**
Why does this network exist? Is there consensus on the purpose of this network, or are there varying interpretations as to what this network does? Could any of the organizations of the network accomplish the network's mission on its own?

2. **What?**
Has the purpose of the network shifted over time? Has the environment forced the network to shift? Has an organization ever left the network? If so, why? Is it because the purposes of the network or of the organization shifted over time?

3. **Who Does What?**
Do all member organizations understand their roles in the network as well as the roles of the other organizations? What happens when new roles emerge? What happens when a dispute occurs over which organization is responsible for a certain task or role? How are disputes over responsibilities resolved?

4. **How?**
How did the network originate? (Did one or a couple of organizations discover that they needed help so they asked others to participate; or did legislation or the environment change and thus force organizations to pull together?)

These questions were developed after reviewing the work of Andrew Van de Ven and Diane Ferry, *Measuring and Assessing Organizations* (New York: John Wiley and Sons, 1980)

Common Purposes in Wildland Fire Suppression

The wildfire suppression common purposes center on the concept of total fire asset mobility in the United States, United States' territories, and countries where the United States maintains international agreements to provide fire support services. The fire suppression purposes are clearly understood in the network as are the divisions of labor among the six federal member organizations and associated state, local, and international fire organizations necessary to accomplish those purposes.

While fire suppression provides common network purposes and divisions of labor, two key issues threaten the cohesiveness of the network. The first issue concerns overall fire management policy. The fire suppression network was not designed to coordinate, and does not always effectively produce, fire science policy outside of suppression. Pre-suppression policy, lands management, and prescribed burning are areas where the network functions more as groups of individual organizations with individual policies, instead of as a collective body with clear priorities. The second issue concerns the increasing use of suppression resources to respond to non-fire related incidents (e.g.: search and rescue; hurricanes) that are still considered public emergencies. The network excels in its narrow fire suppression mission, but expansion of that mission or the addition of purposes would require significant adjustments. It is unclear how the network could adjust to the permanent application of its assets to non-fire related situations.

Common fire suppression purposes arise out of both the external systems change and internal resource allocation models of interorganizational theory. The systems change model provides one framework through which common purposes emerge in the network, while the resource dependence model provided the original justification behind the emergence of the network in the 1950's.

The systems change model is evident in many of the network's contemporary initiatives. The Joint Fire Science Program is one such initiative. Legislated by Congress in 1998 to develop a nationally consistent assessment of the nation's fuels (combustible living and dead material) management and a comprehensive analytical system to provide improved decision support, this program is one of many designed to prevent, or lessen the severity of, disasters.[72] Program goals were developed as a result of system change in that Congress justified its legislation based on growing recognition that fire management policies in recent history were fragmented, ambiguous, and filled with negative human and environmental value outcomes.[73] System change occurred on two levels to create a common purpose through a network of organizations: (1)authoritative legislation forced collaboration in a joint program (i.e.: organizations had no choice in order to remain law abiding in their fire management practices); and (2)the disparate, fragmented fire management community produced varying standards, practices, and procedures without oversight, and this situation resulted in disastrous wildfire scenarios in some areas. On their own, independent organizations in dispersed geographic areas with different resources could not effectively develop common standards. Fragmented policies threatened portions of public and private domain and resulted in the need for an external shock to the system.

With the Joint Fire Science Program in place, the common purpose has been enforced. Each of the wildfire member organizations is represented in the program, so all voices are heard in the development of fire suppression policy, implementation, and evaluation. The common purpose created by the legislation now acts as a collective reinforcing mechanism in the network. Agencies are required to:

---

[72]National Interagency Fire Center, *Joint Fire Sciences Program Online [Internet]*, National Interagency Fire Center Webmaster, WWW: http://www.nifc.gov/joint_fire_sci/ JointFire.html#Introduction, June 1998.

[73]Ibid.

(1)   develop the same interagency fuels mapping and inventory classification and procedures;

(2)   practice similar fuels treatment practices and techniques;

(3)   coordinate with each other for treatment scheduling (to ensure that schedules are environmentally sound); and

(4)   establish common monitoring and evaluation techniques.[74]

The resource dependence model also helps to explain the suppression alliance, and it was this model that provided the original justification for the network to form in 1965. Several organizations provided the resource dependence model's role of single actor attractor for more organizations to fill needs that the single actor could not fill on its own. One actor, the U.S. Forest Service, recognized that it needed an air center for forest fire suppression and realized it would not get one on its own.[75] Another actor, the Weather Bureau (now the National Weather Service) recognized that it could gain a way to improve its weather forecasting during national emergencies through the use of air assets but could not attain the additional forecasting capability alone.[76] After an original interagency agreement (that also included the Bureau of Land Management), the success of the air center venture led the National Park Service, Bureau of Indian Affairs, and Fish and Wildlife Service to request and gain membership in the network.[77] So, while the external systems change model effectively creates common purposes through joint programs, the resource dependence model provided the original motivation for member

---

[74]Ibid.

[75]*National Interagency Fire Center Online [Internet]*, National Interagency Fire Center Webmaster, WWW: http://www.nifc.doi.gov/NifcInfo.html, June 1998.

[76]National Interagency Fire Center, *Lifeline to the Fireline* (Boise: National Interagency Fire Center, 1994), 3.

[77]Ibid.

organizations to form the network in the first place. Both models have made contributions to explain why six disparate organizations come together under common purposes to form a national asset.

Today, the systems change and resource dependence models act to reinforce the strength of the network, but the daily maintenance of the interorganizational relationships produces dynamics that allow the network to function as a separate entity existing in a unique way on its own. The U.S. Forest Service's Tom Frey says that the driving cohesiveness factor among the organizations is not forced changes brought on by the environment or self-interested organizations seeking gains from coopera- tion; instead, it is the joint agreement of all parties on a few key issues. These issues, while having been slightly altered over time, provide a set of stable purposes for the organizations to work together.

External influence through system change led to...
joint programs, training, and standards

...while internal influence through resource dependence led to...
the original pooling of aircraft, weather operations, land management, water resources, and water resources among four organizations

...to the point where...
both internal and external factors strengthen the network together today

---

One of these key issues is a common recognition that coordination is necessary to fight and win the battle against wildfire. It is clear to all member organizations that no single organization can harness all of the people, assets, budgetary authority, and other resources necessary to manage the monumental challenges that wildfires bring in sheer numbers, intensity, and scope every year.

A second issue that contributes to cooperation and coordination across agencies is the jurisdictional reciprocation in fire management. Since a fire today could land on U.S. Park Service property but one tomorrow could just as likely fall on state or local property, prioritization of resources at local, state, regional, and federal levels is commonly viewed by all participants as an effective and efficient wildfire process.[78] Member organizations and jurisdictions can easily see that helping one's neighbor agency or government today could result in reciprocation at some point in the future.

There are self-interest elements in both the recognition that no single organization can handle the enormity and complexity of annual wildfires alone and the jurisdictional turf issue that helps all organizations and levels of government to recognize that a single prioritization system based on standards must hold across the network. As Tom Frey points out, however, it is as important to see the purely collective aspects to what these organizations see in the network, because it is the collective agreements that make the network unique and allow it to cooperate in ways unfamiliar to most other networks.

Two areas where common purposes are clearly identified are in the network's prioritization scheme and division of organizational labors. These areas detail not just what is agreed upon, but how and why collective understandings are reached.

Prioritization

Each of the network's federal agencies/departments willingly pools assets from their immediate jurisdictional needs in the wildfire arena. The wildfire

---

[78]Tom Frey, U.S. Forest Service, interview by author, 14 July 1998, Washington, D.C., notes with author.

prioritization system is based on the understanding that competing demands for resources develop at local, state, or federal levels depending on the severity of the fire. In order to avoid parochial jurisdictional struggles, organizational conflicts during crises, or unequal distribution of resources to one area over another, the network's Multi-Agency Coordination (MAC) Group establishes priorities during a crisis. The MAC Group varies in design, depending on the level being studied, but it is typically representative of the jurisdictional leadership of all concerned agencies, government, and departments in a fire scenario. At the national level, the MAC Group is composed of a representative from all six NIFC member organizations and other rotating organizations.

The priorities that a MAC Group must consider in a crisis are nationally established and collective. They are (in priority order):

(1)   the potential to destroy human life;

(2)   the potential to destroy property and resources (with values assigned based on historical, environmental, and legislated significance);

(3)   social, political, and economic consequences; and

(4)   resistance to control (e.g.: fire growth potential; difficulty of terrain).[79]

The issue of prioritization as a driving factor towards collectivization, or a willingness to subordinate individual organizational interests for the larger whole, speaks to the uniqueness of a crisis network over other forms of network organization witnessed in government or business. Timeliness is

---

[79]National Interagency Fire Center, *National Interagency Mobilization Guide* (Boise: National Interagency Coordination Center, 1997).

essential to everything that this network performs, from the ordering of supplies to the issuance of orders on the fireline.[80] Individual organizational interests must be surrendered to a central (but representative) authority in prioritization, purchasing, and facilitation in order to react quickly and respond to the rapidly changing demands of a wildland fire situation. Other network forms have the luxury of debate, negotiation, and compromise; but in a wildfire crisis, the priorities must be established, the power to act must be granted to the appropriate authority, and the resources and personnel must be mobilized. All of these functions must occur together in a timely, coordinated manner. These common needs are jointly recognized by all of the network organizations, and it is the common recognition of timeliness and teamwork that helps to bind strong network affiliation, purpose, and mutual support.

Divisions of Organizational Labor

A second tenet of wildfire suppression common purposes is its organizational division of labor. One way that this network provides for a clear match of its organizations and tasks is through the issuance of written forms of verification, such as memorandums of understanding or interagency agreements. Such agreements extend beyond internal wildfire member relations to the network's relations in larger associations among foreign governments, state governments, and outside federal agencies. Written agreements allow each organization (or government) to debate, compromise, and agree upon every parties' interests *before* a wildfire crisis erupts. They also provide the wildland fire network with both internal and external clarity of support in any fire contingency.

---

[80]Tom Frey, U.S. Forest Service, interview by author, 14 July 1998, Washington, D.C., notes with author.

An example of external clarity through written verification is witnessed in international agreements. The Governments of Canada and the United States have agreed to operational guidelines that assure both parties of assistance from the other in wildfire suppression. The two key executive agents in the agreement are the National Interagency Fire Center (NIFC) and its Canadian equivalent, the Canadian Interagency Forest Fire Center (CIFC).[81] This intergovernmental agreement covers supporting expectations of salaries, resources, death gratuities, equipment, personnel, and all other requirements involved in the tasking of one government by another to help resolve wildfire situations that grow beyond the means of one government's resources to resolve.[82] The agreement leaves no question as to how the request, operations support, and repercussions of the support will be handled, so that when truly disastrous calamities unfold, both the CIFC and the NIFC know exactly what they have to do and on whom they can depend.

Interagency agreements between the NIFC and federal agencies external to the network also clarify divisions of labor and increase task clarity. The interagency agreement between the Department of Defense and the NIFC is an example of a non-NIFC member's role in the network's collective efforts. The memorandum of understanding between the Department of Defense and the NIFC secures military helicopters and crews for emergency assistance during wildland fire situations that require airborne support beyond the capabilities of the NIFC fleet.[83] This agreement clearly describes the specific demands of each request (i.e.: number of helicopter missions, sorties, cargoes, weights, distances, pilots, etc.); the expectations of pilot adherence to professional standards, flight

---

[81]National Interagency Fire Center, *National Interagency Mobilization Guide* (Boise: National Interagency Coordination Center, 1987), 103.

[82]Ibid.

[83]National Interagency Fire Center, *National Interagency Mobilization Guide* (Boise: National Interagency Coordination Center, 1997), 114.

qualifications, and safety practices; and procedures to resolve disagreements between the agencies at the administrative and operational level.[84]

Written agreements also establish and maintain relations among the member organizations within the NIFC network as well. The NIFC agencies have a standing *Interagency Agreement for Fire Management*, which solidifies the programs, statements of work, and other general provisions expected of each member of the network in preparation for, resolution of, and recovery from, wildland fires.[85] This memorandum lays out the specific understanding of the nature and details of internal NIFC member organizations' responsibilities to the larger whole.

The *Interagency Agreement for Fire Management* also covers the authority and objectives of the network to assign organizational missions.[86] Drawing precedent from legislation dating back to such laws as the Protection Act of 1922 (U.S.C. 594), the Reciprocal Fire Protection Act of 1955 (U.S.C. 1856a), and the Disaster Relief Act of 1974; the NIFC first substantiated its ability to define its interagency agreement with a foundation in public law. From that foundation in law, it set a rationally constructed objective among the members to provide a basis for wildland fire suppression and to facilitate the exchange of personnel, equipment, supplies, services, and funds between the agencies.[87]

The NIFC agreements on the division of labor in wildfire management is both internal and external to the network. The division of labor is established from a foundation in public law, and it is clearly recognized in writing by the parties responsible to provide the labor as well as the parties in receipt of the labor. Portions of the agreements also hold some activities

---

[84]Ibid.
[85]Ibid., 118-122.
[86]Ibid., 118-119.
[87]Ibid., 119.

as collective provisions that all members must provide. These activities include: preventing human caused fires whenever possible; training personnel to common wildfire standards; performing presuppression techniques; suppressing wildfires; rehabilitating areas destroyed by wildfires; developing and exchanging new technologies; developing and distributing cost information; performing fuels management; establishing interagency fire management resources; developing annual fire plans, research, and management priorities.[88] The division of labor has been established as a successful way for this network to understand itself, its member organizations' duties, and its relations with outside governments and agencies.

Threats to Common Purposes

As has been shown throughout this section, commonly agreed upon collective purposes are a unifying principle behind the wildfire interorganizational community. These purposes, solid since the NIFC's inception and strengthened over time, now show signs of breaking down (in the perception of some members) based on a shift in some new purposes proposed for the network. Outside forces, which bring organizations together under the systems change model,[89] have also been witnessed as a factor that might possibly splinter network organizations.

The first assault is the increasing use of wildfire assets for non-fire activities. The concepts that have provided the foundations for operational success—common resource allocation based on centralized prioritization; the Incident Command System (which is the NIFC's operational organizing architecture and will be discussed at length later in this section); and the

---

[88]Ibid.
[89]Warren, 44.

total mobility concept—are being employed in services unrelated to wildfire management. The *Incident* in Incident Command System has been used to draw the wildfire organizations and other related groups into programs, policies, and initiatives that are beyond the original scope of the network, its founding charter, its interagency agreements, and its international agreements. The universally agreed upon success of the Incident Command System in firefighting has led to the consideration of its use for many other public needs.[90] These additional missions and objectives, which include federal search and rescue missions, protection and transport duties for public functions, and other safety, but non-fire related initiatives, may or may not work against the network's cohesiveness, depending on how acceptable they are to member organizations and how well the network performs in these new missions.

The addition of new responsibilities poses a great threat to five decades of stability and cohesiveness. At the individual level, employees have mixed feelings about serving in non-fire roles under the Incident Command System or allowing equipment to be used from shared supply caches to support non-fire related activities.[91] One example of the problem's messiness is found in the shared radio cache at Boise, Idaho. If wildfire radios are pulled from the central warehouse or approved for use by the MAC Group, how can member organizations object? While each organization has representation at the NIFC in the National MAC Group, dissenting organizations might lose a fight (or be forced to succumb to higher political pressures) against the new missions. An extreme move after such a loss would be to weigh costs and benefits of membership in the network if the new missions became a significant part of the NIFC's operations. If

---

[90]Tom Frey, U.S. Forest Service, interview by author, 14 July 1998, Washington, D.C., notes with author.

[91]Ibid.

the new missions are accepted, they could begin to erode the once solid collective network mindset into a group of individually self-interested organizations. Self-interest and collectivization currently work hand-in-hand to give the network its meaning, but if the collective purposes become muddled or unclear, the cohesiveness will dissolve, leaving only self-interest maximizing organizations behind. Long-term systemic problems could result in this network, just as they do in other networks (such as the military) when networks are asked to perform roles and responsibilities beyond their core mandates.

A real example of the perceived siphoning of resources for non-fire suppression activity is in non-fire declared disaster situations. Such a non-fire activity occurred in September 1998, when five of the NIFC's eighteen Incident Management Teams were tasked by FEMA to support Hurricane Georges relief efforts in Puerto Rico, Florida, and Alabama. The use of NIFC assets in such cases is authorized under the U.S. Federal Response Plan as supporting functions for emergency management efforts. Hurricane support by Incident Management Teams may be "O.K." in stable fire summers, such as 1998, but such support might be impossible in busy fire years, when Incident Management Teams are already overtasked and exhausted from performing their primary firefighting functions.[92] If new missions are to become central to the network's common purposes, then they must be captured in policy, incorporated in training, cemented in the prioritization system, and accepted in the divisions of labor (just as the fire suppression purposes are today). Non-fire missions are currently handled on an ad hoc basis which is not healthy for long term network viability.

----

[92]Ibid.

The second issue facing the wildfire network is the influence of overall lands management issues on a system designed for only one small portion of lands management: fire suppression. For example, fire policy is sometimes, but not always, made at NIFC, because individual federal organizations and states have different fire management needs based on the different types of lands that they manage. The differences in fire management policy, based on individual organizational and lands management disparities, are not easily incorporated into a collective structure for decision making.

One of many examples of fire policy discrepancies is seen in Alaska's prescribed burn methods. According to the Bureau of Land Management's (BLM's) Ed Lewis, federal agencies prefer a natural course of burning in harmony with nature's cycle of growth and destruction.[93] The Alaskan state government prefers to limit the destruction of wildland property because fires encroach on state and private property and produce enormous levels of smoke in the air. Whereas in fire suppression, the priorities of the wildland network are clear, the Alaskan fire management case illustrates the fact that competing priorities outside of suppression could wreak havoc on a network not currently designed to resolve them.

---

[93]Ed Lewis, Bureau of Land Management, interview by author, 5 October 1998, Boise, Idaho, notes with author.

Common Purposes in Wildland Fire Suppression? It wasn't always so.

On August 5, 1949, the actions of 15 elite firefighters heroically made the case for a coordinated national fire suppression system through 12 of their deaths in what became a symbolic case of fundamental, systematic crisis response problems. In his award-winning 1992 book, *Young Men and Fire*, Norman Maclean recounts the tragedy that took place in the Montana wilderness, now known as the Mann *Gulch Fire*. At Mann Gulch, the firefighters had little common understanding of their daunting fire task; they differed on their views of how to combat and survive the particular disaster they faced; and they possessed varying levels of experience for the positions held on August 5.

Young Men and Fire highlights issues central to any crisis response: (1) in the 1940's, responders (i.e.: "smokejumpers," elite airborne firefighters) did not train under standard groups or leaders as do law enforcement and military personnel, (2) as a result, the Forest Service (note: the *Mann Gulch Fire* preceded formation of the National Interagency Fire Center and the other interagency groups) had instituted a three-week training course at the beginning of each fire season in which crew members worked together under common training standards, (3) however, the leader of the fire on August 5 had not attended the training, (4) the leader subsequently ordered his men to perform a tactical maneuver that neither he nor his men had attempted in the past, (5) some of his men did not hear him and others did not obey him, (6) there were not enough firefighters to support the needs of two fires in the same vicinity, thus volunteers from the local community were called, (6) the crisis experienced on that day-a "blowup"- was not officially identified as a special crisis situation until the 1950's, (7) the crew assigned to the fire was practically devoid of experience in large fires, (8) the radio assigned to the crew was crushed in the initial airborne jump to the fire and nothing in the operational plans signaled such an event as a problem, (9) and, as a result, through the combination of these factors and others, two-thirds of the team perished while fighting the fire.

Changes made since *Mann Gulch* have resulted in one of the safest, most effective crisis response records in the past fifty years. *Mann Gulch* is used as the example of what not to do in fire fighting. The disaster led to many life-saving improvements to include ten common standing orders that all firefighters from all organizations are expected to know at any scene. They cover knowledge of weather, instructions, task prioritization, escape planning, scouting, communications, alertness, lookout, discipline, and supervision. As witnessed through the efforts of the National Interagency Fire Center, National Interagency Coordination Center, National Wildfire Coordinating Group, the six federal agencies/departments, and state government firefighting organizations, commonalties in training, standards, communications, and response procedures are now in place as an example for other response communities. *Mann Gulch* shows that it was not always so.

The Alaskan discrepancy is one of only many in burn, presuppression, and suppression policies that have occurred between states, federal agencies, and other countries. These discrepancies, although they do not appear to directly undermine the network's ability to do what it does well—fight fires based on recognized priorities—they do raise issues about which priorities should govern U.S. fire policy. To date, such policy is fragmented, and it is handled on a case-by-case basis. Some of the NIFC's personnel believe that fire policy should be fragmented to reflect the individual circumstances faced in different regions of the nation, while another group believes that the only way the network can remain cohesive is to adopt a standard national set of policies, practices, and procedures regarding overall wildfire management.

Emergency Management and Common Purposes

The Delaware emergency management network also displays both collective and division of labor properties. Its collective characteristics are shaped by the wide variety of threats posed in its external environment and the political paths driven by the American federal system. The division of labor characteristics are evident at three levels of the network: in the organization of emergency management; by geographical jurisdiction; and through the separation of Delaware's state bureaucracy roles and missions.

The Influence of Geography

Delaware's environment dictates a state-run apparatus to coordinate a response for emergencies that plague the residents and communities of the state. The emergency management network is driven by the nature of its environment. Natural disasters, radiological power plant leaks, chemical hazards, and terrorist attacks are threats that run beyond a single organization's or geographic jurisdiction's capacity to respond. At the state level, these multi-organizational responses must be coordinated and facilitated (but not directly managed) in a network architecture.

Delaware's geographic environment also dictates a state coordinated apparatus that stands as a hub at the center of many types and levels of emergency response organizations. As a peninsular state neighbored by three other states and partially surrounded by three bodies of water, Delaware is a natural region for collective decision making, because environmental and man-made hazards potentially impact the entire peninsula. Whereas some state governments draw their collective properties purely from legislative gerrymandering that empowers political rule within a specific area, the Delaware government has the additional attribute of representing a geographic area affected by the same circumstances.

The collective properties of Delaware as a natural collection point for political organization were evident in the planning and reaction to Hurricane Bonnie in August 1998. Response organizations recognized the potential danger of Bonnie, and they also knew that the central point of the planning and response was in the DEMA emergency operations center.

Through use of an emergency management "Bridgline" call system, 60 mid-Atlantic departments and agencies participated with DEMA in regional strategy meetings. The centrality of the state government was evident in the strategy sessions. Daily calls at the federal, regional, and local levels put the state government, not other levels of government or organizations outside of government, at the middle of the response. A daily DELMARVA (Delaware, Maryland, Virginia) peninsula call was coordinated by DEMA to get the purposes of the response clear, the characteristics of the threat appraised, and the support from other states clarified. Following the regional call, daily calls were held between DEMA and Delaware's local county and city emergency management directors to coordinate the specific actions that would be taken around the state in order to prepare for the hurricane. In calls and meetings throughout the crisis, DEMA, as the state's emergency arm, was the center of the response. It was through this center that the common purposes of the network were identified and understood by its members throughout the hurricane threat in August 1998.

The Influence of Politics

As a body of people, Delaware's citizens feel a sense of community in their state which empowers DEMA and the state's other agencies to act as facilitators in their areas of expertise. According to DEMA's Radiological Programs Administrator, Emily Falone (a 19 year DEMA employee), Delaware exhibits different political characteristics than other states. She says it is often difficult to distinguish between political parties in Delaware, and mudslinging is not accepted as a proper form of campaigning.[94] Director Mulhern echoes Falone's description of Delaware politics by referring to the political process as "no nonsense" and practical. The collective purposes of emergency management are deeply rooted in the sense of community felt in all aspects of Delaware government, and such a feeling cannot be said to describe the collective properties of larger, more fragmented states.

The political framework of the American federal system also empowers the state government as the appropriate level for emergency response purposes to be coordinated. Above the network is the federal government, with the Federal Emergency Management Agency (FEMA) as its emergency arm, providing a central organization for funding and national

---

[94]Radiological Programs Administrator, Emily Falone, Delaware Emergency Management Agency, interview by author, 24 August 1998, New Castle, Delaware, notes with author.

resource prioritization. FEMA, however, is restricted from fully coordinating a crisis management network at the local level because of two
factors: (1)inefficiencies in federal administration of issues impacting
states and localities;[95] and (2)the need to balance its support between total
neglect, which was perceived in 1992 during Hurricane Andrew, and
complete domination, which would not be tolerated by state and local
officials and citizens. As a result, FEMA is available for disaster funding
support, regional coordination, and national prioritization of resources,
but it is not the appropriate level of government to set the collective
purposes of an emergency response in Delaware.

The common purposes of the jurisdictional, functional, and "special"
organizations are determined at the state level. At the jurisdictional level,
counties look to benefit from DEMA's network as they seek resource
support, a broader range of information surrounding threats, assistance
from other state agencies, and a way of organizing their efforts to align
with a larger whole. At the functional level, organizations such as fire,
police, EMS, agriculture, prisons, public safety, and health services are
state-coordinated on a daily basis in Delaware,[96] so they naturally turn to
a state sponsor for their collective purposes in a crisis. Finally, special
network organizations, such as the many corporations that are headquar-
tered in Delaware, its National Guard, and its many voluntary agencies
tend to tie their allegiances at the state level, not at local or federal levels.
It is the state's coordinating body in Delaware that provides the place
where others look to receive their guidance during a crisis.

95As described in the functional theory of federalism in Paul E. Peterson's, *The Price of Federalism*
(Washington, D.C.: The Brookings Institution, 1995), 21.

96The close state coordination of Delaware's public safety systems through the state fire school and
state police is not characteristic of most state public safety systems. As seen in states such as
Ohio, many state public safety systems are controlled at the metropolitan and county levels,
thereby making state level coordination much more difficult. It is also noted that Delaware's tiny
population plays a role in its governmental structure.

Planning for Common Purposes

DEMA's network of crisis management organizations understands its collective role on a daily basis through interpretation of the Delaware Emergency Operations Plan (DEOP). The DEOP is used to clarify the state's goals and objectives in emergency management, as well as to provide organizational roles and responsibilities in supporting the state's goals and objectives.[97] Seminars, exercises, and training about the DEOP are used to disseminate the state's needs as a whole and the organizations' missions to meet those needs.

The DEOP sets three major collective purposes for Delaware's emergency management network:

(1)   protection of the lives and property of Delaware's citizens immediately before, during, and after emergencies;

(2)   coordination of statewide resources and logistical operations through Emergency Support Functions (ESF's);

(3)   procedures and responsibilities for specific potential manmade and natural disasters.[98]

These purposes are provided to respond to specific disasters that the state recognizes as collective threats. These disasters include: fires, floods, droughts, terrorism, tornadoes, sink holes, hurricanes, war attack, northeasters, earthquakes, dam failures, winter storms, civil disorders, radiological incidents, biological contamination, power failures/fuel shortages,

---

[97] State of Delaware, Office of the Governor, *Delaware Emergency Operations Plan* (New Castle, Delaware: Delaware Emergency Management Agency, 1998).

[98] Ibid., BP-1.

hazardous materials incidents, drinking water contamination, and mass casualty/fatality incidents.

The DEOP defines its incidents as having four comprehensive phases that the network's organizations recognize: mitigation, preparedness, response, and recovery. Mitigation involves the elimination, prevention, or reduction of probability of a disaster. Preparedness is the planning, training, and exercising to ensure that network responses minimize damages. Response is the provision of immediate emergency assistance through the coordination of state resources. And, recovery is the return of systems to normal operations. These phases constitute the emergency management network's overarching, collective strategy in disaster management.

Each of the many incidents described in the DEOP has detailed procedures that illustrate the comprehensive approach taken by the entire state to carry out the phases of emergency management. One example of the many incidents is found in the Biological Contamination Section of the DEOP. The following brief description of biological contamination serves as an example of how the network handles one emergency management category through its identification of common purposes and individual organizational activities. The process used in biological contamination is similar to those used for other forms of emergency management.

The DEOP breaks down biological contamination by purpose, situations and assumptions, concept of operations, organization and assignment of responsibilities, continuity of government, administration and logistics, and authority and references. The overall purpose of the network is identified as "to protect and control biological threats and contamination."[99]

---

[99]Ibid., HS 2–1.

Biological contamination is described as "a man-made increase in the process of environmental change." The DEOP's assumptions rest on DEMA's ability to limit the contamination and contact appropriate federal and private authorities for assistance.

The concept of biological contamination operations includes the following options: dispatching of teams from various Delaware state agencies; decontamination of affected areas (if possible); isolation of affected people and livestock; consultation with appropriate authorities; activation of the DEOP; request for federal assistance; and law enforcement procedures.

Delaware's common emergency purposes.. phases...	..lead to..	...common interorganizational planning
• Protection of lives and property • Coordination of statewide resources and functions • Procedures and responsibilities for specific situations		(1) Mitigation (2) Preparation (3) Response (4) Recovery

..that lead to..	...organizational divisions of labor...	..and..	external support through...
	Planning/Facilitation handled by DEMA *Transportation* handled by Department of Transportation *Resource support* handled by Dept of Administrative Services *Mass care* handled by Health/Social Services & Red Cross *Fire* handled by the Fire Service *Public Works* handled by Department of Transportation		--FEMA --Other state agencies --businesses --volunteers --military

The organization and assignment of responsibilities provides several options as well. The Governor of Delaware is given five action alternatives that include: activating the DEOP; making recommendations to the public; declaring a state of emergency; issuing supplementary orders; and/or requesting federal assistance. DEMA and the Department of Public Safety are authorized to take alternative action steps. Perhaps most critical in the organization and assignment of responsibilities is the Emergency Support Functions provided to each agency (these will be covered in the following section).

Other portions of the DEOP describe government's authorization during the Biological Contamination, how administration and logistics are to work, and the authority and references necessary to conduct the planning and operations during a crisis. Such detailed planning in the DEOP provides a collective, comprehensive approach to meeting overall state goals through many organizations' participation in the crisis, and it also ensures that all organizations know the greater goals of the emergency management plan.

Organizational Divisions of Labor

The DEOP also serves as the primary means for organizations in the emergency management network to understand their roles and responsibilities toward serving collective responses to crises. The Emergency Support Functions (ESFs) in the DEOP provide primary and support responsibilities to federal, state, and private organizations. These assignments of responsibility are delineated based on a set of common functions associated with all types of emergencies and the responses required for those emergencies. A sample of the ESF's and their associated primary organizations are provided below:

ESF	Primary Organization
Transportation	Delaware Department of Transportation
Communications	Office of Telecommunications Management
Public Works	Delaware Department of Transportation
Firefighting	Delaware Fire Service; State Fire School
Planning	DEMA
Mass Care	Delaware Health and Social Services; American Red Cross in Delaware
Resource Support	Department of Administrative Services

The ESFs carefully delineate the tasks assigned to the primary and secondary organizations during the event of an emergency. They are organized in the DEOP in the same manner as the many disaster incidents were described. For each ESF, the purpose, situation and assumptions, concept of operations, assignment of responsibilities, and administration and logistics are described to ensure the appropriate division of labor for the task.

Aside from the state and federal organizations that handle the ESFs, local governments are also held responsible for particular duties, of which they are apprised in the DEOP. The counties have 16 specific responsibilities during any emergency, and those responsibilities are:

(1) assist local government with emergency response

(2) perform county emergency response;

(3) assess incorporated and unincorporated county and local requests for assistance;

(4) forward situation reports to the state emergency operations center;

(5) coordinate county support personnel to assist local jurisdictions;

(6) request available county personnel to report to state emergency operations center;

(7) request the county emergency management member to act on behalf of the county in matters relating to the emergency;

(8) provide county personnel to assist with disaster field office staffing;

(9) develop and maintain a county emergency operations plan;

(10) participate in exercises of the DEOP;

(11) ensure emergency notification data currency by regularly transmitting updated information from local and county sources to DEMA;

(12) collect disaster information and forward to the state emergency operations center;

(13) provide damage assessment personnel;

(14) provide emergency communications;

(15) support emergency public information campaigns; and

(16) provide training.[100]

Towns and cities have eight responsibilities which look much like the county responsibilities. Both counties and cities (where appropriate) are also included for responsibilities in the ESFs. One example of such responsibility in a functional area is in transportation, where the counties must coordinate with state agencies for evacuation routes; assist the primary agency (Delaware Department of Transportation) with transportation arteries during a crisis; work with the Department of Health and Social Services for physically impaired evacuations; and coordinate transportation from key areas (such as large businesses or school districts).

The divisions of labor are clearly defined for all organizations of this network. Together with the clear common purposes described in the DEOP (and ingrained through training and exercises), the divisions of labor ensure that all areas of a crisis are handled by a group of primary and secondary response organizations.

---

[100]Ibid., BP-7.

Common Purposes and Columbus Public Safety

The common purposes of a metropolitan public safety system have been generally clear-cut in historical terms: all of the divisions of public safety recognize that the system's mission is to protect the public from forces that would seek to damage or destroy a community's way of life. The organizational division of labor has typically been just as clear-cut for the member organizations of the public safety system: fire departments handle fire incidents; police departments handle criminal incidents; and emergency medical services handle health incidents.

The Columbus Public Safety Department mirrors the historic conceptions of public safety, but there are evidences of change on the horizon for this department that indicate new understandings of its collective purposes. Changes in the environment, technology, and other external forces (such as budgets) have forced the public safety organizations to expand their thinking to regional approaches to public safety, create linkages between police, fire, and emergency medical services, and use nontraditional approaches in public safety that involve the community at-large.

Common Purpose Focal Point

In the Columbus public safety system, the central component on which all of its divisions depend is the 9–1–1 emergency call dispatch center. While exceptions taken by criminal justice experts to this common focal point are discussed later in this chapter (see section on shifting purposes), the centrality of the 9–1–1 dispatch system is recognized by all organizations of public safety in Columbus: fire; police; EMS; and special services (such as bomb squad units or SWATs).

In placing its public safety around the 9–1–1 system, Columbus adheres to an incident-response system. The public safety incident occurs in the community, and the response is triggered by a 9–1–1 call to a dispatcher. The dispatcher then signals cruisers or engines to respond to the call.

With its 1997 adoption of an 800MHz dispatch system, the organizations of public safety in Columbus have solidified their perception of public safety in a common view that efficiency in the incident-response system is the most effective way of delivering public safety. The organizations agree on a common approach to public safety, and their common purpose is to handle the division of the public safety labor that applies to their functional specialty (i.e.: fire, police, etc.). This section describes possible changes in this philosophy, approach, and purpose that could undermine the current perception of public safety and realign or separate the network in the future.

Environmental Forces

In most traditional public safety response cases, all of the organizations recognize which division (i.e.: fire, police, EMS) should handle a given response based on its characteristics. The cases that are most interesting are the ones that involve more than one facet or dimension, such as a fire and hostage situation in the same scenario. Joint responses to such mixed situations could become more prevalent in the future as a result of changed circumstances in the environment.

According to Columbus's Assistant Director for Fire Administration, David Sturtz, a 31-year highway patrolman and six-year inspector general, a public emergency with more than one type of danger involved is a complex situation.[101] Not only does one emergency, such as a fire, need to be handled with timeliness, professionalism, and safety considerations, but a second situation with its own problems must be handled simultaneously.

---

[101] Columbus Assistant Director of Public Safety for Fire Administration David Sturtz, interview by author, 21 July 1998, Columbus, notes with author.

Oftentimes, these complex situations involve functions handled by two or more organizations, such as fire, police, bomb squad, EMS, hazardous materials specialist groups, etc.

In the Columbus system, the hierarchy of response in such dual-dangered situations gives the fire department predominance on-scene.[102] The justification behind the "fire first" mentality is that if fire is not handled appropriately, then the dangers posed by both of the situations will grow out of control (i.e.: fire spreads, hostages die in fire, etc.). It is important to note that in such complex situations, fire and police commanders work together, with neither commander in charge of the entire situation (or of each other). These dual-danger situations are handled by each organization performing its division of the labor, with little need for overlap or concern for duplication of effort or competition for missions.

New Environmental Forces

Aside from traditional situations in which both fire and police have to work together to solve a crisis, the Columbus public safety system is organizing for non-conventional public emergencies, such as the types of complex scenarios posed by Weapons of Mass Destruction (WMD). Acting in line with the external system change model towards network collaboration, the Defense Against Weapons of Mass Destruction Act of 1996 (Public Law 104–201) focused internal public safety coordination.[103]

Columbus was one of 120 public safety systems that participated in Public Law 104–201's mandated Domestic Preparedness Training for Weapons of Mass Destruction (WMD).[104] Columbus participated in six subjects

---

[102]Ibid.

[103]Public Law 104-201 sought to enhance capabilities of public emergency responders to nuclear, biological, and chemical terrorist incidents. Under the law, the U.S. Army Chemical and Biological Defense Command was designated Program Director for Domestic Preparedness to coordinate and execute a municipal preparedness program.

[104]E. Gayle Saunders, *Safety Herald: A Quarterly Publication of the Department of Public Safety* (Columbus: Columbus Department of Public Safety, 1998), 3.

taught by the U.S. Army Chemical and Biological Command: awareness, operations, technician hazardous materials, technician emergency medical service, hospital provider, and incident command.[105] Columbus Public Safety Director Tom Rice said that when his fire, police, and EMS organizations gathered around the table to discuss strategies for dealing with WMD contingencies, he believed it could have been the first time in 30 years that such a joint-organizational strategy session took place.[106] Director Rice sees WMD as a driving factor toward even greater collaborative initiatives between his own organizations, as well as for his system and surrounding regional safety systems.[107]

The approach taken in the WMD training emphasized cooperation and collaboration. In Columbus's quarterly safety newsletter, public safety executive assistant Gayle Saunders said:

> we gathered scores and scores of data, we identified
> potential targets, we assessed our equipment capabil-
> ities and as a result, we determined we would
> conduct our training using a multi-agency, cross
> jurisdictional approach.[108]

Saunders' words could impact the public safety system beyond one program for domestic preparedness, because they point to the interorganizational, public/private, community-based trends that may hold the answers to tomorrow's public safety crises.

---

[105] Ibid.

[106] Columbus Director of Public Safety Tom Rice, interview by author, 20 July 1998, Columbus, notes with author.

[107] Ibid.

[108] E. Gayle Saunders, *Safety Herald: A Quarterly Publication of the Department of Public Safety* (Columbus: Columbus Department of Public Safety, 1998), 3.

Shifting Purposes: Community Public Safety

In its approach to public safety, the Columbus public safety system is straddling two divergent philosophies. The first philosophy is predominant in most public safety systems. It centers on a crisis/response mindset, which places the 9–1–1 dispatch center at the focal point of the system. A fleet of police, fire, and EMS delivery vehicles surround the dispatch service, standing ever ready to respond to emergencies. Out of this philosophy, the focus of the system is on response: responding as quickly as possible, responding with the most effective safety techniques, and responding with the most information at hand. This system of public safety is concerned with efficiency and effectiveness of the response, regardless of the number of types of responses made.

This philosophy and its subsequent approach is the clearly dominant public safety mindset infused throughout the many divisions and organizations that constitute the Columbus system. In every interview conducted for this study, the initiative that recurringly dominated conversation was the city's new 800 MHz dispatch system. One of the most highly regarded members of the public safety team is Communications Director Tom Trufant. Trufant expressed the central focus of the 9–1–1 system in his description of the many new initiatives that the city is introducing to improve the system. In the department's emphasis on response time, interconnectivity with regional partners, and the ability to transfer data to mobile police and fire units, it has centered its attention on the 9–1–1 response as the focus of public safety in the system.[109] Columbus is not alone in its approach to public safety as a

---

[109]Columbus Public Safety Communications Division Director, Tom Trufant, interview by author, 21 July 1998, Columbus, notes with author.

crisis/response model which is continually refined and improved; in fact, it is this model which really solidifies the member organizations as a group committed to the same purpose: getting to a crisis as quickly as possible and employing the most effective, professional techniques to resolve it.

A second philosophy is emerging in the public safety community, and Columbus, while clearly retaining its emphasis on crisis/response, is experiencing a shift in philosophy that could either create a new shared focus for its organizations or unravel the current focus into confusion. This emergent philosophy questions whether response should be the central focus of public safety, when the real commitment should be prevention and deterrence of emergencies. Former New York Police Commissioner, William Bratton, supports the prevention/deterrence model while questioning police departments that "measure their impact not on what crime they (are) preventing but on how fast they (are) responding to it."[110] Another crisis/response critic, criminologist George Kelling states that, "(while) rapidly responding to crime increases citizen satisfaction or arrests…the benefits are very minimal."[111] These critics and others propose a safety philosophy that encourages citizen involvement, empowers commanders with broad responsibilities for specific geographic jurisdictions, and provides police officers with nontraditional training such as problem-solving, community meeting organization, and city agency roles and missions.[112]

This rethinking of public safety is sending shock waves through cities and counties, and it is forcing the public safety community to recognize its need to adopt some of the community safety techniques that take policemen and firemen out of their cars and stations and infuse them into the

---

[110]Howard Goodman, "How a City Reduced Its 911 Calls--and Its Crime Rate," *Philadelphia Inquirer*, 2 August 1998, A26.

[111]Ibid.

[112]Ibid.

heart of the community. Police and fire departments would shift their purposes from being response oriented to being ingrained as members of a community. Such a shift in purpose would move the focal point of public safety from the dispatch office to the individual commanders in specific regions. Regional community public safety members would keep the pulse of citizens, business, and schools, while responding to any emergencies that might arise.

The Columbus Department of Public Safety is adopting some of the points made in the community approach. Assistant Director for Fire Administration, David Sturtz said that being in tune with the community is an essential aspect to successful public safety efforts. He emphasizes the importance of educating the public on the mission and goals of the public safety department

in order to "get the message out."[113] Sturtz believes that there are many venues through which that message is communicated in Columbus. They include: community groups, civic associations, religious gatherings, neighborhood organizations, and other pubic organizations.[114] Sturtz believes that expectations in public safety have risen. All citizens expect, even demand, timely and professional service, and the job of the public safety community is to inform the public of what uniformed professionals can and cannot provide for them.[115]

Some of the top leaders in the City of Columbus reflect Sturtz's belief in public safety community outreach. Director of Public Safety Tom Rice recognizes the importance of getting into the community, speaking with citizens, and fulfilling their needs. Director Rice has been known to travel

---

[113]Columbus Assistant Director of Public Safety for Fire Administration David Sturtz, interview by author, 21 July 1998, Columbus, notes with author.

[114]Ibid.

[115]Ibid.

to homeless shelters in the Columbus area to pray with the men and women who reside there. The Mayor of Columbus, Gregory Lashutka, has taken groups of religious ministers for meetings and retreats in order to build common ground between the city's community leaders and public service professionals. The tone of the city administration is one that promotes citizen contact, outreach, and awareness.

As leaders in the public safety department, Rice and Sturtz convey the type of public safety-citizen interchange that is necessary, but interchange is only one step towards the transition in common purpose sought by community safety believers such as William Bratton or George Kelling. The assumption in Columbus is that dialogue is based on a professional-to-citizen interchange, whereas, in transformed cities, such as San Diego, the new approach has led to a continuous peer-to-peer relationship among citizenry and safety officials where the lines have been blurred between the two groups. San Diego police officers offer training to citizens on tenant screening, licensing, inspections, and even volunteer policing duties for minor-accident reports and other incidentals.[116]

The organizations that comprise the Columbus Public Safety Department have a common understanding of the purposes for which they serve the public, and these organizations also understand the division of labor necessary for each organization to achieve the collective public safety goals. The questions for this city and many other metropolitan ones like it across the country are: (1)are the perceived common purposes the right ones for a public safety community facing complex problems; and (2)does the clear division of labor between traditional fire, police, and EMS functions create situations where interchange and collaboration for complex

---

[116]Howard Goodman, "How a City Reduced Its 911 Calls--and Its Crime Rate," *Philadelphia Inquirer*, 2 August 1998, A26.

situations (e.g.: drugs, WMD, social decay) is limited? As in other public safety communities, Columbus "feels" as though it is in the midst of a transition to handle the emergent threats. Changes in perception of purpose may be essential to effectively protect the public in a new age.

Pulling It All Together

The fire, emergency management, and public safety networks all demonstrate collective and division of labor properties. Factors that lead to possible weakening of either dimension result in decreased network effectiveness, thus further proving the importance of the two properties in an effectively functioning crisis response network.

The organizations that form the NIFC clearly demonstrate their understanding of the network's collective and division of labor properties. Both internal and external forces bring the organizations together. Internally, collective programs and capabilities are provided in the network that would be impossible for any individual organization to provide or possess on its own. The network also forges collective purposes out of its representational, centralized MAC Group prioritization system for resource allocation.

Externally, a network's purposes are forged by the environment it faces and other forces. The wildland fire suppression network's common purposes are simple. They revolve around preventing and fighting wildland fires. These purposes have been evident from the network's inception, and all of its members understand them. Similarly, the divisions of labor are clearly defined through plans, interagency agreements, exercises, and real contingencies. The NIFC organizations avoid one deterrent to the common understanding of the division of labor: competition. They avoid competition, because each primary member has clearly defined jurisdictional authority.

How the International Y2K Crisis Became a Non-Event

The year 1999 will long be remembered for the crisis that never was. Throughout the months preceding the turn of the calendar from 1999 to 2000, people around the world stockpiled water, supplies, foodstuffs, and other basic necessities under the belief that computers would "read" the year 2000 as 1900 would result in phone, power, nuclear, water, and other disasters when clock turned. On January 1, 2000, the forecasted disaster was a non-event. The story is why, and it has much more to do with interorganizational effectiveness than technical computing prowess.

Early in 1998, John Koskinen was appointed as the federal government's Y2K czar. With the seemingly impossible task of coordinating a response to a forthcoming monumental disaster that touched every organization from the common family to IBM to the CIA, Koskinen and his small team of people (which numbered as low as four at times) established themselves as the global hub around which the response would take place. The team aligned a common purpose among traditionally competing corporations, dueling nations, associations, voluntary organizations, and other interest groups. In an interview with *USA Today* after the non-event, Koskinen attributed the project's success to his group's ability to get normally competing organizations to set aside "mutual distrust long enough to recognize the benefits of working together to solve the problem." The key argument that brought the organizations together was Koskinen's insistence that "the world's network would only be as strong as (their) weakest link...telecommunications can't function without power; retail industry fails without banking and transportation systems; 911 emergency systems are useless without fuel and oil to provide a response." Koskinen's efforts are a case study in first rate mitigation unto themselves; his group effectively pulled together thousands of organizations to collectively focus on a common problem and then recognize and implement the organizational divisions of labor tied to that problem. The government team acted as a facilitator, or hub, around which the response unfolded. Instead of relying on traditional government tactics of command and control bureaucracy, his group empowered other organizations, both public and private, with particular areas of expertise to solve the problems related to the crisis for themselves and the network. While spending over $100 billion, the Y2K czar spent it in the right way, not on a large government bureaucracy to manage the incident, but on a small faciliatory team that cajoled, prodded, negotiated, convinced, and contracted with private organizations and nations to do what they did best in service to the common whole. The result was one of, if not the, most effective crisis response mechanisms in the history of the world.

When the purposes and divisions of labor are undermined, such as in a proposal to use the Incident Command System, fire suppression supplies, and network personnel to perform search and rescue missions, the effectiveness of the network must be reevaluated. Aside from the environment, the U.S. Congress legislates some of the network's joint programs and standards, thus pulling the network together through public law.

The DEMA's collective purposes are driven by its environment and maintained by internal forces, and its division of labor understandings are gained through internal operations of the network. The environmental forces that act to create and maintain a network are the disasters faced in Delaware emergency management. These disasters, both natural and man-made, extend across every aspect of the Delaware community and demand a thoroughly integrated response. The peninsular geography of Delaware creates a natural zone for collective action, since most serious disasters have the potential to impact the entire state. Delaware's political system also drives a state-centric network model because of its small size, communal approach, practical politics, relative lack of bureaucracy, and responsiveness to two major industries (i.e.: poultry and tourism) that are severely affected by disasters.

The internal force acting to create and maintain common purposes in Delaware's emergency management network is the Delaware Emergency Operations Plan (DEOP). This document sets the collective purposes of the network, and it is also the administrative manifestation of the governor's constitutional authority to organize the state for emergencies. The DEOP is strengthened through continuous planning, training, exercises, and real world contingencies that emphasize and reinforce the network's common purposes. The DEOP is also the instrument used to identify the common understandings of each organization's role in the division of labor in the network. Emergency Support Functions (ESFs) are used to task member organizations to fill roles in support of the larger whole.

The Columbus public safety system is a network that has traditionally followed common purposes with clear divisions of labor, but external forces are acting on the network to create new purposes and divisions of labor. Columbus's traditional common purposes derive from its public safety philosophy of incident-response. In this model, Columbus public safety organizations understand the 9–1–1 communications center as the central filter through which public safety action emerges. The 9–1–1 dispatchers know the divisions of labor between fire, police, EMS, and special services, and they assign response roles accordingly.

Changing technological, environmental, and philosophical approaches to public safety maintain existing common purposes and divisions of labor, but they are also creating new purposes and divisions. Technological advances are making it easier to provide regional coordination in public safety, thus drawing a more expansive array of functions and jurisdictions into the network. The concept of a metropolitan public safety system might eventually give way to a larger regional approach to public safety with a much broader network. Environmental threats, such as terrorism and WMD force the clear functional divisions of labor to collapse, as more collective mitigation, planning, and response models are necessary between fire, police, and EMS. Finally, a philosophical shift in public safety is occurring, which is moving the entire network away from one that is incident-response in orientation to one that is fully integrated into the community and comprehensively attuned to the complex demands of the environment.

Upon reflection of the interorganizational and crisis response models and description of the three case studies, the following crisis response principle is provided for crisis response networks to follow:

Principle One: Common Purposes

Crisis response networks have shared collective purposes and divisions of labor among member organizations.

Network effectiveness is decreased in two circumstances: (1)when common purposes are unclear or disagreed upon; or (2)when divisions of labor are unclear or competitive among member organizations. Therefore, when organizations can agree on common purposes for coming together and identify which organization will do what for the whole, the foundation for a successful network has been established.

Chapter 4

Principle #2—Authority

The essential question surrounding authority in an interorganizational crisis response network is: from what source does the network derive its ability to function as a whole? The source which provides authority should be sustainable on the norms of society, legality, efficiency/effectiveness, as well as the unique consideration of timeliness in crisis responses. Network relationships can derive authority from hierarchical, collaborative, fragmented, and other authoritative forms. The essence of understanding interorganizational crisis response authority is in the determination of the particular type (or types) of authority that enable the most effective preparation for, resolution of, and recovery from, crisis within the parameters of the prevailing societal system.

The renowned philosopher Carl Friedrich provided one interpretation of the foundation upon which crisis authority rests. He stated that "authority is of decisive importance for every legal and social order…an order cannot be made to function without authority."[117] An order's authority is derived from that entity's original essence, which can be found in the values, norms, and beliefs of the community of people for whom the order functions.[118] The term *authority* is derived from "auctoritas," which translates from an augmentation of judgment by a council of elders, and

---

[117]Carl Friedrich, *The Philosophy of Law in Historical Perspective* (Chicago: The University of Chicago Press, 1963), 200.
[118]Friedrich, 200.

according to Friedrich, was "more than advice and less than command…such as the expert gives the layman…"[119] The source for such "auctoritas" was a level of wisdom, experience, or knowledge beyond common citizens, which provided a more seasoned, reasoned analysis from which judgments could be made.

Friedrich's philosophy of authority is rooted in man's artificial reason that assimilates the will of society through such mediums as the impersonal judge, who makes decisions in the context of legal principles and is knowledgeable of the law. This rational view does not place authority in the law, for the law also needs to be grounded in something as a basis for its rightfulness, and Friedrich saw that the grounding of the law must be based on the "higher reason" of a community's values that express its ideas, beliefs, and morals in a constitutional framework.[120]

This rational view of authority contrasts the view offered by other philosophers, such as Locke or Rousseau, who believed that "the act of will of the sovereign" is the essential and legal act.[121] Friedrich pointed out that legitimacy of an order must also be complemented by its legality, or its groundedness in rightfulness and reasonableness according to fundamental societal values in order for it to be truly authoritative.

In interorganizational crisis response networks, Friedrich's views have substantial implications both for the sources of authority, as well for as the mediums through which authority is exercised. In such networks, authority is used to justify the priorities in a crisis, allocate public resources, and coordinate the response. If these systems are truly authoritative in a Friedrichian sense, then the sources of authority are both legitimate, in

---

[119] Friedrich, 200.

[120] Friedrich, 200.

[121] Friedrich, 201.

that they represent the immediate will of the governed, and also legal, in that their priorities and decisions are in line with the enlightened values, longer-term beliefs, and norms of the community in which they serve.

The great German sociologist, Max Weber also defined authority, and his explanation of *lasting* authority in systems with staying power[122] is exhibited in effective crisis response networks. Weber described three types of authority—rational, traditional, and charismatic—and he concluded that only rational authority sustains the continued, evolutionary progress necessary for the continuance of human systems. Authority established on rational grounds owes its allegiance to a legally established impersonal order. According to Weber, the effectiveness of legal authority rests on the acceptance of the following ideas:

(1)   that legal norms are established; that there is a body...with intentionally established rules applicable to the situation;

(2)   that authority is held in "office," not in a person;

(3)   that persons obeying the authority do so only as members of the group and what they obey is the law; and

(4)   that members obeying the authority do so to follow the impersonal order, not the individual.[123]

Weber's ideas set the foundation for a successful authority structure in a crisis response network: it should be governed by a system with an understandable code of conduct to be followed by member organizations; and that the network's authority rests, not on an individual, but on the strength of the authority inherent in the unique structural

---

[122]Max Weber, *The Theory of Social and Economic Organization, in The Great Writings in Management and Organizational Behavior* (New York: McGraw-Hill, 1987): 6–7.
[123]Weber, 7.

makeup of its organizations. These principles enable the network to out-live its individual members and remain viable as a response mechanism for as long as its crises remain relevant. Weber's grasp of the impersonal concept is critical as well, because in times of crisis, organizational histories, titles, or stature quickly reduce to irrelevancy. The chief qualities that matter in a crisis response are the capabilities organizations bring to the collective network to cope effectively with the problem.

Weber identified two fundamental categories of rational authority that are also important to recognize in modern crisis response networks:

(1)   a continuous organization of official functions bound by rules; and

(2)   a specified sphere of competence that involves obligations of members to perform functions, carrying out the functions with the necessary authority, and the necessary means of compulsion to accomplish the function.[124]

The categories that govern a Weberian network are important because they establish the rules and obligations of a member organization's commitment to the network in a crisis response. The rules that regulate conduct take on both technical and behavioral forms. In an interorganizational network, it is crucial to define the functions to be performed by each member organization, and it is also important to recognize that the overarching network authority (be it a collaboration center, leader, or system of representation) be provided with the enforcement mechanism necessary to ensure that all functions are carried out by member organizations.

---

[124]Weber, 7.

Finally, Weber's description of bureaucracy retains significance in a crisis response network, because his principles apply at an abstract level as readily as they do at the individual and "office" levels about which he wrote. According to Weber, the following criteria apply to bureaucratic functions beneath a supreme authority:

(1)   members are free and subject to authority only with respect to their impersonal official obligations;

(2)   members are organized in spheres of competence;

(3)   member selection is based purely on the ability to accomplish a function for the whole;

(4)   members are allocated resources based on their contribution; and

(5)   members are subject to a discipline system and control in the conduct of their function.[125]

These five principles provide the main points that must be incorporated into the authority system of an interorganizational network. In Weber's first principle (concerning freedom of membership), effective networks recognize that membership in a network might be one of only many obligations of an organization. In fact, it is precisely because of the competency gained in a specific area that an organization might be called to participate in a network in the first place. In Weber's second and third principles, he addresses the importance of competence and the division of task into spheres of expertise. These points lie at the heart of the interorganizational relationship, because the relationship achieves success

---

[125]Weber, 7.

through the synergies gained by plugging different capabilities together to achieve collective synergies. Weber's fourth and fifth principles concern the allocation of resources and the discipline system that governs the relationship. Both are central arguments for healthy interorganizational networks, because these networks must have the ability to apply resources to the areas where they are most needed depending on the specific nature of the crisis at hand. Those organizations that are most in line with the nature of a specific crisis usually receive the lionshare of resources, and that share shifts as the next crisis unfolds if it happens to be different from the previous one. The allocation of resources can also be tied to the reward/punishment system and remain dependent on the contribution that the part makes to the whole of the network.

Authority, as it is discussed on a philosophical level by both Friedrich and Weber, must manifest itself in a visible, workable, observable form. *Webster's New Collegiate Dictionary* describes this practical authority as "the power to influence or command thought, opinion, or behavior."[126] Traditionally, such authority has been associated with a hierarchical or central figure or personality from whom freedom has been granted to perform a given behavior. Friedrich pointed out that such practical definitions must still be rooted in societal values, and that leaders such as Adolph Hitler, who abandon the natural and societal values of human rights and dignities, do not qualify in the practical application of authority.[127] The traditional definition of authority still applies in many parts of the world, and figures of authority, such as most governors and presidents, still act with their traditional "powers to influence." In the context of interorganizational relationships, authority remains essential,

---

[126] *Webster's New Collegiate Dictionary*, rev. ed. (1979).

[127] Friedrich, 202.

and it is still defined as the source from which "the power to influence or command thought, opinion, or behavior" emerges, but it is often less from a "position" of authority and more in line with Friedrich's natural rightfulness and reasonableness that arises from analyses of the situation at hand. Under this definition, the source of authority for interorganizational relations is as likely to emerge from consensus, collaboration, mutual understanding, or network compromise as it is from a central command and control authority superficially imposed in hierarchical structures.

Such a definition of authority sets a framework for the remainder of this chapter, in that it draws on perspectives of principal theorists, while at the same time it applies their theories based on observations of current practices and trends. Authority itself is timeless. It provides human beings the source from which action arises and aligns them with the values of society. But, in every age or in different environments of the same age, the sources and understandings of authority are both historically rooted and dynamic. This section draws upon the great theorists as often as it does from new developments in hopes that the essence of human interaction can be captured for the purposes of interorganizational relationships that form to solve crises at the turn of the twenty-first century.

Rethinking authority from a concept centered on a person in a hierarchical position to a "source" that could come from many different origins is not a novel concept. It is at least as old as Plato's and Aristotle's writings on a "rule of law" rather than a "rule of man." In 1926, Mary Parker Follett blasted en vogue practices of command and exhortation management of front-line workers by stating that "the strength of favorable responses to an order is in inverse ratio to the distance the order travels."[128] Parker Follett

---

[128]Mary Parker Follett, "The Giving of Orders," in *Classic Readings in Organizational Behavior* (Belmont: Wadsworth Publishing Company, 1996): 175-180.

believed that orders were meant to unite disparate or dissociative paths, where the meaning of orders played the role of unifier toward a common goal. The only way to unite divergent paths was to be fully knowledgeable of where the paths were headed, and the only way to see unification of the paths was to be intimately familiar with the situation from which those paths emerged.

Governance of Crisis Response Networks—Keys to Sound Authority Structures

- *Grounded in the "will of the people"; societal values* (Frederich)
- *Run by "offices"; established legal norms and rules; clarified roles and responsibilities; system of discipline and accountability* (Weber)
- *Authority to make decisions is based on the threat at hand by those most capable of analyzing and acting upon it* (Parker Follett)
- *Interorganizational authority can be derived from consensus* (Seiple)

Her source of the "authority" to issue an order came, not from an individual, but from a depersonalized, jointly conducted study of the situation.[129] Parker Follett stated that "one person should not give orders to another person, but both should agree to take their orders from the situation."[130] These words did not often ring true in hierarchical, bureaucratic structures with many layers of "order giving" in them. Today, however, Parker Follett's words are resonating in interorganizational network relationships (particularly in areas of crisis where layers of decision making waste time and only decision makers close to the situation can determine how to solve it) where authority is derived from a careful assessment of the situation between many members who come from widely disparate backgrounds and beliefs.

---

[129]Parker Follett, 175.

[130]Parker Follett, 175.

Because they exist to serve so many different purposes and bring together so many different forms of organization, interorganizational networks can be characterized on a scale of centralization from being very decentralized, where organizations make individual decisions concerning their participation in the network, to being very centralized, where organizations give up their decision making autonomy in favor of network systems, directors, or staffs. A key distinction in the interorganizational literature concerns the degree of authority hierarchy. Centralization concerns the degree of decision making by the network coordination entity (i.e.: system, leader, staff, center) versus the decisions made by the individual, autonomous organizations that comprise the network. Sometimes, a hybrid of the two types of authority emerges where organization members form the coordination entity themselves and make the decisions from a central point but with the representation of individual member organizations. The short point here is: hierarchy, or the lack thereof, matters. It contributes to the character of the network.

Interorganizational authority derived from a collaborative problem-solving approach is witnessed in the emerging humanitarian crisis response relationship between U.S. military organizations and the Non-Governmental Organization (NGO) community.[131] In description of a Civil Military Operations Center (CMOC), peacekeeping expert Chris Seiple describes a crisis response center where the dynamics of collaboration, consensus, and coordination were achieved in the most chaotic of circumstances. Using Operations Sea Angel (Bangladesh) and Support Hope (Rwanda) among others, Seiple showed that the military should not "control" the decisions in a response effort; instead, it should "sit at the table" with NGO's to

---

[131] Chris Seiple, *The U.S. Military/NGO Relationship in Humanitarian Interventions* (Carlisle: U.S. Army War College, 1996).

discover what each NGO can contribute to a situation, how the military itself can best serve in the situation, and collectively, what action should be taken to resolve the situation.

As it turns out in the CMOC, it is often the military's role to provide functions such as logistics, security, foodstuffs, and other resources; while it is often the many different (and often independent and disunited) NGOs' jobs to perform duties such as assessing the local situation, cultural norms, health problems, and moral dimensions of the crisis. In working through a joint collaboration of the situation in a common operating center, Seiple found that "orders" were given, not by command, but by collaborative analysis among many groups, much in a way that Parker Follett would have prescribed so long ago.

There are many forms of interorganizational relationship authority, each with distinct attributes that have emerged from the nature of the problem to be solved and the makeup of the member organizations.

Determining Authority: A Questionnaire for Crisis Response Networks

1. How are decisions made in the network? (negotiation, collaboration, hierarchical leader, mutual agreement, etc.)

2. What happens when one organization sees things one way and another sees it another? Is resolution made by vote, persuasion, compromise, or dictate from an authority figure, legal agreement, or other means?

3. Where does the network get the information on which it acts (central communications hub, sensors in the environment, field reps)?

4. Do different organizations use different means of gathering and analyzing the information used to put the network in motion (individual sensors, separate communications networks or field agents)? If so, how are network decisions made in the face of conflicting information?

5. Can a disgruntled organization refuse to participate in an event?

6. Is a legal authority behind the network? Legislation, directive, Joint Powers Agreement, etc.?

7. When courses of action are considered in a crisis, what are their origins? Does the situation clearly show what needs to be done? Does a communication center report what is going on and then determine actions? Does a single leader get briefed on all of the actions and then dictate tasks? Are representatives of each organization collected into a decision making body with the authority to speak for their group? Or, are things so clear that actions are laid out based on the situation at hand?

Time is an essential ingredient in the evolution and growth of the authority held by a truly collective interorganizational network.[132] In new interorganizational relationships, pooled decision making is usually very weak, because individual organizations maintain their self-interests. As time progresses, experience in interorganizational relations grows, linkages between and among organizations are made, the network organization grows in strength relative to its member organizations, and it begins to take on a collective life of its own.

Authority in Wildland Fire Suppression

Administratively, the authority in national fire suppression derives from foundations in the values of society, and it is firmly rooted in a series of public laws. Operationally, the authority to run the network in performance of its mission is not as straightforward. This type of authority, that of decision making, coordination, and negotiation, is witnessed in many different sources depending on the particular program or activity being analyzed. Authority is dispersed throughout the network depending on the level of the network being discussed (i.e.: administration, operations, special programs); however, those various levels exhibit collective properties.

Administrative Authority

The administrative authority, or the rational justification to operate as a public service provider for society, is based in public law. Wildfire suppression's place in society is secured by the American public's ongoing

---

[132]Roland Warren, Stephen Rose, and Ann Bergunder, *The Structure of Urban Reform* (Toronto: D.C. Heath, 1974).

concern that fire management should be provided to protect both the citizenry and the environment.[133] Recognizing the public's demand for sound fire management protection practices, federal lawmakers legislated suppression roles and responsibilities from no less than ten public documents that include public laws, statutes, and agreements (see Table 4–1).

The foundation provided by public law establishes two key issues of authority from which the network has drawn its ability to function: (1)it established wildland fire security as an important public function; and (2)it empowered select public agencies to perform the fire management function. From these key agencies collective authority is drawn out of their *Interagency Agreement for Fire Management* to provide for a collective, collaborative, approach to wildland fire management.[134]

Table 4-1
Administrative Authority of the Wildland Fire Suppression Network

National Park Service Organic Act of 1916 (16 U.S.C. 1)
Protection Act of 1922 (16 U.S.C. 594)
Economy Act of 1932 (47 Stat. 417; 31 U.S.C. 1535)
1943 Memorandum of Understanding between the U.S. Departments of Interior and Agriculture
Reciprocal Fire Protection Act of 1955 (69 Stat. 66; 42 U.S.C. 1856a)
National Wildlife Refuge System Administrators Act of 1966 (16 U.S.C. 668dd-668ee; 80 Stat. 927)
Disaster Relief Act of 1974
Federal Land Policy and Management Act of 1976 (43 U.S.C. 1702)
Cooperative Forestry Assistance Act of 1978 (16 U.S.C. 2101-2105)
National Indian Forest Resources Management Act of 1990 (25 U.S.C. 3101).

---

[133]National Interagency Fire Center, *National Interagency Mobilization Guide* (Boise: National Interagency Coordination Center, 1997), 118.

[134]Ibid.

Operational Authority

The operational level of wildland fire management is best understood through observation of the two major areas of firefighting support: (1)resource management; and (2)incident management. The authority in each of these two areas is captured in different parts of the network.

Collective resource management is observed through the National Interagency Fire Center's (NIFC's) Multi-Agency Coordination (MAC) Group concept. For the most severe fires, the National MAC Group is responsible to "establish national priorities and national leadership and direction to wildland fire activities."[135] The National MAC Group consists of the National MAC Group Coordinator and representatives from the Bureau of Land Management, Bureau of Indian Affairs, U.S. Forest Service, National Weather Service, National Park Service, Fish and Wildlife Service, and the State Foresters Association.[136] This group establishes resource priorities for the management of national level wildfire emergencies. It has authority over national resources, such as personnel, equipment, and other assets; and it is also the authorization authority for outside contracts with federal agencies and private vendors. At a bare minimum in any fire, this group determines fire management priorities, allocates resources to priority areas from other areas, develops contingency action plans, and issues coordinated situation assessments.[137] The MAC Group concept is used at regional, state, and local levels for fires of smaller size and/or intensity.

In wildfire crises, resourcing decisions flow from the MAC Group.[138] This flow supports the network's total mobility goal by coordinating the transfer

---

[135]Ibid., 91.

[136]Ibid.

[137]Ibid., 93.

[138]Regional and local MAC Groups are used for fires that are managed below the national level.

of resources to the highest priority areas of a fire from centralized sources, outside agencies and vendors, and lower priority areas of a fire. After priorities and resource decisions are coordinated, the MAC Group turns to the National Interagency Coordination Center (or its lower-level equivalent depending on the scope of the fire) (NICC) to fill the orders, negotiate the transfer of assets, and facilitate the mobilization of equipment, aircraft, and personnel needed to meet the crisis. Based on the MAC Group's decisions, the NICC fills resource orders from existing centralized caches and personnel rosters, lower priority areas, and outside contractors when necessary.[139]

Achieving Total Mobility through Collective Fire Authority

National Level

National Multi-Agency Coordinating (MAC) Group
- Determines fire management priorities
- Makes resource allocation determination based on priorities
- Develops contingency action plans
- Issues situation assessments

National Interagency Coordination Center
- Fills contract orders
- Negotiates asset transfers between organizations
- Facilitates equipment, aircraft, and personnel allocations
- Assigns centralized cache assets

Regional Level

Geographic Area Coordination Center
- MAC Group concept at regional level
- Works with national and other regional authorities to coordinate regional priorities and asset facilitation to priorities in its region

---

[139]Tom Frey, U.S. Forest Service, interview by author, 14 July 1998, Washington, D.C., notes with author.

The National MAC Group and NICC are fully activated during large-scale crises, and they are vested with the authority to coordinate resources when the lower levels of fire management, such as local or regional centers, have been exhausted. In accordance with the wildfire suppression philosophy of gradually expanding control, local and regional authorities "resource" their own fires until the situation calls for input from a greater number and type of resources. The MAC concept at the regional level is implemented through Geographic Area Coordination Centers (GACC) and also at most state and local jurisdictions.[140] Local resources are used first in a fire, then regional GACC's make prioritization decisions with regional resources, until finally, national redistribution decisions must be made in the most severe circumstances.

The means of resourcing is not strictly hierarchical. The type of authority displayed in resourcing a fire from the coordination centers is described as a "horse trading" style as opposed to a command and control relationship.[141] The agencies and various state and local governments all voluntarily join the network, so they each retain some autonomy over their individual assets, but each agency and jurisdiction is aware that if it refuses to participate in the resourcing of someone else's fire, it could be stuck without resources when the next fire lands on its turf. The end result is a generally high level of interagency and intergovernmental exchange of resources through the coordination and prioritization hub provided by the interorganizational system.[142]

Incident management is the second type of operational authority witnessed in wildfire system. The management of a fire "incident" on the ground is handled under the same NIFC philosophy seen in resourcing: the local

---

[140]Ibid.
[141]Ibid.
[142]Ibid.

level first attempts to handle the fire on its turf, then cedes authority to state or regional levels when it grows beyond local control efforts, and finally, national level control is provided for the most aggressive wildfires.[143] Two specific tactical forms of fire management are used: (1)the Incident Command System; and (2)the Unified Command System.[144]

The Incident Command System (ICS) is the predominant form of organization for wildland fire management, and this system places authority for a specific fire situation in the hands of one commander. Under singular command, all personnel, resources, and equipment—regardless of their "home" organization—report under one leader for the most effective and efficient incident management.

ICS took hold in the 1970's after several high profile fires led to publicity about vast jurisdictional irregularities between fire standards, management, personnel qualifications, communications, and equipment.[145] Highlighted in the late 1970's movie, *Design for Disaster*, intergovernmental incompetence due to a lack of unified leadership between city, state, and federal firefighters in the fires surrounding Malibu, California drove the creation of ICS as a way of standardizing all wildland fire management techniques.[146]

The implementation of ICS created the opportunity for commonalties in culture, communications, equipment, language, and qualifications among all wildland firefighters.[147] Out of ICS's principle of unity of command,

---

[143]While the ceding of authority is expected in complex fires that grow beyond a local jurisdiction's ability to control, personalities can interfere with the smooth transition of authority to higher levels.

[144]Tom Frey, U.S. Forest Service, interview by author, 14 July 1998, Washington, D.C., notes with author.

[145]Ibid.

[146]Ibid.

[147]Ibid.

all firefighters, regardless of jurisdiction, would fall under one chain of command during a crisis; as a result, they all had to arrive at the scene with common forms of firefighting. This simple change to a unified command structure at the scene of a fire resulted in second and third order changes throughout the wildland fire management community.

ICS has created similarities at many levels to the point where firefighters are virtually interchangeable for assignment across jurisdictions. Today, collaboration in training, qualifications, certification, publications management, and supporting technologies have all spun off of the need to "be the same at the scene."[148] The assurance of commonalties between agencies and jurisdictions has now been institutionalized through the creation of the National Interagency Incident Management System, of which ICS is only a small part. The ICS commander can now count on the following *results* of a completely common, shared system of fire management:

(1)   common standards in organization and procedures;

(2)   application in any emergency;

(3)   application from small to complex incidents;

(4)   provision for organizational expansion (when fire grows);

(5)   adherence to agency autonomy;

(6)   application to all fire protection agencies;

(7)   use of total mobility and nearest forces concepts;

---

[148]Ibid.

(8)   incorporation of new technologies;

(9)   minimization of training and operations costs.[149]

Some of the *attributes* of the system include:

(1)   common terminology (e.g.: radio, on-the-line, rank);

(2)   common functional management (i.e.: command, planning, operations, logistics, finance);

(3)   adherence to management by objectives by using same top/down information flow to line firefighters in every crisis;

(4)   unified command but participation from all agencies and jurisdictions in the operation plan;

(5)   consolidated action plan (i.e.: only one plan with one agenda);

(6)   span of control consistent with 3–5 supervisory rule;

(7)   integrated incident communications infrastructure;

(8)   shared facilities (e.g.: helicopters, landing zones, warehouses, etc.)

(9)   tactical resource management for *single resources* (e.g.: emergency medical services); *task forces* (i.e.: different functions under one leader); and *strike forces* (i.e.: same resources under one leader).[150]

---

[149]National Wildfire Coordinating Group, *The National Interagency Incident Management System: Teamwork in Emergency Management* (Boise: National Interagency Fire Center, 1984).

[150]Ibid., 35.

According to the National Wildfire Coordination Group, what ICS does, as part of a larger National Interagency Incident Management System, is bring disparate agencies together "into a cooperative association previously unknown in emergency services."[151] The tactical authority of an ICS commander, which began as a result of the disaster of the 1970's, has created a system of interchangeable parts and still maintains authority at the lowest possible operating level.

The second model of authority witnessed in wildland fire management is the Unified Command Model (UCM). In this model, each jurisdictional area is represented individually, and the group of separate jurisdictional commanders jointly formulate and follow an operational fire management plan.[152] This model is more difficult to coordinate and implement due to political factors such as "turf" rivalries, negotiations, and the lack of objective prioritization of fire demands.[153] Nonetheless, UCM is still used to fight some wildland fires, and it does ensure representation of all affected jurisdictions.[154] The main reason that UCM is still used is because some jurisdictional public safety officials do not relish relinquishing control to "outsiders" who come from different or higher levels of fire management.[155]

Regardless of the model used, incident management possesses two key traits that describe where authority ultimately resides in a wildfire crisis. First, the MAC Group and NICC set priorities and allocate resources in conjunction with the needs of Incident Commanders, so if on-scene commanders need resources outside of their immediate jurisdiction, the jurisdictional authorities make liaison with the next higher level for coordination. Second, the principle of local control is followed whenever

---

[151]Ibid., 9.

[152]Ibid., 16.

[153]Tom Frey, U.S. Forest Service, interview by author, 14 July 1998, Washington, D.C., notes with author.

[154]The Unified Command Model is actually an alternative form of ICS, but it is not the tactical form of choice

[155]Ibid.

feasible, and only after local constraints prohibit effective fire management, does the authority in the crisis shift to regional or national levels.

Other Forms of Authority

The authority granted for special programs, training and education, and
research and development is different from that in the resource and
operational arenas. In the previously mentioned Fire Sciences Program,
authority is held at the program governing board level. It is the board,
with representation from all member organizations and a NIFC appointed
program manager, that determines the actions of the network organizations. The governing board holds responsibility over process oversight and
evaluation, financial resources, contract approval and administration, and
member organization reporting requirements.[156] While virtually every
aspect of authority is held at the board level, it is important to recognize
the contributions of member organization representatives and other stakeholders as participants who make up the board. In 1998, Fire Sciences
Program Director Bob Clark conducted a collaborative stakeholder
meeting to generate program proposals centered on new ideas, better
practices, cooperative agreements with private industry, and innovation
and experimentation.[157] This meeting included representatives from the
six standing member organizations of the NIFC, five additional federal
agencies, the Western Governor's Association, and the National
Association of State Foresters. As a source of authority, this meeting
produced several initiatives that were then implemented by the program
governor's board for the entire network. At both the stakeholder and
governing board levels, authority is derived by collaboration, discussion,

---

[156]Ibid.

[157]http://www.nifc.gov/joint_fire_sci/JointFire.html#Introduction, 11 July 1998, 1.

and consensus with the understanding that the program manager has the final say.

Authority in Emergency Management

Much like the wildland fire network, the State of Delaware's emergency management has a source of authority from which its collective actions emerge. While both administrative and operational authority exist as different forms in this network, both forms coalesce at the Delaware Emergency Management Agency as the source of authority for emergency response. The administrative authority to form an emergency management network at the state level is held in the Office of the Governor. The Governor is provided with sweeping authority addressed in the State Constitution as: "supreme executive powers of the State."[158] In the area of emergency management, the Governor's authority is even broader than in his daily executive powers, and this authority includes: authorizing the coordination of emergency management activities, "conferring broad emergency powers on state agencies," and providing for mutual aid with other states and the federal government.[159]

In his authority to delegate emergency roles to state agencies, the Governor provides the vast majority of operational emergency decision making to DEMA as his executive agency for emergency management. In the Governor's role to "utilize all available resources of the state government as reasonably necessary to cope with...emergency or disaster,"[160] he

---

[158]*Delaware Constitution*, art. III, sec. 1.

[159]Delaware Code Annotated, title 20, sec. 3101.

[160]Ibid., title 20, sec. 3116.

delegates coordination responsibilities and the power to command state resources to DEMA.

During an officially declared state of emergency, the Governor's powers are virtually all-encompassing, as other branches of government's powers recede until the emergency has subsided. The Delaware Code Annotated provides the Governor with his sweeping authority, and it is also in the Code where the authority and responsibilities of his DEMA-operated Emergency Operations Center are defined.[161] DEMA is granted authority in the Code distinct from the Governor's. DEMA's distinct authority ensures the establishment and maintenance of an Emergency Operations Center and the Delaware Emergency Operations Plan.

During a state of emergency, the DEMA Director assumes operational control of the emergency and reports directly to the Governor for all matters related to its resolution.[162] The authoritative foundations provided in the Code and by the Governor create a network of emergency management with DEMA at the core. DEMA is legally centered as the hub of all of the federal, state, and local assets used to combat emergencies in the state.

Director Mulhern recognizes the vast powers granted to his position and agency during a state of emergency, and he is careful to plan for the use of such power in actual contingencies. His agency becomes the de facto head of state government during such traumatic times, as all state departments, personnel, funds, and resources fall under DEMA's jurisdiction for application in a crisis. Because of the tremendous authority provided in public law, DEMA, under Mulhern's direction, has successfully raised the awareness

---

[161] State of Delaware, Office of the Governor, *Delaware Emergency Operations Plan* (New Castle, Delaware: Delaware Emergency Management Agency, 1998), BP-10.

[162] Director Sean Mulhern, Delaware Emergency Management Agency, interview by author, 24 August 1998, New Castle, Delaware, notes with author.

level of the expectations, roles, and responsibilities that DEMA has of other state agencies in particular types of disasters so that the other agencies are not caught off-guard in a true crisis. The Delaware Emergency Operations Plan (DEOP) provides a listing of responsibilities, so no agency is caught unprepared to assist in the emergency, and periodic exercises are used to further reinforce and institutionalize the expectations over time.

The administrative authority granted DEMA as the central network hub around which all other organizations coordinate and participate for crisis resolution is truly a significant factor in explaining DEMA's collective framework. Unlike other models, where authority is shared, or organizations are empowered to act by different legal standards, this administrative model is unified in its grounding in public law. As a result, the ties between administrative authority (i.e.: what is legal and in accordance with the values of society) and operational authority (i.e.: what is accepted and followed in order to accomplish a task) are tightly bound in the emergency management network.

Aside from using its authority either granted directly by public law or delegated by the Governor, DEMA has further solidified its administrative authority by reaching emergency support agreements with the federal government, other states, businesses, and nonprofit organizations. These agreements solidify the emergency management network so that all organizations know what to expect from the network. The agreements also solidify DEMA as the center of the network through which all coordination and information pass.

One example of the emergency agreements brokered by DEMA is the Emergency Management Assistance Compact signed by twenty state emergency management agencies. This agreement carries out DEMA's role as Delaware's coordinator with other states for emergency support, both in Delaware during emergencies and outside the state, when other states request support. This legally binding compact guarantees that other states support DEMA as partners in the larger state emergency management network, and it also solidifies DEMA's role as the state agency best able to coordinate other Delaware assets for assistance in extra-state emergency affairs.

Operational Authority

The operational authority for actual emergency planning and operations in Delaware's emergency management network is focused in two different areas: incident management and resource allocation. Incident management authority resides at the local (i.e.: city or county) level unless a state of emergency is declared. Under local command of the local emergency management director, local police, fire, EMS, and other functions are organized according to local procedures to resolve the emergency. DEMA works proactively with the local emergency director to assist where necessary in local emergencies, but in order to be officially involved, local officials must ask for state assistance.[163]

The transfer of emergency management authority from the city and county level to the state level occurs quickly during a state of emergency. While the local emergency management directors are still responsible for their jurisdictions, they cease to function alone and coordinate their responses under the authority of DEMA. Such transfers of authority occur quickly. Typically, an incident deemed to be an emergency is brought to the attention of the DEMA director, who contacts the governor with the recommendation to declare a State of Emergency, and the governor subsequently makes the declaration. In such transfers, the official authority

---

[163]Director Sean Mulhern, Delaware Emergency Management Agency, interview by author, 24 August 1998, New Castle, Delaware, notes with author.

of local emergency directors is not lost per se, because the current relationship between the localities and DEMA is one in which the localities address their needs and then ask DEMA for further support or additional assets for employment against local needs as they see fit.

The issue of resourcing in emergency management is different from incident management. Whereas local control is an important concept in incident management, resourcing an emergency moves from local, to state, to regional, to federal levels as the emergency expands beyond each level's ability to respond. The authority of resource coordination and management for Delaware resides at DEMA. DEMA's interagency and intergovernmental agreements allow it to secure resources from other states, secure federal disaster assistance moneys and resources through FEMA and other government agencies, and solicit the assistance of private organizations.

The operational level of authority extends beyond DEMA's legislated authority to coordinate emergency responses for the state, because authority falls to the state as an operational level coordination mechanism between federal resources and local incident management as well. This phenomenon was proven in the early 1990's (before its reorganization) when DEMA repeatedly failed to coordinate crisis management well and did not function effectively as the state's emergency management operations center. DEMA's inability to coordinate led to a state sponsored commission's conclusion that emergency management had shifted from DEMA to "response coordination…centered primarily with personnel in the Department of Natural Resources and Environmental Control."[164] In many networks, when the hub ceases to perform its coordination and collaboration functions, the organizations fall back on individual organizational

---

[164]Fax between Delaware Secretary of Public Safety and Director of Emergency Management, 12 December 1995.

agendas and subsequently form independent ways to secure needs previously met in the network. However, in this case, the operational authority of the state government kept the organizations from falling back to individual agendas, which resulted in the transfer of de facto operational authority to another agency. In this arrangement, DEMA maintained its administrative authority, but the operational authority, that grew out of DEMA's ability to function as the hub of the network, was picked up by another agency that more effectively performed emergency management coordination in the environment.

DEMA's recent reorganization efforts resulted in the alignment of operational and administrative authority for network emergency management. Incident management is maintained at the local level and then transferred to DEMA during a state of emergency, but in the current relationship, DEMA uses the local authorities to manage their jurisdictions, while DEMA sends state and private support resources to meet both state and local needs.

The Double Edged Sword:
Delaware Emergency Management Agency Authority

Administrative
- Legislative (Delaware Code Annotated)
- Delegated (from the Governor)
- Articulated (intergovernmental reciprocation contracts)

Operational
- Information hub (i.e.: weather, safety, emergency, military, law enforcement, radiological, natural disaster reporting through the Emergency Operations Center)
- Coordination hub (federal, state agency, local liasoning)
- Communications hub (Bridgeline; computer network)

Authority in Public Safety

While wildland fire and emergency management authorities are clear-cut, public safety authority is distinguished by the types of crises it faces. At the administrative level, the Columbus city charter distributes powers to particular officeholders and commissions. At the operational level, the type of public safety situation determines which organization or group of organizations have the authority to resolve a crisis. Administrative authority is vested in the city through public law, but other forms of authority are clearly evident in crisis situations.

The administrative authority of the City of Columbus to maintain a public protective function for its citizens is grounded in the *Ohio Constitution*.[165] The *Charter of the City of Columbus* states:

> it (Columbus) shall have all powers that now are, or here-
> after may be granted to municipalities by the constitution
> or laws of Ohio; and all such powers whether expressed
> or implied, shall be exercised and enforced...[166]

Public safety is one of the powers granted by Ohio to its municipalities, thus ensuring Columbus's authority to provide such a service for its citizens. As one of the functions granted by the state to Columbus, public safety is established in the city's charter through a Department of Public Safety.[167] The offices which hold formal authority in the city's public safety system include the mayor, civil service commission, public safety director, police chief, and fire chief. The mayor and civil service commission fall outside of the Department of Public Safety, while the safety

---

[165] *Ohio Constitution*, art. XVIII, sec. 13.

[166] *The Charter of the City of Columbus, Ohio*, sec. 1, C–5.

[167] *The Charter of the City of Columbus, Ohio*, sec. 101, C–15.

director and police and fire chiefs fall within departmental jurisdiction. The city charter distributes the city's public safety authority among these different offices. This unique distribution of authority is essential in understanding the administrative dynamics of the public safety system.

The Mayor of Columbus is ultimately responsible to the people for their safety, and with such responsibility, he is empowered by the city charter to appoint a Director of Public Safety.[168] The powers of the mayor over the public safety director are vast; in fact, they are much greater than the powers held over other mayoral appointments.[169] The mayor retains special authority to remove the director without concurrence of the city council, so the public safety director can be said to serve "at the pleasure of the mayor."[170]

The Director of Public Safety is provided charter authority as the "executive head of the division of fire and police."[171] The director appoints the fire and police chiefs but is prevented from removing them by executive privilege under the terms of the charter.[172] The charter states:

> the director of safety shall have the exclusive right to suspend the chief of the division of police or the chief of the division of fire for incompetence, gross neglect of duty, gross immorality,…if either of such chiefs be so suspended the director of safety shall forthwith certify the fact, together with the cause of such suspension, to the civil service commission, who…shall proceed to

---

[168] *The Charter of the City of Columbus, Ohio*, sec. 60, C–11.

[169] The city charter (sec. 60, C–11) states that mayoral privilege of both appointment and removal of an officeholder is extended only to the public safety and public service directors. All other office removals must follow terms of the charter, which include concurrence of the city council.

[170] *The Charter of the City of Columbus, Ohio*, sec. 60, C–11.

[171] *The Charter of the City of Columbus, Ohio*, sec. 101, C–15.

[172] *The Charter of the City of Columbus, Ohio*, sec. 107, C–15.

hear such charges and render judgment thereon, which
judgment may be suspension, reduction in rank or
dismissal, and shall be final.[173]

The city charter clearly limits the authority of the public safety director to
suspension of division heads but not termination. The authority to termi-
nate rests with the civil service commission, a three-member body
appointed by the mayor (with concurrence of the city council).

The fire and police chiefs are granted authority under the charter to
perform as the leaders of their functions in the safety system. The charter
states that both the fire and police chiefs have control of all of their
stations and substations, as well as the power to transfer uniformed and
civilian personnel in their departments.[174] According to Columbus Public
Safety Director, Tom Rice, this charter provision entitles the fire and
police chiefs to manage all of the day-to-day recruitment, training, operations, and maintenance of their departments.[175]

The sharing of public safety authority between the mayor (who appoints
the public safety director and the civil service commission), public safety
director (who appoints the fire and police chiefs and can suspend them),
civil service commission (that makes final judgments on fire and police
chief rulings), and the fire and police chiefs (who have daily authority for
the operations of their departments), creates a shared powers dynamic that
reverberates through the department. The system of administrative
authority distribution impacts the effectiveness and efficiency of
Columbus's public safety operations.

---

[173] *The Charter of the City of Columbus, Ohio*, sec. 107, C–15.

[174] *The Charter of the City of Columbus, Ohio*, sec. 103–106, C–15.

[175] Columbus Director of Public Safety Tom Rice, interview by author, 20 July 1998, Columbus,
notes with author.

A recent example of the shared authority structure's impact on the public safety system was seen in the attempted removal of the police chief in 1997. After a mayoral investigation into the police department, Public Safety Director Tom Rice brought charges against Police Chief James Jackson on counts of favoritism, ordering the destruction of a police document, and three other charges that were eventually dismissed.[176] Rice believes that the five counts justified Jackson's removal from office, but the Columbus Civil Service Commission found they did not. The commission charged Jackson with only two counts and a five-day suspension.[177] The outcome was a high degree of tension between Rice and Jackson, as well as strained relations between the fire and police commissioner. A typical statement from Jackson regarding his April 1998 release of a report on training and accountability in the police department displays his shaky relationship with the public safety hierarchy: "they'll find some fault with it…I'm sure they will try to blame me for something."[178]

The differences among the leadership of the public safety department result from Columbus's shared authority system. The public safety director must work with a division head whom he believes should have been fired, and the division head must work under a man who does not have confidence in him to perform his duties. This uneasy relationship, when coupled with the fact that the fire and police chiefs do not interact with one another, leads to a department that comes together on very few initiatives at the strategic level.

Fortunately, the influence of leader relations does not always impact the ability of fire, police, and emergency medical service personnel to work together on the street to get the job done. Columbus Assistant Director

---

[176]Erin Marie Medick, "Rice Probes Allegation of Vengeance," *Columbus Dispatch*, 27 December 1997.

[177]Columbus Director of Public Safety Tom Rice, interview by author, 20 July 1998, Columbus, notes with author.

[178]Connie Higgins, "Police Chief Gives Report on Division," *Columbus Dispatch*, 16 April 1998.

for Fire Administration, David Sturtz, says that "street level guys work well together out of a need to make it all work…the breakdown occurs further up the line."[179] Sturtz's comment rings true in many crisis response communities, where figures in formal authority positions struggle in a system of shared powers, while their subordinates work and learn with each other to solve common problems. The problem in the Columbus case is that the environment no longer allows for leadership disputes to disrupt strategic alliances among organizations. Complex problems, such as narcotics trafficking, terrorism, immigration, and weapons of mass destruction are being solved, not by one organization, but by task forces and cooperative groups involving many organizations. The "street level guys" may work well together, but it is also time for them to be brought together to learn how to solve problems together by using the talents and skills of each organization before a crisis forces them to figure out solutions together only as a disaster unfolds.

Operational Authority

In most of the public safety emergencies in Columbus, the divisions of labor between fire, police, EMS, and other units (such as SWAT or bomb squad units) determines who will hold operational authority in a crisis. In the case of police or fire, responsibility for the crisis moves up the chain of command from an individual officer or fire station to a Battalion Chief as the demands of a crisis intensify. In traditional public safety, there is little dispute as to where, or in whom, authority rests to resolve an operational crisis. It is either a law enforcement, fire, medical, or special services

---

[179]Columbus Assistant Director of Public Safety for Fire Administration David Sturtz, interview by author, 21 July 1998, Columbus, notes with author.

problem, so it is the responsibility of that particular division or subdivision (in the case of special services) to resolve the crisis.

When functions overlap, operational authority gets trickier, but it is still relatively straightforward. As related by Assistant Director for Fire Administration, David Sturtz, fire hazards take precedence over law enforcement situations, so the fire commander's needs are met first at the scene.[180] Authority in the situation does not shift to the fire commander over the police commander in any way; instead, both commanders work together to resolve the crisis in each of their separate domains. Functional authority remains in place in these slightly more complicated situations, where two or more public safety threats exist within the same operation.

The situation where a shift in authority is occurring is in the planning, resolution, and recovery from complex contingency operations, such as those posed by terrorism, weapons of mass destruction, or chemical or biological threats. In line with other metropolitan areas, Columbus has considered adoption of the U.S. Army Domestic Preparedness Program's recommendation to use the Incident Command System (ICS) for these types of operations.[181] Under the ICS, authority for operational decision making is vested in one incident commander who is responsible for the overall crisis response.[182] Such a commander has fire, police, EMS, and all other available public safety functions under his/her command in order to most effectively and efficiently respond to the crisis.

Adoption of the ICS's shift of authority to an overarching collaborative model from one that was divided by functions is a monumental change for the public safety community. Police and fire commanders must

---

[180] Columbus Assistant Director of Public Safety for Fire Administration David Sturtz, interview by author, 21 July 1998, Columbus, notes with author.

[181] The ICS is the same concept used by the wildfire suppression network in Chapter 6.

[182] United States Army Chemical and Biological Defense Command, *NBC Domestic Preparedness Training Course Outlines: Incident Command* (Washington, D.C.: United States Army, 1998) 19.

subordinate themselves to the mission and objectives of a higher authority figure in the management of an emergency incident. This commander then has federal, state, and private access links for resources and personnel needed to supplement local emergency response capabilities. In such a unified system, public safety organizations can be used as a set among many organizations in a response. This model, if implemented on a regular basis, should have dramatic implications on the operational command and control of the public safety system in Columbus.

Defining a Principle of Interorganizational Crisis Response Authority

Administrative authority is the grounding of a network in its political, legal, and societal abilities to function. Fire, emergency management, and public safety networks are approved to perform their crisis response roles in the institutional structures that govern the particular environments in which they operate. The networks gain legitimacy from their administrative authority.

The operational authority of a network can reside in the same positions of the network as does its administrative authority, but often, operational authority is held in separate areas of a network. Operational authority comprises the decision-making responsibilities for the network in a crisis situation. It is concerned with who makes decisions, and how those decisions are made, at the point of a crisis. The fire and emergency management networks display a division of operational authority into two distinct levels: incident management and resource allocation. These networks perform effectively when incident-management authority is held at the lowest levels and ceded to higher levels as the crisis grows in severity and intensity. Resource-allocation authority is held at a level removed from incident-management in a way that allows for a broader, more comprehensive analysis of the situation. At a point of a crisis, the two types of authority act in concert with one another: the incident-management authority is focused on a specific situation at hand, while the resource-allocation authority considers the most effective application of resources based on the priorities of the network. The representativeness of member organizations in resource-allocation authority varies.

The wildland fire network's administrative authority is built on a solid foundation of public law, which has been solidified since 1953 to currently include over a dozen acts of federal legislation. These laws, together with interagency and intergovernmental agreements, establish the basis for National Interagency Fire Center (NIFC), National Interagency Coordination Center (NICC), Geographic Area Coordination Centers (GAACs), National Wildfire Coordinating Group (NWCG), and other collective bodies. Operational authority is handled differently for incident and resource management. Incident management is locally controlled in the Incident Command System (although the Unified Command System is still sometimes used), which places authority for a specific fire management situation in the hands of one Incident Commander. Once the fire grows beyond local abilities to control, authority shifts to higher levels of incident command. Resources management is performed in the Multi-Agency Coordination (MAC) Group concept, which emphasizes prioritization of resources to fire management based on agreed upon principles of the NIFC. MAC Groups exist at all levels of fire management, and their distribution of resources begins at the local level MACs and expands all the way to the national level.

The DEMA also possesses both administrative and operational authority, with its operational authority being distinguished between incident management and resource allocation. Administrative authority for Delaware's emergency management network is held in the Office of the Governor of Delaware and the DEMA. The governor is constitutionally empowered to hold supreme executive powers of the state, and the

Delaware Code Annotated authorizes special emergency powers. His delegation of emergency powers to DEMA provides justification for the publication of the Delaware Emergency Operations Plan (DEOP) that sets the network in motion.

Operational authority is held at the local level until emergencies expand beyond local means to control, at which time operational authority resides at the state level. Regardless of the size of the incident, the state's DEMA-run Emergency Operations Center maintains the authority to conduct the response for all jurisdictions under the state of Delaware. Resource allocation is also handled locally and then ceded to the state for broader coordination of state resources, but in extraordinary circumstances that grow beyond the state's capabilities, DEMA has two options. The first resourcing option is to use the authority vested in Delaware as a member of the *State Emergency Management Compact* between 20 state governments to reinforce Delaware state assets with those of compact member states. The second option available to Delaware (both options are usually used in conjunction with each other) is to appeal to FEMA Region III for regional resource and monetary support. In Delaware, the ultimate organization for both administrative and operational authority is currently DEMA, but historical situations have proven that the administrative/operational linkage can be broken.

The Columbus public safety system also possesses both administrative and operational authority, but administrative authority is fragmented and operational authority differs based on the type of problems faced in the environment. The administrative fragmentation displays problems in the Columbus system (not problems for the justification of the revised hypothesis).

Administrative authority for Columbus's public safety is passed from the State of Ohio Constitution to the cities, and it is provided to the mayor and public safety director in the city's charter. The administrative limitations placed on the system include separate lines of authority for the fire and police chiefs, which place them in a separate chain of authority for removal from office. This fragmentation of authority limits the unification of the public safety system and splits it into three camps: political leadership (i.e. mayor and public safety director); fire chief; and police chief. The effectiveness of the network is limited by its failure to align administrative authority into a common source, and this limitation is witnessed in the current disputes between the police chief and public safety director.

Operational authority is held at the incident level by the commander of the appropriate fire, police, or EMS function, depending on the type of safety incident. When functions overlap at the scene of the same crisis, overall jurisdiction over different functions is not established, but fire responses are recognized as the first priority in all complex situations. Currently, the different functions work among themselves in such complex situations, which describes a shared, collaborative model of operational authority that works well because of the clear differentiation of roles between law, fire, and EMS organizations. Operational authority is changing, however, as a result of complex contingency planning witnessed in WMD preparation. WMD planning has centered on the Incident Command System form of organization, which would place all functions under one line of operational authority in a crisis.

Upon evaluation of the crisis response literature and the use of wildland fire, emergency management, and public safety authorities, the following general principle applies to crisis response networks:

Principle Two: Authority

> *Crisis response networks possess administrative and operational authority. Administrative authority legitimizes a network through its provision of a societal, political, and legal foundation. Operational authority is the decision making responsibility at the point of crisis resolution.*

Operational authority is effective when it functions on two levels: incident management and resource allocation. Incident management concerns the authority to make decisions "on the ground" with the resources at hand. Resource allocation concerns the bigger picture: allocating limited resources based on a broad understanding of the situation and overall network priorities.

Chapter 5

Principle #3—Incentives

Interorganizational relationships must attract and remain attractive to organizational members of the relationship. Organizations find networks attractive that serve certain needs that the organization may not be able to meet outside of a cooperative arrangement. These needs act as incentives to join and stay in a network relationship. Types of incentives include resource (i.e.: money, space, equipment), information, or moral attractors. This chapter examines some of the reciprocity and exchange that occurs among network organizations.

As far back as 1977, organizational behavior expert Karen Cook identified interorganizational networks as interlocking systems of exchange relationships negotiated between members of different organizations to shape external environments.[183] She recognized that political negotiation and social definition determine the collective network, dictate its work rules, and form its options.[184] Collective bargaining, compromise, and political maneuver define the interorganizational working relationships, and, over time, they produce the norms, customs, and laws that form the rules of the collective entity. Such negotiations are driven by organizational self-interests served by resource attraction to gain access to new opportunities,

---

[183] Karen Cook, "Exchange and Power in Networks of Interorganizational Relations," in Kenneth Benson (ed.) *Organizational Analysis: Critique and Innovation* (Beverly Hills: Sage, 1977), 64–84.

[184] Cook, 64–84.

accelerate the pace of entry into new ventures, share research and development or other costs, or learn new capabilities.[185]

Chief among the incentives for participation are the allocation of resources in the network; it is how resources are allocated that contributes to the character of the network. Resource flows (i.e.: money, equipment, staff, customers or clients, and other goods or services) are the units of value that move among the network's organizations.[186] The three major dimensions used to measure resource flows are *direction, amount, and variability*. These dimensions determine the type and strength of the network. The number and types of resource flows, or even the guarantee that flow will occur in a disaster, provide the links that hold the interorganizational relationship together. A measurement of the resource links determines the relative strength of the network.[187]

Direction

As a function of network strength, direction can be quantitatively measured on a scale of interdependency variables.[188] Directional strength is correlated with dependence from three sources: parent resources, local resources, and host institutions.[189] Organizational "buy-in" to an interorganizational relationship can be determined through the amount of resources being delivered to and from an individual organizational relationship to the interorganizational whole. Key directional forms include: (1)*bottom-up—* resources flow from individual organizations into the center of a network

---

[185]Rajan Varadarajan and Margaret Cunningham, "Strategic Alliances: A Synthesis of Conceptual Foundations," *Journal of the Academy of Marketing Science* 23 (Fall 1995): 282–296.

[186]Van de Ven and Ferry, 302.

[187]Van de Ven and Ferry, 302.

[188]John Hannon, Ing-Chung Huang, and Bih-Shiaw Jaw, "International Human Resource Strategy and Its Determinants: The Case of Subsidiaries in Taiwan," *Journal of International Business Studies* 26 (Fall 1995): 531–554.

[189]Hannon et. al, 531–554.

through its "hub"; (2)*top-down*—resources flow from the network down to the organizations; (3)*horizontal*—resources flow across organizations between each other rather than working through a network center; and (4)*combinations* of the first three forms characterize complex network.

Amount

With respect to crisis response, it is important to recognize that centralized, top/down resource flow networks function quite differently than horizontal or individual resource distribution models. The centrality of a network is the degree to which resources are distributed to one or a few organizations in the network at the expense of the others.[190] A decentralized network displays a more equal distribution of resources. Both types of networks could have a coordination entity through which resources flow, but in situations where resources are unequally distributed, the few organizations where the predominance of resources and information flow hold the balance of network power.

Variability

Lacking continual exchanges of resource transactions, networks rarely survive. A response of "we coordinated but nothing happened" is common in the absence of resource exchange between organizations. Incentives to participation are lost when information and resource flows stop or resources fail to flow to priority areas in a crisis, and it is at such times that individual organizations begin to lose sight of the common purposes for which they joined the network.[191] The interchange of resources and information is a

---

[190]Van de Ven and Ferry, 302.

[191]Van de Ven and Ferry.

major consideration in the health of an interorganizational network. It is the foundation upon which the symbiotic gains from association are made.

Incentives: The Glue that Holds Interorganizational Relationships Together

Interorganizational relationships are measured by the attraction and exchange of resources among organizations of the network. Three major resource dimensions affect network strength—direction, amount, and variability.

- The *direction* of resources is concerned with how they are distributed: top-down, bottom-up, between organizations, or combinations of all three methods.
- The *amount* of resources transactions is concerned with the relative exchange of resources compared to the amount of resources used in single organizational missions and the relative distributions among all organizations of the network.
- The *variability* of resources is measures how often and with what frequency resources are exchanged.

When networks do in fact fall apart, their death is largely attributable to a shortage or stoppage of resource flows because the disruption cuts off one of the major incentives to stay united. After joining a network, many organizations find that the costs of association outweigh the benefits of membership.[192] This fact further buttresses the point that self-interest incentives must be met for all of the organizations in the relationship. The costs of membership are often high; therefore, the returns from participation must be high as well. Costs to network membership include: workforce representation at the network level, time and workforce allocations to design and monitor network operations, and functions or expertise that the organization agreed to supply

---

[192]Chris Baughn, John Stevens, Johannes Denekamp, and Richard Osborn, "Protecting Intellectual Capital in International Alliances," *Journal of World Business* 32 (Summer 1997): 103–117.

to the network. All of these resources are outlays to the organization that could have been used in singular organizational missions. The benefits to network participation must be perceived as at least equal to those resource outlays or the network ceases to operate as a going concern.

To determine how incentives influence the character of a particular network, the set of general questions from the box below is helpful:

Questioning Incentives:
to join/stay or leave a crisis response network?

1. What self-interests are served in your particular organization by being a part of the network?
2. Does your organization receive additional money, equipment, or physical assets for being a member?
3. Does your organization have a "moral obligation" or a "sense of duty" that might attract them to serve the network's cause?
4. Does your organization gain public relations, prestige, or political "points" for being involved in this network?
5. Does your organization get access to valuable information or information technologies by being a member of the network?
6. What are the costs of being a member of the network?
7. Does the organization ever wonder if the costs are high?
8. What would the organization do with the assets tied up in the network if it did not participate?
9. Is there a cost/benefit consideration involved?
10. Is the organization legally bound to the network? If so, is legal compliance the only reason why the organization participates in the network?

Incentives in Wildland Fire Suppression

Incentives play a fundamental role in attracting organizations to the wildfire suppression network; they are exhibited in many different types and forms. Some are collective in that they attract all member organizations.

Other incentives satisfy only one organization. Key incentives in the wildfire network include grouped resources that are available to member organizations, shared jurisdictions for economies of scale in fire suppression, special programs that provide such extras as funding and new technologies, and response reciprocity among organizations.

Grouped Resources

Just as it was founded on a need to share assets in order to gain benefits for mutual and self-interest goals (i.e.: the original air facility), the attractiveness of grouped resources continues to play a key role in holding the alliance together. According to the network's statement of organization and mission, "cooperation is the name of the game…with federal resource agencies sharing firefighting equipment, supplies…to make the wildland firefighting task more efficient and cost effective."[193] Cooperation, through its institutional history of pooling assets for collective use, has created a substantial incentive that joins and maintains membership in wildland fire suppression. The vast web of assets attainable through the network is simply too significant for any one of the single organizations to ignore.

Although primarily a coordinating body, the National Interagency Fire Center (NIFC) retains substantial national fire assets that it makes available to member agencies upon request in severe fire situations. Some of the network's national assets include: air tankers that drop fire retardant, "hot shot" and "smokejumper" crews that perform special missions, and radios.[194] Under the total mobility concept, grouped resources, as well as

---

[193]National Interagency Fire Center, *Joint Fire Sciences Program Online [Internet]*, National Interagency Fire Center Webmaster, WWW: http://www.nifc.gov/joint_fire_sci/ jfsprop.html#anchor1652465, June 1998.

[194]National Interagency Fire Center, *Lifeline to the Fireline* (Boise: National Interagency Fire Center, 1994), 1.

the authority to prioritize and distribute them, makes the NIFC one of the attractive features of network membership.

Helicopters represent an example of one highly sought after grouped resource accessed through network membership. They are available for geographical reassignment through the National Interagency Coordination Center (NICC).[195] As an integral, yet expensive fire suppression asset, helicopters are an attractive resource that help bind jurisdictions and agencies into the network. Typically, a request for helicopters through the NICC will be approved by one of two helicopter sponsor agencies that control most of the assets: the U.S. Department of Interior or the U.S. Forest Service.[196] Requests for service are filled on a contract basis, and funding for use of the helicopters, to include personnel and maintenance costs, is paid by the requesting agency.[197]

Shared Jurisdictions

The management of U.S. lands is divided among federal and state property. Federal property is divided among the NIFC's member organizations, and state property is managed independently by the state governments. *Fire management* of both federal and state lands, however, is often divided in jurisdictions that do not directly correspond to the geographical distribution of lands between federal agencies and state governments. The distribution of fire management responsibility across jurisdictions to achieve economies of scale creates a collective incentive for all organizations to work together in fire suppression.

---

[195]Tom Frey, U.S. Forest Service, interview by author, 14 July 1998, Washington, D.C., notes with author.

[196]National Interagency Fire Center, *Interagency Call-When-Needed Helicopters* (Boise: U.S. Government Printing Office, 1998), 4.

[197]Ibid., 4–a.

According to the Bureau of Land Management's Ed Lewis, fire management redundancies and inefficiencies would be created if all state and federal agencies managed their lands independently.[198] Sometimes, state and federal lands do not provide smooth boundaries for transitions of authority, where one jurisdiction can begin and end in the space of a few miles. Instead of establishing fire suppression control strictly in line with jurisdictional boundaries, many states are portioned into large segments of fire suppression jurisdictional authority between the federal agencies and state government represented in that state.

California is one example of apportionment between agencies and levels of government. California's lands are divided for fire management purposes between the U.S. Forest Service, Bureau of Land Management, and California Department of Forestry and Fire Protection. Since all three agencies have jurisdictional control over some of the state's lands, the agencies agree to divide the state into three roughly equal regions, with each agency responsible for one region. In each region, the controlling agency actually responds to areas under others' jurisdiction, but for fire management purposes, efficiencies are gained. As a result of a shared lands system, all three of California's responsible agencies have incentives to work together to help each other in wildland fire management.

In Alaska, an even more unique arrangement for fire management exists. Due to its overwhelming amount of federal lands, most of Alaska's fire suppression is provided by the Bureau of Land Management (BLM), regardless of jurisdiction. The BLM provides fire suppression services for the state in many areas (although Alaska now provides some services itself) and bills the Alaska for services rendered at the end of every fiscal year.

---

[198]Ibid., 4–b.

Special Programs

Another collective incentive that ties organizations to the network is the federal budget outlays distributed to specific network programs. These funds are only available to individual organizations based on work performed in special network program capacities. For example, the Joint Fire Sciences Program received a Fiscal Year 1998 budget of $4 million with future budgets to be determined by the program governor's board.[199] In order to receive funds from this program, member organizations submit proposals to the board for approval and then perform the activities in the proposal for the benefit of the network.

Federal budget outlays also provide a major incentive for individual organizations to fill specific niches with highly specialized programs used by the entire network. An example of such a program is the Drill Program managed by the Bureau of Land Management (BLM). The BLM retains a stock of drilling equipment that reseed burned lands below the surface of the earth so that rapid wildlife replenishment can take hold without wind erosion or animal disturbance. Instead of stocking every federal and state agency with such a specialized program, the BLM has been awarded the drill reseeding mission for all jurisdictions. BLM receives operations and maintenance funding for the program from the federal government, and it also collects reimbursements from other organizations that use the seeding services.

---

[199]Ed Lewis, Bureau of Land Management, interview by author, 5 October 1998, Boise, Idaho, notes with author.

Response Reciprocation

The different budgetary pipelines create interesting issues in the wildland fire management community. Budget cutbacks have forced many agencies to understaff or underequip their firefighting forces, and, as a result, these agencies are not as fully equipped to fight fires within their jurisdictions as they previously were.[200] Cutbacks in some agency and state budgets have increasingly led local authorities to request more assistance at regional and national levels. The result of financial limitations harkens the network back to its original incentive to pool assets and lend assistance for fire protection under the Reciprocal Fire Protection Act of 1955 (U.S.C. 1856a).

A related fallout from smaller budgets has been the subsequent rise in mobility of available resources and people to firefights around the country. While shrinking budgets have drained personnel and resources, they have also strengthened the reciprocation bonds between agencies and jurisdictions to meet and work across jurisdictions. Unfortunately, the strain of increased personnel and resource usage is severe, and it has led to personnel and equipment burnout and a decline in the overall capacity of the wildfire management network. Budget cutbacks have contributed to a closer knit network, but one that is less capable overall than it was in the past.

The close working relations between the wildland fire agencies extend beyond the fact that they are forced to work together due to constrained budgets. Reciprocation is at the heart of the network, and it is witnessed in the NIFC's cost sharing concept described as "You Order, You Pay."[201] In other words, regardless of jurisdiction, member organizations will support fire suppression efforts for each other *and pay* their own ways for the

---

[200]National Interagency Fire Center, *Joint Fire Sciences Program Online [Internet]*, National Interagency Fire Center Webmaster, WWW: http://www.nifc.gov/joint_fire_sci/ JointFire.html#Introduction, June 1998.

[201]Ibid.

support. Nonmember organizational costs, such as state governments, the military, or the American Red Cross are captured separately and reimbursed based on whose land was supported, but all member organizations are absorbed by the sending, not the receiving organization. Such a system is based on reciprocity and results in automatic responses uninhibited by concerns of payments or asset exchanges in times of crisis.

Incentives also exist among the NIFC and its external partners. At the international level, Canada and the United States share reciprocation to support each other in border fires. The U.S.-Mexico fire suppression relationship lacks secure reciprocation incentives since the Mexican government's vastly inferior fire management capabilities offer little in terms of fire support on U.S. soil. The incentives that are bringing the U.S. and Mexico close to an interstate agreement for fire suppression are Mexican interest in receiving U.S. fire support and U.S. interest in reducing smoke hazards in U.S. border states from Mexican wildfires. The proposed fire suppression policy between the two nations reflects the different incentives that are drawing them together. The proposal states that the U.S. will pay for its involvement in those Mexican fires that pose a threat to U.S. border states, while Mexico will pay for U.S. involvement in Mexican fires that pose no threat to the U.S.[202] As is clear in the proposed agreement, reciprocation is an ineffective incentive in this arrangement, because Mexico, unlike Canada, has little to offer the U.S. in return for its fire support services. The different incentives that govern the different international fire management agreements support the fact that incentives attract organizations to the NIFC, but they do not have to be the same incentives that join different parts of the network.

---

[202]National Wildfire Coordinating Group, *Interagency Incident Business Management Handbook: NWCG Handbook 2* (Boise: Incident Business Practices Working Team, 1996).

Incentives in Emergency Management

A variety of incentives are used in the Delaware emergency management network to attract organizations to participate. The incentives drawing organizations to the network are varied, and that variety produces the many different forms of relationships between the network and its member organizations. Six types of organizational relationships can be seen in the network, and each type has its own set of incentives. The different relationships are: interstate alliances; federal organizations; local government emergency management offices; the National Guard; other state government agencies; and private organizations such as businesses and nonprofit organizations. A description of each organizational relationship and its accompanying incentives describes the attraction of organizations to Delaware's emergency management network.

Interstate Alliances

The basic incentive that attracts state emergency management agencies to the state emergency management network is reciprocation. As a member of the state emergency management network, Delaware finds it beneficial to participate in other states' emergency networks. Director Mulhern says that Delaware's small size and limited resources leave it particularly vulnerable to a large-scale catastrophe.[203] As a result, he finds it beneficial for Delaware to participate in mutual aid agreements with other states in order to provide security for Delaware in times of serious duress. Providing a little support for another state when DEMA can spare the personnel or resources is reciprocated with support during a Delaware crisis.

---

[203]Director Sean Mulhern, Delaware Emergency Management Agency, interview by author, 24 August 1998, New Castle, Delaware, notes with author.

Two examples of Delaware's commitment to interstate assistance displays mutual aid in action. During an outbreak of wildland fires throughout the south in the summer of 1998, Director Mulhern sent his deputy director to assist the state of Florida for 14 days. With a background in firefighting, the deputy director was able to assist the fire management efforts from the wildfire operations center. In the same summer stretch, Texas was burdened with extreme drought conditions, and Delaware was prepared to send two emergency management experts until rainfall reduced the crisis. These two examples are among the many external contingencies that Delaware supports. Director Mulhern recognizes that DEMA sends more assistance abroad than it ever receives in return, but he believes that the small expenditure of resources in such cases is low in comparison with what would be needed if Delaware ever had to handle a serious emergency on its own. Mulhern views helping other states as a goodwill effort, but he also sees such action as a way to build up credit for a worst case scenario in tiny Delaware.

DEMA's interest in getting a guarantee of future support by providing other states with support when needed is felt by other states as well. The dependence of each state on the others is institutionalized in the *Emergency Management Assistance Compact*.[204] Twenty states reached an agreement that they will provide assistance to each other, just like Delaware does on a continuos basis, in exchange for similar guarantees from fellow member states. The compact, which has risen from inauspicious beginnings in 1949, now provides joint training and exercises, planning and mitigation support, and legal agreements to avoid lawsuits during joint responses.

---

[204]D. P. Munro, *The Emergency Management Assistance Compact Guidebook and Standard Operations Procedures* (Washington, D.C.: Southern Governors Association, 1997), B–2.

DEMA and other emergency management agencies have built outside states into their networks through the reciprocity incentive.

Businesses

Businesses are attracted to Delaware's emergency management network in a number of different ways: (1)traditional fee-for-service arrangements; (2)goodwill support (due in part to the large number of company headquarters in the state of Delaware); and (3)public/private partnerships that benefit both businesses and government agencies.

Traditional fee-for-service arrangements between DEMA and businesses are the most prevalent way that businesses enter and stay in the Delaware emergency management network. One example of this type of relationship is in DEMA's testing and evaluation of environmental threats, which is a capability that the government either cannot or does not want to provide on its own. DEMA used private contractors to perform the state's terrorism risk analysis for the entire state. The state's contractor, *Emergency Response Institute*, solicited citizens, government employees, and public and private leaders for its survey of all public and private facility targets of terrorism.

Another type of fee-for-service arrangement occurs during actual emergencies. Such an arrangement was seen in the February 1998 Noreaster that struck Delaware. The state's capacity to remove water from heavily flooded areas was overwhelmed during the crisis, so DEMA contracted with Godwin Pumps of America to perform much of the pumping of flooded areas during the crisis. Godwin provided six pumps over a week-long period.[205] Businesses such as Godwin are attracted to the emergency

---

[205]Rental contract between DEMA and Godwin Pumps of America, Inc., 19 February 1998.

management network by the financial opportunities that the network creates during times of crisis. These businesses also recognize that DEMA has virtually unlimited spending authority during a State of Emergency.

Goodwill is the second form of business incentives. Several businesses offer services to Delaware during emergencies as gestures to build or maintain roles as "corporate citizens" in the community. One corporation that performs such a role is the ACME food company that provides disaster food banks for citizen use during states of emergency.[206] These supplements keep citizens from starving when roads or vehicles are inoperable due to inclement weather conditions. ACME also keeps a fleet of disaster vehicles on tap to make deliveries in conditions that shut down normal delivery trucks. Many other companies offer financial, personnel, or resource gestures of goodwill during Delaware's crises.

The third form of business attraction is formed in pubic/private partnerships that provide win/win opportunities for Delaware and industry. An example of the partnership arrangement is seen in the agreement between FEMA, DEMA, and Delaware insurance providers. The agreement eliminates multiple insurance contacts between providers, government, and the affected citizens of an emergency. Prior to the agreement, citizens with insurance claims had to answer the same question three times at significant cost to both the insurance agency and state and federal government. The new agreement provides one agent per citizen on behalf of federal and state governments and the insurance industry. FEMA and DEMA pay for insurance information in exchange for access, as well as for the fact that government insurance claims agents are freed for other duties. In such a partnership, both business

---

[206]Director Sean Mulhern, Delaware Emergency Management Agency, interview by author, 24 August 1998, New Castle, Delaware, notes with author.

and government prosper from the efficiencies of working together in the emergency management network.

Federal Agencies

While 26 federal departments and agencies have roles in emergency management, FEMA is the agency most directly linked to the state emergency management network. As the federal agency charged with disaster mitigation, preparation, response, and recovery, FEMA is ultimately accountable for disaster management in the United States. While DEMA and other state emergency management agencies are quick to mention state responsibility for their own crises, FEMA knows its responsibility to assist the states in any way that it can. According to Delaware's FEMA liaison officer, Nelson Wiles, the federal role in emergency management was driven home in the public's response to Hurricane Andrew in 1992. Throughout Hurricane Andrew, FEMA patiently waited for the State of Florida to request federal assistance, but Florida never did ask for assistance and was wrecked by the hurricane. The public was incensed over the incident, but the brunt of public aggression was directed not at Florida for failing to ask but at FEMA for failing to act.[207]

FEMA Director James Lee Witt instituted a new philosophy. He says, "we're much more proactive…instead of waiting on the hurricane…we get there, pre-position everybody."[208] Witt's philosophy is reiterated at the field level by agents like Wiles, who says that although states' desires during a crisis are important, FEMA also has a very real public-image incentive to participate in the resolution of state crises. If necessary, Wiles says that FEMA is prepared to work alone if states ignore the necessity of federal participation during intense disasters. FEMA has a strong political

---

[207]State Liaison Officer, Nelson Wiles, Federal Emergency Management Agency, interview by author, 26 August 1998, New Castle, Delaware, notes with author.

[208]Edward Walsh, "It Took a County Judge to Bail Out FEMA: James Lee Witt's Arkansas Experience Reshaped Agency and Its Approach to Disaster," *The Washington Post*, 9 August 1998, A–19.

incentive to be involved in disaster management that is linked to the very survival of the agency.

Local Governments

The four local governments with emergency management officers (i.e.: three counties and one city) in Delaware have substantial incentives to participate in Delaware's state emergency management network. They receive resources, personnel, and money from DEMA for emergency mitigation, planning, operations, and recovery. The local governments' emergency management sections can request a state liaison from DEMA to facilitate resource and information requests during a crisis. During Hurricane Bonnie, both Sussex and Kent Counties received such assistance. The liaisons helped secure thousands of sandbags from the Delaware National Guard and the Delaware Water Conservation and Treatment Plant during the hurricane. State resources such as these keep local governments in contact with the network. The government's emergency operations center at DEMA is looked up to by local governments as the appropriate level from which additional resources can be obtained once local resources are exhausted.

Other Delaware Government Agencies

The other Delaware state government agencies have either legal or legislated responsibilities to support DEMA when a state of emergency is declared. Director Mulhern becomes the coordinator of all state employees, facilities, and resources during an emergency, so the incentive in such situations is to comply with state law in support of state emergency management.[209] The DEOP describes the expectations

---

[209]The constitutional and Delaware Code Annotated authority of the Governor and the DEMA Director over the state agencies was detailed in this chapter's discussion on authority.

of each state agency in different types of states of emergency, and the agencies have an opportunity to address their capabilities before it is signed.

Although it can be considered a quasi-state agency, the Delaware National Guard's incentives to join the emergency management network are different from those of other state agencies. The Guard serves a dual mission to the federal and state governments, with Delaware gaining control over the organization only during a declared state of emergency. As a result of this peculiar arrangement, decisions on the Guard's support of emergency management are handled in a unique manner. For effective use, the Guard must be incorporated not only in declared emergencies but also in planning and training for such emergencies.

Agreements to support emergency management are made between the Delaware National Guard Adjutant General and state government leaders, such as the DEMA Director or the Director of Public Safety.[210] In the Delaware government, the Adjutant General is a cabinet member, which provides him a position not afforded many other state adjutants general. As a result of this position, the roles of the Guard in the emergency management network are determined through political agreements among the agency heads. The Guard's incentives can be interpreted and set through the motives of its leader.

Other factors also serve as incentives for the Guard. The Guard is interested in serving state missions where it can, because the state pays for the salaries and resources used in such training or missions. Also, the Guard enjoys its status as a respected community member that is available to serve the state during emergencies. Like other state agencies, the Guard also has a legislated

---

[210]Major Dallas Wingate, Delaware National Guard, interview by author, 26 August 1998, New Castle, Delaware, notes with author.

incentive to comply with the law in supporting the Governor's designated coordination center (i.e.: DEMA) during a State of Emergency.

Incentives in Public Safety

The Greater Columbus public safety system is much larger than its jurisdictional metropolitan lines on a state map. As a safety network, it includes, not only its internal divisions, but also an expanded association of neighboring towns, counties, villages, and cities.[211] These associations are critical to the safety of Columbus and its surrounding communities because of the rapid rates of growth in the area. The city's terrain is open and flat, which causes growth problems unknown to Ohio's other cities, such as land and water blocked Cincinnati and Cleveland. In recent years, Columbus has expanded through geographical, jut-like "fingers" that have usurped former township and village areas through annexation. The unprecedented and uneven growth has forced Columbus safety officials to work closely with neighboring areas to avoid jurisdictional disputes.

Columbus's growth led the city's mayor, Gregory Lashutka, to pursue an incentive-based "buy-in" strategy with neighboring towns, villages, and counties. One shining example of his strategy is witnessed in the water and sewage services. Reversing traditionally heavy-handed, "carrot and stick" approaches in municipal services, Columbus no longer requires smaller jurisdictions to surrender their sovereignty to become part of the city in order to receive city water and sewage services.[212] Being too small to build water and sewage treatment facilities, these smaller jurisdictions

---

[211]Columbus Director of Public Safety Tom Rice, interview by author, 20 July 1998, Columbus, notes with author.

[212]Columbus Director of Public Safety Tom Rice, interview by author, 20 July 1998, Columbus, notes with author.

were previously forced into annexation in return for services. Lashutka's strategy has encouraged these jurisdictions to buy water and sewage services from Columbus, and thus retain independence while in receipt of vital services. Instead of having additional citizens requiring public services who do not really want to be part of his city, the mayor now has a contented set of neighboring jurisdictions who have incentives to see the city prosper.

The initial outreach services created opportunities for the construction of many other network-based alliances, several of which involve regional approaches to public safety. Two major changes in the delivery of public safety have affected the relations of the region, and both have led to increased effectiveness and efficiency for the citizens.

Technological Incentives

The first type of changes to the public service structure have been driven by technological innovations. The recently installed 800MHz voice (with limited data) dispatching system has created a huge incentive towards a network alliance for public safety. The city and its surrounding Franklin County teamed together to share the new dispatch system, and this alliance has grown to many other smaller partners. Mayor Lashutka, with Director Rice as his point man, had to be very careful to create the proper incentives for neighboring communities to join in the new dispatch system.

According to Rice, sovereignty became a big issue in getting participation from smaller areas. He said that "Columbus was very careful…groups of suburbs could have their own dispatch services and still be on the system."[213]

---

[213]Ibid.

Recognizing that Columbus would have to fund most of the system's installation costs, Mayor Lashutka saw a bigger network picture forming and permitted the city to take the short term financial hit.

The 800MHz system is an impressive incentive, if viewed from the vantage point of a small surrounding town or village. A 28 channel communications system, the 800MHz system efficiently places 17 emergency channels on the Columbus side of the system and 9 non-emergency service channels on the Franklin County side. Smaller jurisdictions access all 28 channels and communicate with regional organizations linked to the network. These jurisdictions and other connected regional organizations might never have afforded the extensive coverage, collaboration, and interorganizational linkages on their own.

The communications system is also pulling functions of public safety together at the same time that it is pulling regions together. Fire, police, EMS, and special services (such as hazardous materials units) can speak with each other on the network; and each of these functions must use similar communications while on the network, so cultural communications differences between, say fire and police, are being broken down due to the need to speak with one another through the communications system. Federal, state, and interstate links are established as well, so the resources available to Columbus public safety have grown exponentially as a result of the investment in cutting-edge technology.

Service Incentives

Columbus offers a number of services to other jurisdictions in its regional public safety network. These services act as attractive incentives for small towns and villages to associate with the city in a cooperative safety alliance. The services also aid Columbus because spin-offs from alliances that began through incentivized services have led to other forms of reciprocity in the relationship.

One example of the network's service structure is seen in the agreement between Columbus and a neighboring jurisdiction, Upper Arlington. Columbus provides Upper Arlington (and many other surrounding jurisdictions) with a critical public safety function: bomb-squad services. As a result of the bomb-squad agreement, Columbus Fire Division personnel must respond across the entire city of Upper Arlington for any bomb related crises. Upper Arlington, on the other hand, reciprocates for Columbus by participating in the region's "automatic response" program. This program is an agreement between fire departments, that, regardless of jurisdiction, the closest fire engine to the scene of an emergency will respond. In the course of a year, Upper Arlington assists Columbus many more times than vice versa, but, in return, Upper Arlington is freed of the fixed costs associated with the recruitment, training, and equipment of a bomb squad. As the lead actor in the Central Ohio region, Columbus has used attractive services to draw its fellow jurisdictions into a regional public safety network.

Types of Network Incentives
- Grouped resources
- Special programs available only through the network
- Response reciprocation
- Profit
- Goodwill
- Economies of scale through partnerships
- Access to technologies
- Access to pooled information
- Public mandate; public law
- Public opinion
- Services exchange; "tit-for-tat"

Summarizing Incentives as an Interorganizational Crisis Response Principle

Wildland fire, emergency management, and public safety exhibit incentive structures for both collective and individual organizational purposes. The wildfire network's two biggest attractors are resources and reciprocity. Resources provide member organizations opportunities inaccessible outside of the network. Network resources also provide a supply system based on common equipment for all organizations which insures a steady stock of resources as well as the removal of significant supply cache management demands from member organizations. Reciprocity is evident throughout the network as member organizations assist other members which guarantees mutual support for all wildland fire jurisdictions.

In emergency management at least seven different types of incentives attract organizations. Legal incentives to comply with state law attract Delaware's state agencies to participate. Response reciprocation attracts over 20 states to support their fellow state emergency management agencies. Businesses are attracted by money, goodwill, and win/win partnerships. Federal agencies, such as FEMA, have political incentives and responsibilities to participate. Finally, access to information serves as one of many incentives for local governments to participate in the Delaware emergency management network.

Three incentives dominate pubic safety. The first is an attraction to power that successful metropolitan centers such as Columbus use with smaller surrounding jurisdictions. Columbus's attraction is a result of leadership through a conscious "buy-in" strategy designed to bring an entire region into a common public safety network in areas such as dispatch communications and WMD training and development. Peripheral jurisdictions are attracted to the central power because of the number of programs and technologies that Columbus funds on behalf of all regional members.

The second incentive is reciprocation. This incentive is observed in public safety services exchange, such as in the provision of bomb squad services by Columbus for its neighboring jurisdictions. The neighbors, in return, provide automatic response support in fire services in Columbus and vice versa. There are many different forms of reciprocation in public safety arrangements.

The third incentive is access to information. Columbus's 800Mhz dispatch system allows for regional peers to expand their communications systems. All organizations also receive access to channels and databases that previously would have been out of the reach of their individual systems. Access to information through the enhanced capabilities of technology, is a critical incentive driving the consolidation of public safety systems around the country.

It is clearly evident that interorganizational incentives are critical to the formation and survival of crisis response networks. Through the incentives structure, each member organization meets self-interest needs. The structure and delivery of incentives vary, and as a result, they contribute to the unique character of each unique network. Such needs range from moral (i.e.: goodwill) to material (i.e.: money). While the incentives vary, the principle of interorganizational incentives is constant. As a result, the following principle can be said to apply to interorganizational crisis response networks:

Principle Three: Incentives

Incentives attract member organizations to participate in a network, and they contribute to the strength, character, and structure of the network. These incentives are varied in type, and organizations in the same network may be attracted to different types of incentives. Incentives also vary in flow based on the direction, amount, and variability of resource distribution among a network's organizations.

Chapter 6

Principle #4—Culture

"If planning is normalized, i.e., made a part of daily life and organizational activity, then an emergency is not a disjointed, abrupt departure from everyday life."[214]

—Staff Report to
the President's Commission
on the Accident at Three Mile Island

As previously stated, interorganizational relationships take on a unique identity separate from the identities of other networks or individual organizations.[215] This network identity is a result of the unique demands of the crisis to which two or more organizations perceive it necessary to prepare and respond together. With a distinct identity, interorganizational relationships possess distinct cultures, that in large part, form the character and "feel" of the crisis response.

Renowned MIT psychologist Edgar Schein's definition of organizational culture describes precisely why an interorganizational relationship possesses a distinct identity:

---

[214]Staff Report to the President's Commission on the Accident at Three Mile Island, "Report of the Emergency Preparedness and Response Task Force," 27, in Chris Seiple, "Crisis Management Theory and the Lessons of Three Mile Island," 10 December 1999.

[215]Van de Ven and Ferry, 299.

the pattern of basic assumptions that a given group has invented, discovered, or developed in learning to cope with its problems of external adaptation and internal integration, and that have worked well enough to be considered valid, and therefore, to be taught to new members as the correct way to perceive, think, and feel in relation to those problems.[216]

Coping with external adaptation, internal integration, and teaching new members how to relate to the crises they face are exactly why interorganizational networks develop. When external factors cannot be solved by one organization, internal integration must occur among the organizations in order to work together for crisis resolution.

Three levels of culture form the unique identity of an organization. They are: *visible* (e.g.: symbols, art, manner of dress, audible behavior patterns, public documents, employee orientation materials, identifiable behavior patterns); *values* (i.e.: espoused and accepted reasons for behavior; "core values" statements); and basic *assumptions* (i.e.: unconscious assumptions that determine how group members perceive, think, and feel; learned responses; taken for granted).[217]

While the first cultural level, the visible, is readily apparent because it is "visible," values and basic assumptions are more difficult to understand. To see how the values of a network contribute to its success, it is essential to define the various types of values that exist. Organizational values typically fall into five categories: (1)mastery (e.g.: task, power); (2)self-development (e.g.: growth, challenge, creativity); (3)relationship (e.g.: working with others,

---

[216]Edgar H. Schein, "Coming to a New Awareness of Organizational Culture," in *The Great Writings in Management and Organizational Behavior* (New York: McGregor-Hill, 1987), 445.

[217]Schein, 445. Schein uses basic assumptions as they apply at the singular organization level; in this study, they are applied at the crisis response network level.

sharing experience); (4)continuity (e.g.: tradition, status quo, control, predictability); and (5)people (e.g.: how others should be treated).[218]

If left unimpeded, these values can compete and conflict with one another, producing harmful repercussions that would hinder the ability to resolve crises. Healthy organizational cultures exhibit alignment of values with mission and personal needs to ensure that a balance is maintained. The values most prevalent in 200 leading organizations are: integrity, competence, teamwork, communication, autonomy, creativity, and personal growth.[219] These values transcend the crisis response community to include many different types of organizations. They must be taught, reinforced, and rewarded/punished to ensure compliance. The role of the network is to make sure that such values are instilled as thoroughly as possible in organizational recruitment and network training, education, simulations, and exercises. The network's roles in building culture are critical because member organizations that resolve crises pledge their employees' lives in the process. Between and among the network's organizations, agreement on fundamental values that produce complete commitment to the cause must be present in order for the network to function effectively.

The deepest level, the basic assumptions, are fundamental, deeply ingrained, and they drive the organizational entity. Basic assumptions define the following organizing tenets:

---

[218]Dennis Jaffe and Cynthia Scott, "How to Link Personal Values with Team Values," *Training and Development* 52 (March 1998): 26.

[219]Jaffe and Scott, 26.

(1) *how members view the relationship of the network in its envi-ronment* (e.g.: is it one of dominance, submission, niche);

(2) *how reality and trust are determined* (e.g.: what is real and what is not; what is fact; property as communal or individual; time as linear or cyclical);

(3) *how human nature is viewed in the network* (e.g.: attributes; good and evil; Theory X or Theory Y);

(4) *how human beings should act* (e.g.: active, passive, self-developmental, fatalistic); and

(5) *how human beings relate to each other in the network* (e.g.: cooperation, competition, individualistic, group collabo-rative, communal, lineal authority, law, charisma). [220]

When the unique demands of a crisis response network are considered, its underlying assumptions should look quite different from a typical interor-ganizational, or "macro," culture that exist in business or management. Crisis usually means "life and death," so Schein's five questions surrounding the network's most basic assumptions about itself will tell quite a bit about how effective the network really is.

The visible, values, and basic assumption aspects of interorganizational culture are formed and sustained through mediums such as language, devotion, and education and training. The characteristics define how and what crisis response organizations communicate to each other, how committed the organizations are to network purposes, and how people are indoctrinated into the crisis response community.

---

[220]Schein, 445.

Language

Network language, or how people speak with one another, is an interorganizational culture factor that leads to increased collaboration for decision making, common understandings of complex operations, and definitions for the unique work performed by the network as it compares to other networks or organizations. Regardless of the specific community being discussed, crisis response networks that work well together speak the same special language together.

For example, a study of interorganizational emergency service delivery systems found interorganizational dialogue to be a key factor in service delivery improvement.[221] The service delivery network was established in response to consumer complaints of poor responses to emergency needs, and as a result, the experimentation with interorganizational dialogue was uncovered. The delivery system network identified people, groups, and agencies relevant to the problem; it established a board to vet proposals, ideas, and solutions, and it implemented the results of the findings. Dialogue was concluded as (1)a metaphor for organization, (2)a clinical, collaborative method of inquiry for interorganizational fields, (3)a change agent for interorganizational relations, and (4)a liberating process for human systems.[222]

The dialogue observed in the example above and in countless other networks is a specific type of language tailored to the nature of the problems solved. Sometimes called crisis *genre*, this dialogue organizes communications structures that shape, and are shaped by, emergency actions. Effective interorganizational workers develop a rich, varied array

---

[221] Mary Ann Hazen, "A Radical Humanist Perspective of Interorganizational Relations," *Human Relations* 47, no. 4 (April 1994): 393–415.

[222] Ibid.

of unique communicative genre in response to community norms, specific projects, and pressures of crises.[223]

One form of crisis genre is the acronym. Acronyms distinguish one interorganizational relationship from another and assist people from different organizations to work together at the point of a crisis. In crisis management cultures, such as in police and fire departments, this popular form of communication breaks down complex ideas into easily transmittable jargon for recall and action in tense situations. The level of understanding one has of an acronym or sets of acronyms in an organization or network is a good indicator of the depth of knowledge an employee has of his or her environment.

Acronyms relate to key elements of content, accomplish end-state objectives (e.g.: familiarization of important concepts), and are tailored to fit the needs of the response population.[224] They are used as props, metaphors, and pictures that convey information in ways that enhance attention and retention of knowledge specific to the demands of the situation.[225] If acronyms in an organization or network are used correctly, then they should provide a useful reference guide to understanding what is important, what is valued, and what is remembered as critical in a particular organizational or interorganizational culture.

Devotion

Devotion is an interorganizational component pervasive in crisis response communities. It is composed of attributes such as trust, ethos, civicism, esprit, and a sense of duty. Such attributes provide a moral imperative

---

[223]Wanda Orlikowski and JoAnne Yates, "Genre Repertoire: The Structuring of Communicative Practices in Organizations," *Administrative Science Quarterly* 39, no. 4 (1994): 541–574.

[224]Diane Ullius, "Art: Acronyms Reinforce Training," *Training and Development* 51, no. 2 (February 1997): 9.

[225]Ullius, 9.

throughout an organization or network that results in the ability to overcome what Clausewitz called the "confounding elements of friction," to resolve crises. At the network level, since organizations must work inside, alongside, and for other organizations to accomplish common purposes, a unique form of network esprit should emerge to allow for individual organizational mission accomplishment within the confines of a particular expertise, while also enabling organizations to count on each other in situations when their roles come together at the point of crisis resolution.

One example of the many ways that individual crisis response organizations develop and instill this unique devotion to duty is seen in the United States Marine Corps, which is a premier expeditionary crisis response force. The Marine Corps lives by principles of leadership which embody the concepts central to being a Marine: seeking self improvement, setting an example for other Marines to follow regardless of rank, developing a confident presence in the face of adversity, living with determination and tenacity, articulating the spoken and written word in a professional manner, encouraging and teaching others to achieve their highest potential, and maintaining physical fitness.[226] These concepts have been hallmarked in the Marine Corps throughout its historical and contemporary affairs.

As in most cultures, the Marine Corps's key cultural embodiments have been symbolically cemented and affirmed through routine, as can be seen in Marine names and monikers. Daily traded nicknames of Marines include terms such as "Devil Dogs," which was coined by the Germans in World War I for the Marines' tenacity in battle; "Band of Brothers" which exemplifies the familial traits of the Corps (that is characterized by friendships, mentorships, discipline for misconduct, and a deep sense

---

[226]Kenneth Estes, *The Marine Officer's Guide* (Annapolis: Naval Institute Press, 1985), 294.

of responsibility for each other); and the Corps' motto, "Semper Fidelis," which translates from Latin to "always faithful" and attests to the strong Marine commitment to the organization, the Naval service, and the country. With these cultural symbols, it is not surprising that this crisis response organization has answered the nation's call to crises with resounding successes. The Corps preaches, practices, and disciplines against its principles.

The Marine Corps's core values of honor, courage, and commitment reinforce the cultural devotion to its crisis response cause. The Corps's 31st Commandant, General Charles Krulak, opened his four year reign in 1995 with a statement to Marines about their core values:

> There is no room for situational ethics or situational morality; those found wanting will be held account-able...I expect Marines to epitomize that which is good about our nation and to personify the ideals upon which it was founded. I do not intend for honor, courage, and commitment to be just words; I expect them to frame the way we live and act as Marines.[227]

In this statement, General Krulak reinforced a notion that has guided the organization throughout its history: Marines operate in a world of ethical black and white, right and wrong, because in the crises Marines are expected to quell, they have no time to ponder whether the guy in the next foxhole will do his job or save his buddy. They have to instinctively know heroism to be true, and this deeply intuitive cultural instinct starts

---

[227]U.S. Marine Corps, Office of the Commandant of the Marine Corps, *Commandant's Planning Guidance* (Washington, D.C.: U.S. Marine Corps, 1995).

with the symbolic messages and is reinforced with the core values that help to shape men and women as the nation's crisis resolvers.

While an historical institution such as the Marine Corps relies on its heritage, strong education and training, and deeply reinforced values to produce its crisis response culture, some other systems find that cultures must be built from scratch, restructured due to changes in purpose, or even assembled "just-in-time" among organizations that must pull together at a moment's notice to quell an unforeseen emergency situation. In such circumstances, trust, cohesion, and devotion must still be present to resolve the crisis, but functions must be performed without a rich heritage, continual reinforcement, and deep personal ties. The networks that best manage to pull together in the face of such shortfalls are the ones that are successful in resolving their particular crises.

Education, Training, and Simulation

Education and training are both important components of crisis response culture. They are the teaching mechanisms that inculcate in new members the correct ways to perceive, think, and feel in relation to the problems faced in the environment.[228] Crisis response networks rely on training and education to practice, perform, and perfect techniques among a variety of different organizational members. Many education and training methods are used to indoctrinate members into the interorganizational network and update methods from previous experience and new insights.

Training expert Carol Steinfeld describes two levels of training that are incorporated into building strong teams: level one training is designed to

---

[228]Schein, 445.

build trust among the members of a network; and level two training seeks to teach the technical proficiencies needed for the network to achieve its objectives.[229] Steinfeld's model for team building among organizations unfamiliar with each other is essential for establishing and maintaining interorganizational working relationships. The Steinfeld model provides four elements essential in training activity: references, safety, qualified facilitators, and facilities.[230] References are important because they consider the background and experience of a group before training goals and objectives are constructed or measured. Safety refers to the standards that must be maintained to build trust in participants and to ensure that health and comfort expectations of the group are met.[231] Facilitation techniques are important because group dynamics and development, course mechanics, and overall network objectives must all be met in the training package. Only qualified instructors in all three domains are capable of providing top quality training. Finally, the facilities used for the training must adequately cover the needs of the training. The facility must be realistic, safe, and flexible enough to encompass the many different structures that training can take.

Crisis management training seminars are especially important in the development of interorganizational culture because they set the tone, establish the operating procedures, and provide the roles and missions centered on activities that save lives. The Baltimore Police Department's scenario-based simulations seminar is an industry standard of how culture is bred in its teaching of sergeants to supervise and resolve hostage situations. The Baltimore simulator provides three essential elements found in effective training programs:

---

[229]Carol Steinfeld, "Challenge Courses Can Build Strong Teams," *Training and Development* 51, no. 4 (1997): 12.

[230]Steinfeld, 13.

[231]Interorganizational networks will vary in their degree of safety standard risk depending on the nature of the crises that led to the formation of the network.

(1) a mechanism for practicing how to do something;

(2) a helpful environment where participants learn how to plan for different crisis scenarios; and

(3) an assessment system where participants' crisis prevention and resolution skills are graded and measured for improvement.[232]

The success of the Baltimore simulator is due to specialized staff skills and cutting edge technologies essential to run the program. Simulations skills include: expertise in situational analysis; research capabilities that are topic-specific; the ability to write comprehensive, accurate, easy-to-understand rules; the ability to recruit and enthuse people about their tasks; and the persistence to update the simulation to keep it relevant and accurate.[233] The Baltimore simulation team recently provided a decision making model based on hundreds of actual incidents, and this model now provides novices with a checklist to emphasize the importance of a measured, controlled, and comprehensive response to a crisis.[234]

In the 21st Century, simulations are becoming even more important because technology now provides alternatives to on-site exercises and other forms of training, where many "virtual" benefits can be gained without bringing geographically separated members from different organizations together. While these types of training do not take the place of personal interactions between two members of different organizations that must resolve a crisis together, they have been shown to facilitate sharing of knowledge, increase common learning, and build common educational bases among organizations.

---

[232]John F. Reintzell, "When Training Saves Lives," *Training and Development* 51, no. 1 (January 1997): 41.

[233]Reintzell, 41.

[234]Reintzell, 41.

Electronic meetings have also assisted interorganizational learning. In 1991, a series of computer assisted interorganizational planning meetings were held in New Zealand to develop opportunities for channeling that country's competitiveness in world markets.[235] Follow-up results showed that, not only did the electronic meetings redirect the country's long-term strategic vision, but they also proved that interorganizational learning was promoted and sustained among groups previously characterized by dysfunctional conflict.[236]

Formal education to improve interorganizational learning has also been conducted using interactive technology. A virtual learning concept developed by Roger Schank provides a look at how interactive learning takes place to accomplish the goals of formal organizational learning. Schank's model calls for detailed scenario building; failure and corrective actions built in at difficult stages of the virtual learning process; help-desk availability, goal achievement, and credible feedback mechanisms.[237] The *Training and Development* journal's editorial staff supports models such as Schank's and believes that separation of time and space should not inhibit formal learning programs for organizations.[238]

Learning is clearly one of the drivers bringing organizations closer together to solve common problems, and interorganizational learning is increasingly being driven by technological advances. Some of the benefits from the best

---

[235] Jim Sheffield and Brent Gallupe, "Using Group Support Systems to Improve the New Zealand Economy--Part II: Follow-up Results," *Journal of Management Information Systems* 11, no. 3 (Winter 1994/95): 135–153.

[236] Jim Sheffield and Brent Gallupe, "Using Group Support Systems to Improve the New Zealand Economy--Part II: Follow-up Results," *Journal of Management Information Systems* 11, no. 3 (Winter 1994/95): 135–153.

[237] Roger Schank, "Virtual Learning: A Revolutionary Approach to Building a Highly Skilled Workforce," *Training and Development* 51, no. 11 (November 1997): 88–89.

[238] Unattributed, "A Start-Up Guide to Distance Learning," *Training and Development* 51, no. 12 (December 1997): 39–47.

technological learning programs include: cuts in training costs; increased productivity; reduction in trainee backlogs; increased access to subject matter experts; flexibility in training; and access to alternative instructional options. These advances, possessing so many advantages for interorganizational purposes, have broken down the barriers between organizations and have helped networks to build common knowledge, skills, and training bases from which they can move on to handle such complex problems as disaster or crises in a complex modern society.

All crisis response networks must be capable of self-evaluation that spans levels of culture (i.e.: visible, values, basic assumptions) and factors of culture (i.e.: language, education/training, devotion). In order to evaluate a specific network culture, the set of questions in the box below is useful.

Determining a Network's Macroculture

1. *The Visible*

   Are there visible signs that distinguish the network from its member organizations or other networks?
   Symbols?
   Uniforms?
   Acronyms?
   Manuals?
   Orientation books for new network members?
   Behavioral patterns?
   Art, artifacts, or visible bumper stickers?

2. *The Values*

   Does the network share distinctive values that are different from its member organizations or other networks? Or, do the organizations all come to the network with their own values? If so, do the differences between the organizations cause problems in the network?
   Do people from different organizations have to adjust to each other during a crisis?
   Do values among the organizations conflict and thereby cause problems in solving the crisis together?
   Network Core Values?
   Jargon?
   Vocalized Esprit or Pride in Network Membership?
   Is Allegiance Tied to the Network?
   Does a statement or set of statements convey network values?
   Are there assumptions that are so basic that they are taken for granted in the network (an example of this would be the assumption in America is to treat your neighbor as you would like to be treated yourself)?
   Are organizations mandated to participate through law or decree? If so, do all organizations value membership in the network?
   Do the network's organizations trust each other?
   Are network missions sought after by the organizations and viewed as critical? Or are they viewed as secondary assignments next to the organizations' everyday responsibilities as a singular entity?

3. *The Environment*

   What is the relationship of the network to its environment?
   Does the network dominate, fill a specific need, or respond to the environment?
   How are resources handled in the network?
   Are property and resources individual to member organizations or shared by all? Or, is only some property shared? If so, is the shared property a substantial portion of overall resources to each organization—substantial to some but inconsequential to others?

4. *The People*

   How are people of the network viewed?
   Are there differences between how members of one organization are viewed as opposed to another?
   When contributing to network missions, are people in the network generally viewed as go-getters or just doing their jobs?
   How are people expected to act in the network?
   Are they supposed to accomplish the mission, follow regulations, listen to their boss? What is the method through which people take action?
   How do people relate with one another in the network? Do they cooperate, compete, act as a group or an individual, do they follow rules or just work to get a common job finished?
   Are network missions tied to career success or viewed as secondary assignments by members?

Interorganizational Fire Suppression Culture

A macroculture is pervasive throughout the wildfire network. The need to fight fires together is a driving factor in the consolidation of education, standards and procedures, and communications methods and means. One gauge of the closeknit cultural norms that dictate the behavior of this network is the results compiled in the "Wildland Firefighter Safety Awareness Study." The safety study was aimed at the identification and improvement of wildfire culture to effectively align the network's organizations with the needs of wildfire suppression.[239] It identified three cultural traits and eight cultural factors that distinguish the network as an effective crisis response system. These traits and factors set the foundations upon which the network can even further improve its operations for the future.[240]

Culture Traits

The cultural traits present throughout the network are: a continuous change mindset, leadership, and accountability.[241] Continuous change is evident in simultaneous "bottom-up" and "top-down" approaches that work in concert with each other. Because the intense demands of dangerous working environments are most often felt by those on its front lines, such members are respected as trained professionals who are oftentimes the impetus for new ideas, concepts, and innovations. Unusual in widespread organizational practice and praised in those organizations where it exists, "bottom-up" appreciation creates a unifying spirit and commonly held "all-for-one" approach. The Wildland Firefighter Safety Awareness Study

---

[239]NIFC Wildland Firefighter Awareness Study, 1
[240]Ibid
[241]Ibid

indicated that the network should embark on even further "concentrated, systematic efforts to involve all people from all levels in determining the details of the strategies to be pursued."[242]

The network's leadership is viewed as a series of small steps taken on a daily basis to build expertise, trust, and accomplish the mission by "walking the walk," leading by example, soliciting input from subordinates, and making tough and demanding decisions. While this form of leadership is evident in the network, the future network culture will incorporate stronger technical expertise in leadership positions, closer alignment of experience and formal testing/evaluation among leaders across the six federal organizations and a greater emphasis on the behavioral side of leadership.[243] While leadership is a culturally distinguishing feature, that same culture also exhibits recurring leadership shortfalls that need to be addressed, such as technically inferior leaders or technically competent, but behaviorally inept, leaders. As a cultural identifier, leadership is exhibited mainly for its cross-agency strengths, but it must be recognized that the interorganizational culture is also defined by some persistent leadership shortfalls as well.

Leadership is jointly developed and ingrained in firefighters, regardless of organizational affiliation, through the courses and certification of the National Wildfire Coordination Group (NWCG). Providing courses, catalogs, and certification in essential areas to all firefighters, this common training and certification system creates a unified cultural indoctrination to fire management. The NWCG's education system includes some of the following courses: Incident Command System National Training; Prescribed Fire Techniques and Procedures; Fire Prevention Planning and Determination; Suppression Skills Training at

---

[242] Ibid
[243] Ibid., 5.

the Firefighter, Crew and Supervisory Levels; and Special Skill Training (e.g.: base camp manager; ordering manager; air support manager).[244] The educational system offers joint training and certification in every specialty or occupation of wildfire management.

One example of the many cross-agency training courses that create common leadership patterns throughout the network is seen in the network approach to public relations manager training. The NWCG course on public relations covers the intent of wildfire public relations as it relates to the firefighting cause. It is titled, "Strategic Communications for Wildland Fire Management," and its course description displays how thorough the NIFC is in one very narrow aspect of firefighting:

> Strategic Communications for Wildland Fire Management was specifically designed to help wildland managers and spokespeople in their efforts to deal with today's media...while the concepts presented are of special interest to full-time public information personnel, the entire program has been designed to meet the needs of a wide range of wildland fire managers and agency administrators who might find themselves in a position of making tough communications decisions, or acting as a spokesperson during a difficult situation.[245]

---

[244]Ibid., viii.

[245]National Wildfire Coordinating Group, *National Fire Equipment System--Catalog Part 2: Publications* (Boise: U.S. Government Printing Office, 1998), 7–8.

A Macrocultural Perspective of the Wildland Fire Suppression Network

Culture Traits

(1) Continuos Change

Exhibited Through:
"Bottom-up innovation"
--front line workers add ideas, innovations
--produces "all-for-one" approach

(2) Leadership

Promotion from within; "been there"
Common courses, catalogs, training, certification
Technical leadership expertise
Behavioral leadership expertise

(3) Accountability

"Life and Death" profession
Performance evaluations; safety standards
Objective investigations into wrongdoing; negligence

Culture Practices

(1) Risk Management

Fire qualification standards
Decision skills training
Common firefighter training across organizations
Refresher training
Safety center for lessons learned

(2) Retention of Experience

Symbolic pride
"Us versus them"

(3) Emphasis on Training/Certification

"Red Card" qualification

(4) Human Communications

Common technical systems; shared interorganizational radio cache
Refined emergency jargon
Respectful subordinate questioning of orders

(5) Human Factors

Anti-fatigue campaign (work/rest guides; shift rotation; sleep)
Anti-machismo campaign (safety first)

(6) Professionalism

Fire as a science
Industry standards
Fire suppression as a career

(7) Safety Attitude/Incident Reporting

Protective procedures; anonymous reporting; investigative arm

This one course description provides a good example of the common education provided throughout the wildfire network. As a driving factor in the creation and maintenance of a macroculture, education indoctrinates managers and firefighters in the procedures and policies that are accepted across organizations throughout the network. Firefighters from different walks of life are taught in the same manner, given the same objectives and behaviors in a given area, and evaluated in the same way on their mastery of the subject matter.

Accountability is the third cultural trait that distinguishes fire suppression. It is also an area recommended for higher standards as a "culture setter" for the future network. In the hazardous wildfire environment, crew members, managers, staff, and even administrators are held strictly accountable for the decisions they make. Performance evaluations, safety standards, budget and program decisions, and general competence are all scrutinized in this network that holds lives in the balance.[246] The Wildland Firefighter Safety Awareness Study recognized this somewhat unique commitment to accountability and called for even more stringent standards. The study suggested a paid leave policy for members under investigation to put firefighter accountability standards on par with military and aviation communities. The study also found accountability lax in some areas when compared to how the system should operate (according to procedures). The result of such lax conduct is the occurrence (albeit infrequent) of an untrained firefighter or poorly prepared supervisor fighting some of the most difficult wildland fires that confront the network.

Culture Practices

The three traits, at the same time both evident and in need of improvement, describe how members are viewed in the system, how leaders are supposed to function, and how standards are to govern member conduct. The traits are realized through performance of eight culture practices. These eight practices are: risk management, retention of experience, emphasis on training and certification, human communications, human factors, professionalism, safety attitude and incident reporting, and external factors.[247] The Wildland

---

[246]Ibid., 59.
[247]Ibid., vi.

Firefighter Safety Awareness Study recognized each of these practices as a "pillar of wisdom" and included them as forming the path to further strengthen the three key cultural traits in the future.

Risk management practices center on the training, education, and evaluation of fire management officers against minimum fire qualification standards.[248] Many of the standards are interagency-common to ensure training integration occurs across the network. The risk management practices rely heavily on network-common training and education standards that include shared fire management courses at the National Advanced Resource Training Center in Merana, Arizona.[249] A new feature included for future training is the proposed "Decision Skills Training" that will place leaders in intense pressure, tactical decision making situations, and communications exercises under noise, heat, and time constraints. This type of simulation training is designed to produce intuitive, learned common responses across the wildfire network organizations so that operations are virtually identical and personnel are interchangeable.

While the proposed decision skills will further refine a common macro-culture, several initiatives are already in the training pipeline to correct cultural shortcomings. These initiatives will be expanded upon in the future to create a tighter, more cohesive interagency approach to wildfire responses. Several problems were identified in the safety awareness study and have now been targeted for change. They include: a lack of adequate seasonal firefighter training, a shortage of human relations training, and a lack of realistic training.[250] Several corrective steps have been taken. On-the-job training is one way that seasonal firefighters are brought into the system, and new recruits or rusty veterans are mentored by

---

[248]Ibid., vii.

[249]Ibid.

[250]Ibid., ix

seasoned supervisors during "teachable moments" of an actual wildland fire response.[251] Rather than teaching, which is a technique already used in the classroom, on-the-job training allows for trial and error, self-confidence enhancement, and the benefits of long-term relationships.

Refresher training has also been instituted. Seasonal firefighters have other "lives" away from the network's operations, so they have to be reinculcated with procedure, safety, and new techniques to remain part of the wildfire culture.[252] A new Safety Center for Lessons Learned is being established to use case studies and interactive learning to impart field lessons, training procedures, and innovations for those who have been off the fireline completely, as well as for those who have been in staff or administrative positions for lengthy periods of time.

Retention of experienced personnel is the second cultural practice in the network. Experience is viewed as an invaluable asset to crisis management and is recognized across wildfire organizations. Retention is valued in both word and deed through pay, certification, media, and award recognition, and these areas are targeted for even further attempts to aggressively identify and pursue veteran firefighters.[253] One cultural weakness in this practice is recognition that senior firefighters leave for a variety of reasons. Attempts are being made to incentivize them to come back.[254]

An integral part of the training program as a cultural unifier is the certification process that results in the "red-card" qualification. The red-card is the ultimate cultural symbol in the network, and it distinguishes those who meet the criteria to be a wildland firefighter from those who do not. The process to receive a red card is a vital indoctrination tool that pulls

---

[251] Ibid., xiii.

[252] National Wildfire Coordinating Group, *Interagency Incident Business Management Handbook: NWCG Handbook 2* (Boise: Incident Business Practices Working Team, 1996).

[253] Ibid., xv.

[254] Ibid., xii.

firefighters together into a common "us versus them" category and encourages all "wannabe" firefighters to meet the standards of membership. Unfortunately, evidence shows that sabotage of the red-card system exists through misrepresentation of credentials, verbal vouches, and other forms of certification circumvention. These situations are handled with severe penalties, and they must be reported because they undermine a key element of the fire suppression macroculture.

Communication is a third practice that distinguishes the NIFC. The network is striving to further refine its communications jargon and content to meet its operational needs.[255] The goal of communications is to make information transmittable with the least amount of verbiage that still clearly makes the point. Taking existing jargon from military, law enforcement, and aviation communities, the wildfire network developed a means of communication that simply states a message, repeats it when necessary, and confirms or denies it in as few words as possible.[256] Examples from one firefighting manual include: "copied" to respond to a piece of information; "understood, dig creek line east" to comply and repeat intended action; and, "we dig east until wind shift, then we use escape route east" to signify compliance and clarification of complex instructions.

Other language identifiers in the wildland firefighter community focus on every member's role as a communicator of information. An open system is evident in the fire suppression environment where subordinates can legitimately ask questions and demand clarifications to orders, and where leaders can ask the advice of subordinates without embarrassment. This openness is most evident in the areas of safety that surround the network.

---

[255] Ibid., xiii.
[256] Ibid., xvii.

"Respectful interaction" is the process taught to subordinates to point out safety issues or areas of concern.[257]

Human factors also represent essential cultural practices, because it is ultimately human beings who resolve crises. Research shows fatigue as a leading factor in operational casualty lists, so a new campaign has been implemented to determine how to develop and enforce common work/rest guidelines, complete with shift rotation scheduling, sleep, and noise/heat/light minimization procedures.[258] Included in a concern for the human element is the cultural emphasis on accurately reporting health conditions of unit members. Although machismo, devotion, and dedication to duty encourage deceptive health reporting, the fire culture has shifted and now punishes violators in the best interests of its members. Leaders can be severely punished for violating the integrity of the health status reporting guidelines.

The final cultural practice, a commitment to safety, is evident throughout the wildfire network, and this practice results in the ability to: keep more fighters on the front line, build trust among all members that their well-being is highly considered, and maintain a delicate balance against "machismo," "daring," and "guts" that are natural elements in a crisis response environment. The culture is moving away from one that was characterized by risk taking and toward one that is better described as professional.[259] A profession has rules, guidelines, and standards that govern member conduct, and it is in the area of safety that professionalism is expected to be even further exemplified. Safe behavior in the fire culture includes: reporting "near-misses," pointing out safety violations, and determining the smartest, safest solutions for wildfire tactical

---

[257]Ibid.
[258]Ibid., xviii.
[259]Ibid., xx.

situations.[260] The Wildland Firefighter Safety Awareness Study captures the cultural shift by stating:

> ...two or three decades ago, firefighters were considered macho and professional if they went into burning buildings to rescue people without using breathing apparatus and wearing protective clothing. Today, they would be considered foolish and unprofessional, unable to do their job effectively unless properly attired and equipped.[261]

To solidify the move to a professional network from a loose assemblage of "heroes," the fire network may adopt a comprehensive, multi-agency injury and near-miss reporting system. A safety system such as the one being created will track common problems that crop up throughout the network, allow for anonymous reporting to ensure compliance, and develop plans to correct recurring problems.[262] Following from the safety system, an interagency investigatory arm has been proposed to explore the many dimensions of serious incidents in hopes that knowing why dangerous situations exist might help to prevent more of them from occurring in the future.

Other Culture Factors

The NIFC traits and principles describe many of the macroculture factors that bring its organizations together into a tightly knit network, but there are a few other reasons why this particular culture is unique in interorganizational relations. The commonalties observed in several key points of

---

[260]Ibid., xxii.

[261]Ibid., xxiii.

[262]Ibid.

the network drive shared practices, principles, and beliefs. These commonalties are observed in the resourcing practices, supply management, and personnel management, all of which are essential areas of any network. It is interesting to see that all three areas are common throughout the system.

Because major member organizations (i.e.: six federal agencies) use the same system to provide resources and fight fires, the rest of the network is forced to adopt similar practices and procedures. The practice of resourcing first locally, then regionally, and only last nationally is a shared cultural practice that brings all agencies and jurisdictions together in a shared view of how the network must function to meet the demands of its environment. Directly tied to the concept of gradually expanding geographical control is the total mobility concept. This cultural belief is infused throughout the system and acts as the facilitator of resource movement across jurisdictional and agency lines. The cultural belief in prioritization based on a few fundamental, agreed upon points, such as risk of life, property, and legislated significance, is another related cultural practice that goes so far as to hinder some jurisdictions if their land happens to fall short on the resourcing list. Central resourcing, gradual expansion of control, total mobility, and prioritization are cultural drivers that bring disparate organizations into a true community where they hold a few sacred shared beliefs. It is those beliefs that lead the network into so many further shared practices.

The supply system is another cultural driver. As witnessed in other crisis response communities, such as the military and search and rescue outfits, the supplies and equipment used to respond to a crisis contribute significantly to the tactics, organization, and people used to quell the crisis. In direct opposition to either of the just mentioned communities, the network uses virtually identical supplies and equipment regardless of agency, department, or jurisdiction.

The supply system is one congruous, identical process, and it produces the same result if a part or tool is ordered from an Indian Reservation in Oklahoma or the Yosemite National Park. Publications from the interagency National Wildfire Coordinating Group list the thousands of supplies and equipment available to the network. Bags, batteries, helmets, jeans, and administrative forms are all standard issue items among the thousands of other related products available through the supply catalogs.[263] The catalogs provide cost, unit of issue, stock order number, and pictures of the items to be ordered.[264]

A standardized supply system contributes to the network's ability to meet other cultural requirements, such as training. All firefighters, staff members, and special function personnel use the same equipment for their trade, receive training in the same tactical procedures, and replenish and replace their equipment through the same channels. This system also allows for vending and contracting centralization of new items, rapid dissemination of new materials into the firefighting supply and training pipelines, and identification of new technologies and research and development techniques.

One example of a shared supply asset is the radios used in the wildfire communications system. Having communications centralization at the Boise National Incident Radio Cache keeps member organizations from buying radios that cannot communicate with other organizations, and it also encourages organizations to develop common training, radio jargon, and other communications techniques. All of the different radio assets used in wildland fire management are intermingled at the radio cache, and they are tied directly into the MAC Group priority ordering system.[265] By centralizing the reserves of a key asset, community practices are ensured throughout the network.

---

[263]Ibid., xxiv.

[264]National Wildfire Coordination Group, *National Fire Equipment System--Catalog Part 1: Fire Supplies and Equipment* (Boise: National Interagency Fire Center, 1998).

[265]Ibid.

Differences in supplies do exist in the system. Budget drawbacks have forced some departments and agencies to limit the quantities of supplies on-hand, while other groups have plentiful reserves. This disparity, although unfortunate, does not lead to differences in training, education, or tactical approaches. The disparity actually contributes to even further cross fertilization of people and resources, because increased mobility of assets occur with fewer on-hand resources immediately available to front-line commanders.

People are the final cultural component that create a shared macroculture. Unlike many crisis response organizations, firefighters do not join their organizations to be members of that particular organization; instead, they join because they want to be firefighters. This attribute is reflected across the network and creates a strong cross-organizational bond within the firefighting community. At the most fundamental level throughout this network, regardless of organizational affiliation, people are fulfilling similar human needs of association in a very demanding public service trade. Even more closely aligned than the U.S. military personnel (i.e.: a U.S. Marine does not typically join the Marine Corps because he wants to be an infantryman just like a U.S. Army soldier—he wants to be a Marine first), these individuals in different organizations first align themselves as firefighters, "smoke jumpers," or "hot shots," well before they call them-selves members of the U.S. Park Service or Department of Interior. This basic distinction between trade and organizational affiliation displays a cross-cultural bond that helps the wildfire suppression network maintain its close interorganizational ties.

People in these organizations do not become firefighters for exactly the same reasons.[266] The U.S. Park Service's Tom Frey says that, while most

---

[266]Tom Frey, U.S. Forest Service, interview by author.

firefighters seek thrills, excitement, and adventure, others begin the trade for practical reasons such as paying for college.[267] Throughout his career, Frey has observed Type A and B personalities in the network, and often the only observable similarities between two different firefighters are their shared professional attributes held as members of the wildland fire management community. The Joint Fire Science Program pointed out that a shared professionalism based on training, certification, and leadership qualifications are critical to the success of this network. So, while the network takes people of all shapes, sizes, and temperaments, it also molds the firefighters into a common professional character that allows them to perform together and claim affiliation outside of any particular agency to the larger community of wildland firefighters.

Firefighters distinguish themselves as professionals. They are all different upon arrival to the network, and the wildfire macroculture "creates" a shared ethos in the men and women in the fire suppression system. Unlike a "natural" cultural attribute that is selected in the recruitment and training of like minded people,[268] the human characteristics in the wildland firefighter community are a result of a professional system designed to create similarities in organization through a standard National Mobilization Guide; in tactical response through the Incident Command System; and through supplies and materials through the centralized cataloging, warehousing, and caching system.

---

[267] Ibid.

[268] Ibid.

The Emergency Management Macroculture

A macroculture is pervasive throughout the Delaware emergency management network. This culture is attributable to four distinct factors that distinguish Delaware from other states and crisis response networks. The four factors are: the unique characteristics of the state; a network philosophy of information sharing in emergency management; the comprehensive approach to emergency response as a result of the complex emergencies faced in the environment; and the alignment of functions and jurisdictions into a larger conception of public safety.

Delaware's Unique Characteristics

Delaware is a closely knit community where most key decision makers are friends, grew up together, served in a public capacity together, or at least know each other. Size, for the purposes of emergency management, does in fact matter. Delaware's small size allows it to prepare for and react to crises more quickly than other states. Having only three counties and one major city makes it much easier to coordinate for emergencies than neighboring sixty county Pennsylvania. Delaware can be traversed from one end to another in an afternoon, which makes state support for localities much easier than in more expansive states. With a population approaching only 1.5 million residents, people in Delaware perceive they are held to a higher level of responsibility, because the leaders actually know, live among, and answer to the people whom they serve.

Being geographically small and sparsely populated raises several other important issues. Being small means having less to worry about. The Governor of Delaware personally observes emergency management training exercises. In a small state, the personal touch is expected. Emergency management training exercises led by the Delaware Emergency

Management Agency (DEMA) are often "the only game in town." Being small also restricts the numbers of things Delaware can do well as a state economy. A few key industries have arisen in Delaware, and two of them—poultry and tourism—are directly linked to the natural environment. As a result, emergency management is a top priority. Without a lot of competing industries, emergency management is emphasized almost by default in Delaware.

Aside from cultural characteristics attributable to its size, Delaware also conducts its public business in a way that contributes to its tightly knit emergency management community. The state is described by those who work in it as one that is entrepreneurial and non-bureaucratic, which are two essential characteristics of emergency management. For example, the Governor of Delaware has fewer levels between him and lower decision makers as compared with the bureaucracies of other state governments. When working on a *Joint Hurricane Task Force* initiative between Virginia, Maryland, and Delaware, the channels of bureaucracy played a large role in the policy process. The Governor of Delaware was briefed quickly on the subject and signed the initiative, but the Virginia government could not move the initiative out of its bureaucracy for the governor to sign prior to 1998's Hurricane Bonnie.

The entrepreneurial nature of Delaware government also plays an important role in the culture of the state. Due to its lack of resources in comparison with other states, Delaware government officials often are forced to use unconventional means to accomplish state goals. Instead of conducting large-scale studies, programs, or analyses, DEMA usually "piggybacks" off of other states' efforts in these areas by tailoring existing reports to meet its particular needs. One example of this approach to "doing more with less" is evident in the state's Weapons of Mass Destruction (WMD) preparation. DEMA's Radiological Section Administrator, Emily Falone, decided to wait on WMD planning because of the many other states and federal agencies already working exhaustively on the issue. She then used the existing number of studies from other sources as a foundation for her Delaware's domestic preparedness planning at a very low cost to taxpayers.

Delaware's unique geographical location also shapes its culture as a state and has significant implications for emergency management. Being a neighbor to four states and three bodies of water has forced Delaware to move into regional alliances in almost every area of governance. Regional issues impact the peninsular state on a daily basis, and as a result, a significant portion of government workers' time is spent on regional coordination and collaboration. Such close ties with neighboring states, and particularly those on the DELMARVA (Delaware, Maryland, and Virginia) Peninsula, has helped in providing a government culture conducive to networking in emergency management.

Several daily examples of interstate collaboration exist in emergency management itself, which serve to effectively bind Delaware into a regional emergency management network. One example of the close regional ties between Delaware and its regional state peers is seen in the area of nuclear power. New Jersey provides the Mid-Atlantic with nuclear power, and, as a result, it must work with Delaware and other neighboring states to provide information, emergency planning, and training drills on nuclear outbreak possibilities.

Natural hazards are also a significant shaper of culture for Delaware as a regional partner. In the planning and response for Hurricane Bonnie, Delaware coordinated its action plans with Virginia and Maryland on a daily basis. During a February 1998 Noreaster, the states of Pennsylvania and Delaware were closely linked in their planning processes. These two states also coordinate planning for water emergencies on the Delaware River they share. Delaware officials are vigilantly aware of the state's position in and around other states and bodies of water. Working outside of its own state is a natural process for DEMA and all of the other agencies of the state government, which is advantageous for the state in preparing for the types of emergencies and crises that are most likely to threaten Delaware in the future.

Information as Culture

The philosophy, functions, and jurisdictions in Delaware exhibit macro-cultural characteristics as well. One overriding philosophical approach to Delaware emergency management is in the information sharing between levels of government and across functions of emergency management. The emphasis on information dissemination grew out of a Governor-commissioned report in the early 1990's that stated "the Delaware Emergency Management Agency is viewed as an agency 'planning in isolation' and is perceived to be an ineffective response coordinator during emergency situations."[269] The report pointed out that natural emergencies were actually coordinated in other state agencies due to DEMA's "perceived and actual inadequacies," "internal disorganization," failure to tie plans to implementation, and failure to coordinate properly with other state agencies.[270]

As a result of the report, a reorganization was ordered, and one of the first acts in the new agency was the installation of a new director. Subsequently, the new director, Sean Mulhern reestablished DEMA as the state hub in emergency management. He put DEMA at the center by emphasizing information sharing as a key tenet. From the director's guidance, several information sharing initiatives grew into a DEMA-centric model where

---

[269]Fax from Delaware Secretary of Public Safety to Director of DEMA, 12 December 1995.
[270]Ibid.

the agency acts as the go-between for levels of government, as well as functions of government, in any matter related to an emergency.

The first initiative to create the information sharing network was the installation of DEMA's Bridgeline phone system. This system links 60 agencies on the DELMARVA peninsula, to include federal, state, and local participants. The Bridgeline is the information sharing hub before, during, and after a crisis strikes, and DEMA leads the effort by maintaining the line, coordinating the calls, establishing the protocol, and adding and deleting participants as an emergency evolves.

A typical Bridgeline call occurred on August 24, 1998 to prepare for Hurricane Bonnie, which at that time, was located 18 hours off of the coast of Delaware. DEMA Natural Hazards Section Planner, Lloyd Stoebner chaired the call by taking roll call, asking for a National Weather Service update on Hurricane Bonnie, coordinating the external requirements from any Bridgeline members (e.g.: shelters, resources), and establishing the next gathering time. In this particular call it was clear that regional representatives from all three states appreciated and counted on the information that the Bridgeline provided; they asked probing questions at each stage of the call; and they used the information to coordinate their crisis management planning and actions. Unlike other crisis management communities, the DEMA centric culture is one of openness, critical inquiry, and unabashed honesty. The Bridgeline has created a network through which it is so easy to communicate that the various organizations are comfortable with the process and each other.

From the regional Bridgeline call system, the information sharing has expanded to Delaware-specific calls on the same network. Immediately after the August 24 Hurricane Bonnie call, the DEMA Natural Hazards Section then huddled around the speaker phone to coordinate planning with Delaware's three counties and city emergency management authorities. At both the regional and local levels, information was passed and acted upon as a result of the Bridgeline call. This situation stands in stark contrast to the "planning in isolation" cited earlier in the decade.

Director Mulhern's second area of emphasis in the information sharing campaign has been to include the larger Delaware community in the process. According to DEMA Radiological Programs Administrator, Emily Falone, DEMA views all of Delaware's citizens as being affected by emergencies. As a result they all have stakes in emergency management. Such thinking led to a DEMA information campaign that informs the public on individual citizen roles in emergency mitigation, planning, and response.

The information campaign is heavily laden with literature for citizens to use in their emergency management roles. For example, "How to Prepare for a Hurricane" details citizen responsibilities in before, "watch," warning, evacuation, and recovery stages of a hurricane.[271] This guide provides telephone points of contact, public shelter and food bank storage areas, and "safe step" procedures that citizens use to lesson their individual potential for disaster.

In its information campaign, DEMA also targets certain audiences because of the special roles they play in providing a safe environment. Farmers are constituents who directly influence the health of the citizens and constitute a major portion of the state economy. For the farming community, DEMA supplies radiological information packages that provide human and animal ingestion information, crop radiation warning and detection signs, and land protection procedures in radiation incidents.[272] To further incorporate farmers into the emergency culture, DEMA also conducts exercises in farming pastures and fields, where field

---

[271]Delaware Emergency Management Agency, *How to Prepare for a Hurricane* (New Castle, Delaware: Delaware Emergency Management Agency, 1998).

[272]U.S. Department of Agriculture, *Radiological Emergency Information for Farmers, Processors, and Distributors* (Washington, D.C.: U.S. Government Printing Office, 1989)

monitoring teams measure radiation levels in animals, milk, water, and crops. Animal staging plans are also tested to keep livestock out of severe radiological exposure. Such practical exercises and informational publications pull a large, important block of stakeholders into the emergency management process. Delaware's emergency management culture is most clearly defined as one based on the exchange of information in an open, multi-channeled way that puts DEMA at the center as the emergency information conduit for the state.

An additional information based feature contributes to DEMA's open exchange philosophy, but it is not the product of Director Mulhern's initiative; instead, it is a key feature of the Public Safety Department. Delaware's 800MHz communications system puts all state and local emergency response agencies on the same dispatch network. This system is also capable of expansion during crises to include other states communications as well as federal agencies. Such a system provides a shared method and language of communication among fire, police, EMS, public safety, and emergency management organizations from the state all the way down to the county levels. Delaware's integrated emergency communications culture breaks down only when it finds neighboring states not nearly as collective in their efforts and stalled in their abilities to work together to solve complex problems.

Environmental Factors in Network Culture

The types of emergencies to which the Delaware emergency management network prepares and responds require a comprehensive approach. These types of emergencies and the corresponding approach differ greatly from clearly delineated problems best suited for functional organizations to handle alone. Delaware's network cooperation and coordination in radiological emergencies and weapons of mass destruction are two areas where a comprehensive network approach is clearly displayed.

A radiological event touches virtually every organization and community in Delaware, and the different local and state agencies, along with private organizations, have learned to work in and among each other to solve such tremendous public problems. Delaware's *Radiological Emergency Plan* conveys the comprehensive network purpose behind a type of emergency that runs across the responsibilities of jurisdictions, functions, and levels of government:

> The purpose of the Radiological Emergency Plan is to coordinate and implement a comprehensive state and county response to protect the public from the hazards of a radiological emergency...[273]

The "comprehensive state and county response" required for such an event involves health, agriculture, water, military, police, media, and citizen organizations in critical capacities that must overlap, coordinate, and respond together.

These organizations work well with each other in such circumstances because they annually plan, train, and implement the comprehensive techniques together. Personnel from all state agencies and local governments participate in several different types of radiological courses in order to develop a shared understanding for the types of problems faced in radiological emergencies. The Radiological Planning Course is designed for planners, program administrators, and specialists to learn the off-site effects of nuclear accidents. The Radiological Accident Assessment Course is attended by the National Guard, DEMA's radiological section representatives, and field monitoring team members in order to provide a common

---

[273]State of Delaware, *Radiological Emergency Plan* (New Castle: Delaware Emergency Management Agency, 1998), 2–1.

understanding of technical aspects of nuclear and health physics. The Delaware Radiological Emergency Plan Course is designed as a legal, assessment, and recovery primer for all state and local employees. Other courses highlight specific portions of emergency response to provide the same type of comprehensive understanding of radiological emergencies across organizations. Finally, the courses are implemented in week-long training exercises that test knowledge and organizational compatibilities for actual emergency situations.

The comprehensiveness of the preparation and training for radiological disasters is also evident in the network's approach to Weapons of Mass Destruction (WMD) training. DEMA has instituted a five step process to handle this emergent threat: (1)Survey for WMD risks in conjunction with all affected functions, to include fire, police, and emergency management organizations; (2)Conduct intelligence and environmental assessment on highly vulnerable areas to mitigate against severe threats; (3)Establish WMD plan; (4)Train and exercise against plan; (5)Implement plan when and where necessary.[274]

In the fight against WMD, the emergency management network is working among its organizations to identify its environment, weaknesses, and plans to prevent or recover from a broad assault on Delaware's communities. In such an effort, the emergency community has even grown to incorporate new members. State and local agencies and private businesses associated with garbage collection have willingly participated in WMD training to fill newly identified roles as debris removal specialists. The collective WMD approach also includes psychological services and assessment centers to handle the human impacts of such a traumatic experience.

---

[274]Radiological Programs Administrator, Emily Falone, Delaware Emergency Management Agency, interview by author, 26 August 1998, New Castle, Delaware, notes with author.

The finding from this extensive network is that Delaware emergency management is a comprehensive process among many organizations, and it is a process built from the needs of the environment in which the emergency network operates. The broad range of characteristics faced in environmental threats, such as those posed by radiological accidents or WMD attacks, force the network to develop a macroculture perspective that includes collaboration in all aspects of a response: planning, training, exercising, and organizing in a collective effort to protect the community.

Functional and Jurisdictional Alignment

Unlike situations in some states, the functional organizations responsible for Delaware emergency management (such as county emergency management officials and state and local fire and police organizations) exhibit a remarkable amount of goodwill towards each other and work closely together to solve common problems. Part of this goodwill is due to the characteristics of the state mentioned earlier, but part of it also has to do with the consolidation of public safety services into one statewide department of public safety.

In Delaware, the traditional cultural disparities between state, county, and metropolitan police organizations do not exist, because the divisions of responsibility are clear. The state police have most of the criminal law enforcement authority, and the counties handle local issues and administrative processes such as parking and speeding tickets.

In fire management, a statewide fire training academy ensures common training standards and qualifications in the firefighting community. While the fire departments in Delaware's four major cities are run by local authorities, their firefighters abide by the same standards as those set by the state fire school. Local fire marshals also meet periodically with the state fire marshal to review polices, practices, and procedures.

A recent example of inter-functional cooperation took place in the area of WMD training. The fire school received a FEMA grant for a terrorism awareness course for its "first responders," or those personnel who would arrive first to the scene of a crisis. Instead of filling the course with firefighters, the fire school opened up its training to the state police, national guard, EMS, and DEMA personnel.[275] Since the WMD instruction is provided in a "train the trainer" environment, the participation of so many organizations ensures that the entire emergency management network will eventually be trained through the representatives who accepted the fire school's invitation.

Such interorganizational cooperation in training is common in Delaware, and the close relationships that result help in the creation of cross-organizational operating procedures, language, and communications. Over time, such cross-organizational linkages have been institutionalized. An injection pathway exercise in 1996 illustrates the collective mindset in Delaware's agencies and departments. The event was coordinated by DEMA as a radiological simulation of a nuclear leak from one of New Jersey's power plants. Dozens of federal and Delaware state agencies, other states' agencies, and Delaware's county representatives worked under Delaware's Emergency Operations Plan to plan, respond to, recover from, and reenter after, the feigned disaster. The scenario displayed an entire network institutionalized to train together in emergency response. The fact that so many organizations support interorganizational training is a testament to DEMA's ability to conduct a quality, well planned exercise that puts all actors in the same scenario and asks them to work together to respond to it.

---

[275]Delaware Emergency Management Agency, Radiological Programs Administrator, Emily Falone, interview by author, 26 August 1998, New Castle, Delaware, notes with author.

Future Cultural Factors

DEMA's commitment to information sharing and dissemination is being taken to a new level as the agency cements itself as the hub for the entire emergency management community. In 1999, DEMA moved into a new $9 million emergency operations center, which provides technological, communications, and functional interoperability between federal, state, and local government authorities, as well as with key business and nonprofit organizations.

The heart of the new network is the center's Emergency Information System (EIS), which will provide: 23 emergency related databases; Global Information System (GIS) geographic, topographic, and positioning capabilities through satellite links; the most current natural, chemical, and radiological monitoring software and systems; 800Mhz communications links; and emergency management network email.[276] This system provides every source gathering intelligence system in one shared network at DEMA's headquarters, and also accesses outside links to federal and local officials. EIS also generates administrative harmony between agencies and governments because supply, fiscal, personnel, and logistics databases are centralized. DEMA's funding sources, such as FEMA, the state legislature, and private businesses, track exactly how and where money is spent in a crisis. Such a completely integrated information management network is creating even stronger cross-organizational, cross-jurisdictional approaches to emergency management to allow for every aspect of a crisis to be fought from a common vantage point.

---

[276]Communications Operations Administrator, Carol Spencer, Delaware Emergency Management Agency, interview by author, 26 August 1998, New Castle, Delaware, notes with author.

The Public Safety Macroculture

The Columbus public safety system is dominated by functionally distinct organizational cultures, but a macroculture exists and distinguishes itself as a separate identity from two existing cultural forms in the metropolitan pubic safety community: (1)the tightly knit cultures of individual functions (i.e.: fire, police, EMS) that compose the public safety network; and (2)macrocultures that exist in other metropolitan public safety communities.

In Columbus, it is apparent that the most prominent cultural features exist at the functional level, and it is the strong single organizational features that sometimes inhibit larger cultural association at the network level. The situation can be explained by the clear divisions of organizational labor in this network, where overlap of organizational responsibilities is rare, and the need to collaborate and coordinate between functions has traditionally been minimal.

A macroculture is emerging in the face of functional organizational dynamics that discourage it. The macroculture is a result of: complex threats in the environment (i.e.: Weapons of Mass Destruction; drug trafficking; terrorism; urban decay) that force interorganizational coordination, new public safety technologies that create interorganizational commonalties (i.e.: radio communications, dispatch services, email), and regional approaches to public safety that are pulling jurisdictions closer together in efforts to realize effectiveness and efficiency gains.

Functional Culture Disparities: Columbus Police and Fire Departments

The Columbus Police Division's culture influences its ability to enter into larger regional alliances with other police departments in the State of Ohio and other divisions of public safety, such as the fire and EMS communities. At both the regional and divisional levels, the Columbus Police Division has a much more tenuous connection to its surrounding public safety communities than do its counterparts in fire and emergency services. The reasons for the police's lack of regional outreach and cooperation is due in part to three factors: the legal repercussions of police actions in modern society, the nature of police work, and the current leadership philosophy of the Columbus Police Division.

The legal repercussions of police work grow out of two legal strains in American society: governance under federal and state constitutions, and the power of the individual to press lawsuits in an increasingly litigious system. Policemen in Columbus operate under these two strains by adhering to strict, detailed guidelines that impose careful, professional conduct in the performance of duty. The guidelines meet the demands of the governing laws and protect the police from litigation.[277] Compared to other crisis response communities, such as those that fight wars, recover from natural disasters, or fight fires, the conduct of the police community is much more regulated by guidelines, laws, and procedures.

Public Safety Director Tom Rice states that Columbus police procedures flow directly from the individual rights guaranteed in the U.S. and Ohio Constitutions, and federal and state level judicial decisions. The laws and statutes of specific localities, such as those that govern the City of Columbus, also impact the policies and procedures of the police department. As a result, police jurisdictions are carefully observed, and actions taken to ensure public safety outside of one's own jurisdiction can be an infringement of the law. Outreach to other organizations, can, in effect, be stifled by the law.

---

[277]Columbus Director of Public Safety Tom Rice, interview by author, 20 July 1998, Columbus, notes with author.

Director Rice uses Ohio's Lucasville Prison riot as one example of how the legal system steers institutional police behavior into the narrow confines of individual organizational cultures. In the Lucasville riot, the highest of consequences in the American political system were at stake: the prisoners had taken the life of one correctional facility officer and had threatened to kill more, and several wounded guards and inmates needed attention. The Lucasville Incident Commander was forced with one of the most difficult combinations of legal, policing, and safety decisions: should he follow the criminal procedure hostage guidelines and immediately enter the hostile compound with force due to potential loss of life; or should he go with his gut instinct drawn from communications with the hostage-takers and broker a deal that might save lives that could be lost in an invasion. Regardless of the decision made (he waited and brokered a deal), the Incident Commander was forced into a narrow decision set dictated by his legal jurisdiction, training and education in the criminal justice system, and the unique demands of the situation. The forces that shaped his decision are features of an organizational culture uniquely suited to a specific political, legal, law enforcement, and safety system that cannot easily adapt to a dramatically different set of cultural norms. Such a rigidly formed cultural identification makes association in a macroculture difficult.

A second cultural outgrowth of the Columbus Police Division is a reflection of the nature of its work, which is a unique alignment of the law enforcement function in the outside world it serves. Columbus police officers most often encounter citizens when they are likely to be in one of three states of mind or action: grieving, breaking the law, or being victimized. In such states of mind or action, citizens are generally unhappy, and the way that they treat and judge police officers is affected by the perceptions triggered in their abnormal states of mind. People deal with police when they have, or are the cause of, a problem, and they often do not objectively judge police efforts on timeliness or quality of service measures.

As a result of its unique contact with the world that it serves, the Columbus Police Division (and police departments in general) tends to take a very insular, "us versus them" approach to its profession. Columbus Equal Opportunity Officer, Aaron Wheeler says that the police officer mentality is one of defensiveness and protection of both himself and the department. This mentality results from having to cope in a work environment that is generally hostile, uncaring of police service, and unsatisfied with police performance.

Another cultural factor related to the nature of police work that limits the police department from interacting in network organizational forms is the individuality of police duty. The police culture is not team-based like other crisis response organizations. The nature of the work dictates individual effort, such as homicide investigations, undercover stings, and internal investigations. When police do work in teams, they are usually with only one partner on a beat, stakeout, or watch, and this partner is a dependable ally. It is a much rarer occurrence to find police officers working in and among large associations to solve common problems.

The Columbus Police Division is focused on solving the individual problems that plague its community, with most problems requiring solitary or paired efforts. The outcome of such work is an organization that operates as a group of individuals, promotes and rewards based on individual effort, and retains members that succeed in solitary work environments. With an organization composed of individually focused members, it cannot come as a surprise that the Columbus Police Division has difficulty in working with outside networks on complex problems. Its members are simply not trained to work in that manner.

The third major cultural factor that keeps the Columbus Police Department focused internally is the leadership philosophy set by Police Chief James Jackson. While Director Rice is firmly supportive of collective approaches, alliances, and collaboration to meet threats to public safety, Chief Jackson can be described as more of an "old school" police officer. Chief Jackson's commitment to traditional law enforcement has set the tone in his department.

Lacking leader-driven support, it is unlikely that the police division will wholeheartedly approach network alliances between functions in Columbus or at the regional level with other police organizations. Jackson has a history of retaliating against uniformed personnel who do not follow his tone and message in the division. He has most recently been accused of retaliation by Lt. Tom Fisher for Fisher's service on the mayor's investigative team that looked into Chief Jackson's conduct in office. Fisher's case shows that, if the chief does not want something to happen in his department, he will go to extreme lengths to insure that it does not in fact occur. Chief Jackson's traditional enforcement approach contributes to the police division's independent and compartmentalized stance towards public safety.

Fire Culture

The Columbus Fire Division's culture is completely different from the insular environment witnessed in the Columbus Police Division. The fire division has been on the cutting edge of network approaches to solve common problems for a long time. The ability of the fire department to engage in such interorganizational relations, where the police department has not, is attributable to their cultural differences. The cultural factors that contribute to the fire department's ability to join networks are: the nature of its work, its team orientation, and its strong cross-functional history.

Fire fighting demands a much different type of service than does law enforcement. The Columbus Fire Division is not inhibited from performing the vast majority of its duties by the Constitution, judicial decisions, or local statutes. The result of such freedom of action is a professional organization that clearly understands its mission in public service and goes out and does it.

Public opinion polls routinely rank the Columbus fire department at the top of local public services list.[278] Why? One reason is that people are in a much different frame of mind when they see firefighters: they want their fire put out and loved ones saved, and they see brave men and women arriving in a loud, visible way to perform such heroic roles. The relationship between the fire and police divisions and the community can be described in the public perceptions from two common images of each community: (1)a firefighter bravely rescuing a baby from a second story window; and (2)the Los Angeles Police Department stomping over Rodney King and his civil liberties. Neither picture accurately depicts reality, but the public perception of each function influences how these departments see themselves as part of their larger environments. Whereas Columbus Equal Employment Opportunity Director Aaron Wheeler describes the police department as "defensive and protective," he sees the fire department as a "let's just get the job done" organization.[279] Both organization's cultures reflect the nature of their work and their perceptions in society.

The second cultural factor in the fire division that leads it into network alliances is its team orientation. The structure of a fire response is conducive to teamwork, esprit, dependence on others, and commitment towards common goals. Unlike police officers, who often work alone or in pairs on different duties from their peers, firefighters work long, 24 hour shifts together in firehouses.[280] While each member on a fire shift has his/her own duties, the project of a firefight is collective in nature, the work of a group in motion. Firefighters are clearly oriented to group

---

[278]Columbus Director of Public Safety Tom Rice, interview by author, 20 July 1998, Columbus, notes with author.

[279]Columbus Public Safety Equal Employment Opportunity Officer, Aaron Wheeler, interview by author, 21 July 1998, Columbus, notes with author.

[280]Columbus Director of Public Safety Tom Rice, interview by author, 20 July 1998, Columbus, notes with author.

behavior—eating, sleeping, and relaxing together—as well as training, exercising, and responding to crises together. One reason why the fire department adjusts well to a network-styled architecture is because its own internal organizational behavior mirrors the network effort at a lower level: one common purpose with each individual member fulfilling a specific role toward a common, clearly identifiable end.

Both the nature of the Columbus Fire Division's work and its team orientation contribute to the third cultural factor which enables it to operate in a network association: it has a strong history of cross-functional experiences. The Columbus Fire Division is used to working with other organizations toward common goals because it works alongside another public safety function, the Columbus Emergency Medical Service (EMS), on a daily basis. Having progressed as a collective effort over the years, fire and EMS are virtually "interchangeable parts in the same system," according to Assistant Director for Fire Administration, David Sturtz.[281]

The combination of fire and EMS has provided a number of positive advantages for Columbus. Over 500 firefighters (almost one-third of the force) are paramedically qualified, and every firefighter has at least basic emergency medical training.[282] If health crises arise on the fire line, they can be handled by firefighters in the normal course of their duties, which is not typical of all fire departments.

Joint certification between divisions extends beyond personnel to include equipment and mobile assets as well. Columbus realizes tremendous budget savings in EMS equipment by equipping fire engines with EMS

---

[281]Columbus Assistant Director for Fire Administration, David Sturtz, interview by author, 21 July 1998, Columbus, notes with author.

[282]Columbus Director of Public Safety Tom Rice, interview by author, 20 July 1998, Columbus, notes with author.

capabilities.[283] Having EMS capable fire engines creates flexibility for emergency dispatches, because the dispatchers can send the closest asset—engine or EMS unit—to the scene of a health emergency.

Working in and among other areas of pubic safety enables the fire division to engage in outside networks, partly because it already knows how to operate in another function's culture. Unlike the police division, the fire division is on familiar ground when working with other facets of the public safety system. Working together with other groups is ingrained in Columbus firefighters.

Another cross-functional advantage of fire culture that aids its adjustment to networks is its "automatic response" agreements with other fire departments in the region. Whereas the police division is hindered by legal limitations between jurisdictions (as well as political limitations posed by sheriff/police jurisdictional rifts), the Columbus Fire Division has standing cooperative agreements to support other fire departments in the surrounding region. This "first on the scene" mentality in the region's fire departments is built on a cultural commitment to do the job wherever it needs to be done, regardless of whose turf it is on. This cultural commitment is just another reason why the fire division is able to participate in so many of the opportunities that the police division simply cannot.

---

[283]Ibid.

Macroculture Factors

While the majority of public safety missions are handled by a single function (e.g.: fire division handles fires; police division handles law enforcement), which leads to strong cultural predominance at the functional (or single organizational) level, some complex emergent threats have forced a macrocultural semblance in the Columbus public safety environment. As a result of a need to work together on some key interorganizational issues, the following characteristics of a macroculture exist in the Columbus public safety network: common communications system and language, common training, common workplace rules and regulations, and common commitments to equal opportunity in the crisis response work environment.

Communications System and Language

The 800MHz dispatching system creates a shared public safety communications infrastructure for safety functions and regions in the Columbus area. Since the system puts all users on the same network, all users speak to each other in talk groups and broadcast messages. Speaking on the same system is forcing organizations and regions that previously used individual radio jargon to develop a common jargon. Tom Trufant, the Columbus Public Safety Assistant Director for Communications, says that police and fire organizations used to speak completely different radio languages during emergencies: police with their "10 codes" and fire with a more English-language styled jargon.[284] Over the course of his career, Trufant also noticed severe language disparities between independent police forces. Each force developed variations of the "10 code" system over time

---

[284]Columbus Public Safety Communications Division Director, Tom Trufant, interview by author, 21 July 1998, Columbus, notes with author.

to the point where officers from different jurisdictions could not communicate on the radio in the Central Ohio region.[285] These differences in emergency communications created obvious problems during crises, because public safety personnel could communicate and coordinate responses only within their isolated functions.

Today, police and fire divisions operate autonomously for most message traffic on their new shared system. They use different channels, talk groups, and dispatchers from each other, but over time, Trufant believes that the language and dispatch barriers will be broken completely.[286] Trufant thinks that the public safety department and the surrounding region is headed toward one dispatch center with one language spoken across the entire network.[287]

The road to a common language and emergency dispatch hub is a long one. When the new system was created, both the fire and police departments insisted on a physical wall of separation between their dispatchers in a dispatch complex housing the 800MHz system.[288] Director Rice also had to assure regionally connected local jurisdictions that they would not lose their dispatch authority in the new system.[289] Dispatch separation is an inauspicious start to a lofty goal of communications coordination and information sharing. Even so, public safety technology and leadership have driven functions and regions together. The next step toward macro-communications will be the implementation of Trufant's vision to digitally track all public service vehicles—buses, trains, police cruisers, fire engines, cabs, and EMS units—on one central screen in the dispatch

---

[285] Ibid.
[286] Ibid.
[287] Ibid.
[288] Ibid.
[289] Ibid.

center.[290] Such a tracking system would allow a computerized dispatch of the closest asset to an emergency. In order to implement such a system, functional and regional systems would have to be pulled even closer together in shared communications, dispatch, and training services.

Common Training

In 1998, the public safety department participated in the U.S. Government's Program for Domestic Preparedness, which was headed by the U.S. Army Chemical and Biological Defense Command. This training highlights the complex threats and subsequent cross-organizational methods of preparedness that are breaking down traditional public safety divisions of fire, police, emergency medical, and special services. As one example of how communities are preparing for complex threats of modern society, the Army's Weapons of Mass Destruction training was run in Columbus as a shared preparation, training, and response network that included several regions and functions. It even incorporated some nontraditional actors, such as private companies. This network training initiative is one example in a growing number of signs that point to a macrocultural approach to public safety in Columbus and around the nation.

The Domestic Preparedness Program is helping Columbus to coordinate, integrate, and execute a program to enhance preparedness for nuclear, chemical, and biological terrorism or attack.[291] It consists of 21 perform-ance objectives that Columbus public safety personnel will meet upon completion of the training. The performance objectives are met through intense instruction to key personnel in eight different courses:

---

[290]Columbus Public Safety Communications Division Director, Tom Trufant, interview by author, 21 July 1998, Columbus, notes with author.

[291]United States Army Chemical and Biological Defense Command, *Training History to Include Nunn-Lugar-Domenici Legislation* (Washington, D.C.: United States Army, 1998), 1.

Course	Personnel
Senior Officials Workshop	Mayor and cabinet
Incident Command	Incident commanders
Basic Awareness	All employees
Responder Awareness	Fire, police, EMS, personnel
Responder Operations	Incident response teams
Technician—HAZMAT	HAZMAT employees
Technician—EMS	EMTs and paramedics
Technician—Hospital Provider	Emergency department physicians/nurses.

The courses differ in three important ways in comparison to how public safety personnel have traditionally been trained in Columbus: (1) they integrate personnel from different divisions in the training; (2) they include nontraditional public safety bureaucracies such as hospital employees and some key businesses; and (3) they emphasize the collective effort among all organizations to work toward a common goal of consequence management. Traditional public safety training occurs in fire and police academies and stations for the division of labor responsibilities that each function handles in the system. What the Army emphasizes in its WMD training is that the threat does not provide clear roles and missions, and that organizations must work together under strategic political leadership and tactical incident commanders to accomplish the overall public safety objectives in the crisis response.

Examples of the collective training begin with its instruction for Columbus's senior political leadership, the Senior Officials Workshop. This course set the city in a mindset of "integrated planning, training, and exercising among all local jurisdictions and its mutual aid partners."[292] This course brought together all public safety organization leaders to set a collective strategy for handling the WMD threat. Columbus does not typically address such overarching goals and objectives among its public safety organizations.

At the lowest level of the training chart is the Basic Awareness Course that most Columbus public safety employees will have completed by the end of the program. It also shows differences between traditional approaches to public safety and the new approaches being used to combat complex threats. This course emphasizes every person's individual role (regardless of civilian or uniformed agency or status) in knowing the potential, signs, unusual trends, and response infrastructure associated with WMD incidents.[293] By bringing all employees together for common training, the Basic Awareness Course provides a common learning environment outside of functional organizations to show public safety personnel that they have tasks that go beyond their everyday work responsibilities in a particular division.

At the heart of the course schedule is the Incident Command Course. This course establishes common management of WMD incidents, regardless of regional or functional affiliation. The Incident Command System is critical in the alignment of common tactical objectives to gain common under-standings of a crisis response. It imposes the same procedures on all commanders in areas of site management, coordination of response assets, casualty management, decontamination, and federal response requests. The federal response requests are important because they force incident commanders into the same procedures when soliciting assets, personnel, or federal support structures in times of crises. The Incident Command

---

[292]U.S. Army Chemical and Biological Defense Command, NBC Domestic Preparedness Training Course Outlines, Senior Officials Workshop, 23.
[293]Ibid., 5.

System, which proved so successful in the wildland firefighting community that it was adopted for WMD training, could lead to a truly streamlined, collective approach to public safety among all levels of government, just as it did in the wildland firefighting community in the late 1970's.

The WMD training is designed to achieve performance objectives in a public safety system, not in any one agency or division of public safety. Its objectives are communal, in that they recognize that a WMD attack is a threat to the entire City of Columbus and its surrounding regional community. Out of this training, common languages, management procedures, resourcing processes, and exercises will emerge beyond the organizational level to help sustain a public safety macroculture in the Central Ohio area.

Common Workplace Rules and Regulations

A macroculture is clearly evident in the area of employment relations across fire, police, and emergency medical services. The vast majority of public safety members are covered under contracts by one of the following three unions: International Association of Firefighters; Fraternal Order of Police; and Association of City and Municipal Employees. The only public safety department members not covered by one of these three unions are: the fire chief and assistant chief; the police chief and five deputies; and the public safety director and assistant directors.

The cultural disparities witnessed between the fire and police divisions are mirrored in their unions. The differences in the nature of police and fire work keeps the unions in disagreement with each other on several major issues. The International Association of Firefighters believes that police wages are higher than fire wages, while the Fraternal Order of Police believe that police officers work harder and thus deserve the higher wage. According to the Assistant Director for Support Services, Robert Hartsell, both organizations are incorrect in their perception that a compensation gap exists at all, because fire compensation is structured differently in terms of wages and benefits. Hartsell believes that the plans turn out to be roughly the same.[294]

Hartsell says that the unions' animosity over wages is unwarranted at another level as well. Police and fire contracts are negotiated 18 months apart, so the two communities do not even negotiate over "the same dollar."[295] Contracts vary according to the city's revenue, public safety budget, expected inflation, and other factors.

At the working level, the public safety employees operate in a macroculture due to the influence of the unions in the work environment. The simple fact that every employee is covered by a union means that work hours, rules, and terms are clear in all of the crisis environments. Both fire and police personnel are limited in terms of functions and hours that they can work. Overtime is paid for special shifts, such as those that fall on holidays. A stiff adherence to seniority is followed in considerations for promotion and special assignments. All of these factors contribute to a pubic safety culture that operates under the watchful oversight of a union, and it is a much different culture than exists in nonunionized crisis response communities.

Common Commitment to Equal Opportunity

In employment relations, both the police and fire divisions have had historical animosity toward minorities, and it is that history that has served as the impetus behind the public safety department's attempt to refocus employment relations on teamwork, trust, and integrity among

---

[294]Columbus Public Safety Assistant Director for Support Services, Robert Hartsell, interview by author, 21 July 1998, Columbus, notes with author.
[295]Ibid.

all employees. The department has a long way to go, and its current macrocultural acceptance of all races is high professionally in the work environment but much lower beneath the surface. This area of macroculture is one in transition.

Historic discrimination in the Columbus Police Division culminated with the 1989 U.S. District Court case, *Police Officers for Equal Rights, et al.-vs-City of Columbus, et al.* This case found systematic discrimination against black Columbus police officers in areas of promotion, station and squad assignment, and shift rotation.[296] Two court orders grew out of the court's findings; one of these orders was a short-term fix to historical discrimination against black officers, while the other order had far reaching, systemic implications that continue to influence the public safety culture in Columbus today. The first order mandated the immediate assignment of black officers to the robbery, homicide, crime scene, search, auto, SWAT, and helicopter squads.[297] The second order mandated the establishment of the Office of Equal Employment Opportunity.[298]

The second court order identified the functions of the Equal Employment Office:

> The EEO office is charged with the responsibility for ensuring within the Columbus Division of Police with all federal and state anti-discrimination laws, decisions of the court and City anti-discrimination regulations. The EEO office shall address claims of unlawful employment discrimination within the Columbus Division of Police and work to prevent the occurrence

---

[296] *Police Officers for Equal Rights, et al. v. City of Columbus, et al.*, C–2–78–394 (6th Cir., 1989).

[297] *Police Officers for Equal Rights, et al. v. City of Columbus, et al.*, C–2–78–394, Interim Court Order No. 10 (6th Cir., 1989).

[298] *Police Officers for Equal Rights, et al. v. City of Columbus, et al.*, C–2–78–394, Interim Court Order No. 12 (6th Cir., 1989).

of discrimination on the basis of sex, handicap, or national origin.[299]

Since the establishment of the office, both the fire and police divisions have been placed under its purview, because the fire division faced similar discrimination problems in its employment relations and Columbus did not need another court case to prompt changes.

Progress has been made since the court cases were enacted almost ten years ago, but further changes remain to be made. One of Columbus's two EEO officers, Aaron Wheeler, says that in comparison to the equal employment environment he experienced in Little Rock, Arkansas, Columbus is way ahead.[300] Wheeler states that, where discrimination was once "openly hostile" in Columbus public safety, it is now a "hidden prejudice."[301]

According to Wheeler, the progress made in moving discrimination from the open to beneath the surface is the same type of progress being made to eliminate it altogether. Under Director Rice's regime, 16 hours of diversity training are required for each new recruit and four refresher hours are mandated every year after recruit graduation.[302] Wheeler believes that Rice's leadership has played an instrumental role in moving public safety culture from one that discriminated to one that accepts diversity. He says that "it's not the (EEO) program…it's the man (Rice)."[303] Wheeler feels that Rice is one of the fairest men he has ever met.

The current employment relations culture reflects Rice's leadership, but improvements still need to be made for complete acceptance of all

---

[299] *Police Officers for Equal Rights, et al. v. City of Columbus*, et al., C–2–78–394 Interim Court Order No. 12 (6th Cir., 1989).

[300] Columbus Public Safety Equal Employment Opportunity Officer, Aaron Wheeler, interview by author, 21 July 1998, Columbus, notes with author.

[301] Ibid.

[302] Ibid.

[303] Ibid.

employees in the system. Two recent cases illustrate "under the surface" discrimination problems that plague the department. The first case involves the Spring 1998 exchange of racially charged information in the Columbus African American Firefighters Association's (CAAFA) newsletter article titled, "White Men Make Better Firefighters" and the underground newsletter called "The Worm." CAAFA President Wes Fullen (who is also a Columbus Fire Division Lieutenant) hurt the feelings of many personnel with comments about perceived differences between black and white firefighters.[304] Fullen's letter was answered in "The Worm" newsletter's second edition, in which the author or authors (identity unknown) stated that black firefighters were "hired by court order" and alluded to the fact that many black firefighters have criminal records.[305] This exchange of racial complaints shows that, while Columbus safety personnel can perform their professional duties well together, tensions still exist along racial lines.

The second case that illustrates the current racial climate is one described by Wheeler of a female African American firefighter with 16 years of service. Her case embodies the progress of the racial hostility from a culture that openly supported discrimination to one that is more subtle today. When she entered the force as a young woman, this firefighter had a mouse placed in her boots by male members of her fire station to indicate their low tolerance and prejudice towards women firefighters.[306] Having survived that openly hostile climate and persevering through a 16-year career, the firefighter recently applied for a promotion that was well within her qualifications. The promotion application was purposely found to have been held up in interoffice mail, so she was denied while someone

---

[304] Ibid.

[305] Aaron Wheeler, *Closure to the "Worm" Newsletter Investigation* (memorandum to Director of Public Safety, Thomas Rice), May 15, 1998.

[306] Ibid.

with less experience was promoted. The difference between her "mouse" days and today, however, is that she petitioned the EEO Office and won back the promotion to which she was entitled.[307]

In the last ten years since the U.S. District Court decision, progress in employment relations has been made at the macrocultural level. Wheeler says that he observes fire, police, and EMS employees of all races going beyond the call of duty together to engage in fun and creating off-duty work relationships together.[308] Discrimination still exists, to be sure, but it has moved underground and is believed to be the work of only a small number of public safety personnel. The court decision, the subsequent establishment and workings of the EEO office, and the director's leadership have all contributed to a public safety macrocultural shift that will hopefully remove discrimination from its last vestige of power in an underground form.

Macroculture as an Interorganizational Crisis Response Principle

Fire, emergency management, and public safety each exhibit macrocultural features, but the influence of the macroculture varies among the three networks based on the characteristics of the crises faced. A macroculture that extends beyond the organizational level is seen in response to crises that require interorganizational responses. When the vast majority of a network's problems are handled by single organizations acting alone, then the predominant cultural characteristics remain at the

---

[307] Aaron Wheeler, Closure to the "Worm" *Newsletter Investigation* (memorandum to Director of Public Safety, Thomas Rice), May 15, 1998.
[308] Ibid.

organizational level. When the problems extend beyond the ability of one organization to respond, the macroculture is strong in comparison to the individual cultures.

The wildfire network possesses a strong macroculture of shared symbols, traits, and practices, which are used to promote values in the system. These shared cultural characteristics extend across all of the organizations and produce a common set of beliefs about wildfire management. Out of these shared beliefs, common training, equipment, communications, language, exercises, and standards emerge. The macroculture produces a unified system of wildfire management that results in the ideal situation where firefighters from completely different network organizations can stand next to each other on the fireline with the same capabilities to engage a crisis. While the network typically agrees upon its macrocultural traits and practices, small differences do sometimes appear. These differences are a result of the organizations' relationships that exist in their "other lives" outside of the network in other networks or in serving other organizational missions.

The Delaware emergency management network also possesses a strong macroculture that has been built on the state's unique communal characteristics, a DEMA leadership philosophy based on open sharing of information, a comprehensive approach to problem-solving, and an alignment of functions and jurisdictions in the state's political system. This network's culture is shaped by information sharing, common planning and training, and continual real world contingencies that are resolved through the network. All of the factors combine to produce a network of emergency management that has similar structures, language and communications, and operating procedures, regardless of level or agency of government.

The Columbus public safety system possesses a relatively weaker macroculture (in comparison with the other two cases), and it is dominated by functionally distinct organizational cultures. The strong single organizational dominance is attributed to the traditional environmental distinctions between law, fire, and public health that are handled by police, fire, and EMS organizations. A public safety macroculture does exist, however, and it is most evident in areas of public safety that require cross-organizational expertise, such as in WMD planning and training. A macroculture also exists among the jurisdictions of public safety that is a result of automatic response and mutual aid agreements to work together. The future macroculture for Columbus will be significantly strengthened by the influence of new technology, which is pushing all public safety functions to adopt similar language, communications, training, dispatch, email, and response systems.

Combining the interorganizational literature with the wildfire, emergency management, and public safety observations, the following interorganizational principle can be said to apply to crisis response networks:

Principle Four: Macroculture

A network possesses a macroculture that distinguishes it from the identities of its members or other networks. The strength of a network is attributable to two variables: (1)the characteristics of the crises it faces in the environment; and (2)the relative dominance of the network in the roles and missions of its member organizations. If the crises predominately dictate responses handled by single organizations, then the network macroculture will be relatively low in comparison with single organizational cultures of member organizations. If the crises in the environment demand integrated network responses, then the network macroculture will be relatively strong in comparison with single organizational cultures of member organizations. If the network comprises the predominance of its member organizations' responsibilities, then the macroculture will be relatively strong. If the network comprises only a portion of member organizations' responsibilities, then macroculture will be relatively weak.

Chapter 7

Principle #5—Structure

Types of Network Structure

Interorganizational networks can be structured as dyads, sets, or networks.[309] A dyad is a pair of organizations that work together to solve a common problem. A set consists of separate organizations with a central focal point. The focal point focuses relations through a central hub to solve the problem between the individual organizations without cross-organizational coordination. Since all coordination occurs in a hub and spoke arrangement around a central focal point, a set actually functions as a series of independent dyad relationships which are coordinated at the center. A network is a "total pattern of interrelationships among a cluster of organizations that are meshed together as a social system to attain collective and self-interest goals or to resolve specific problems for a target population."[310] Crisis response networks can take on characteristics of all three forms, and they can also possess elements of all three forms within the same network. For example, the public safety system exhibits a dyadic relationship when fire and police arrive together on scene to handle a crisis that involves both public health and law enforcement issues; public safety acts as a set around the 9–1–1 emergency call system with the dispatcher

---

[309]Van de Ven and Ferry.
[310]Van de Ven and Ferry.

serving as the central hub with little interorganizational communication; and public safety is beginning to act as a truly integrated network to coordinate the planning and responses to WMD scenarios.

Each framework, whether it be a dyad, set, or network, attains its goals as a unit, and this unit is organized according to its structure and process for organizing the activities of its members. Interorganizational theorists Andrew Van de Ven and Mathew Ferry state that "structure refers to the administrative arrangements that are established to define the role relationships among its members."[311] Process is the flow of activities in direction and frequency of resource and information through the structure. Structure and process combine in different arrangements according to the type of interorganizational relationship.

Four major characteristics of network structure are associated with the organizing activities of the members: *formalization, complexity, centralization, and intensity.*[312] *Formalization* is the degree to which policies, rules, and procedures govern the relationships of the organizations in the network. Two indicators of formalization are contracts (or agreements, memorandums of understanding, etc.) and procedures (i.e.: minutes at meetings, schedules, forms). *Complexity* refers to the number of different elements that are integrated into the network, as well as the number of different resource transactions taking place in the network. Sub-interorganizational cliques, units, and arrangements characterize complex structural networks.[313] *Centralization* refers to the centrality in decision making of information and resource flows. *Intensity* is the volume of resource transitions that occur against the number of agencies in the network.

---

[311]Van de Ven and Ferry, 301

[312]Van de Ven and Ferry, 301.

[313]Richard Hall, *Organizations, Structure, and Process* (Englewood Cliffs, N.J.: Prentice-Hall, 1972).

Oftentimes, the framework for an interorganizational network will be unclear to the outside world, and it may also be confusing to those people working inside the network itself. A well ordered, clearly designed wiring diagram is often not flexible enough to meet the demands of a crisis. While such network arrangements appear to be unclear, confusing, or jumbled, they may have a distinct order and structure specifically tailored for the situation and organizational players involved.

In his 1992 book, *Complexity,* W. Mitchell Waldrop describes a theory of self-organization from research that spans from molecular biology to macro-economics. In complex systems, Waldrop describes self-organization as:

> matter's incessant attempts to organize itself into ever
> more complex structures, even in the face of dissolution
> described by the second law of thermodynamics.[314]

Waldrop uses the recurring tension between life's increasing complexity and ability to break down to explain the inherent order that arises out of seeming disorder. Out of the order/disorder construct, a natural science "law" emerges in complex systems.[315] The principles behind such a "law" apply in interconnected networks. Technological increases return the connections through more communication, better products, and higher complexity in the system.[316] While increasing connections occur, at the same time, the old dissolution tensions force older network arrangements based on other technologies and forms of organization to fade and die as a result of the new gains from the more effective system.

Waldrop's research applies to interorganizational crisis response networks because of the way that such networks tend to self-organize. Whether the

---

[314]W. Mitchell Waldrop, *Complexity: The Emerging Science at the Edge of Chaos* (New York: Bantam Books, 1992), 102.

[315]Waldrop, 112.

[316]Waldrop, 119.

organization occurs because of circumstances under the internal resource allocation model or the external systems change model, each model can be explained as examples of "people consciously or even unconsciously organizing without anyone being in charge or consciously planning it."[317] Challenges facing a single organization (i.e.: resource allocation model) or changes in the environment (i.e.: structure change model) both lead "organisms (to) constantly adapt to each other through evolution," thereby organizing themselves into a workable system. In this regard, organizations are no different from other living forms. They constantly adapt structure to meet the environment and change to meet new crises, threats, and opportunities. In each case, Waldrop says:

> groups of agents seeking mutual accommodation and self-consistency somehow manage to transcend themselves, acquiring collective properties such as life, thought, and purpose that they might never have possessed individually.[318]

It is for the self and collective interests that organizations come together to build network structures that meet the needs of both the organizations in them and the environments to which they must respond. These systems are adaptive and do not passively stand by as the world changes around them; they "turn what happens to their advantage...constantly reconnecting and reorganizing...connections to learn from experience.[319]

The structure of an interorganizational network varies according to the demands of the situation that it faces and the organizations involved. The situation could be a one-time crisis or crises could recur periodically; it

---

[317]Waldrop, 11.

[318]Waldrop, 11.

[319]Waldrop, 11.

could be the same form of crisis or it could be a drastically different one to which the network must respond. The organizations might be the same ones over extended periods of time; or the network might be one that infuses new organizations to meet new demands while discarding organizations that no longer serve its needs. Waldrop's thesis should not be missed in all of these different structural alternatives, and the thesis is that patterns appear in the order of life, so as functioning systems, crisis response frameworks have their own patterns unique to their situation and its players. It is these patterns that are essential, and it is essentially the elements in the pattern which this book attempts to uncover in order to explain the common characteristics among interorganizational crisis response networks.

Structured Failure: The Interorganizational Response to Three Mile Island

In his December 1999 report, "Crisis Management Theory and the Lessons of Three Mile Island," Chris Seiple recaps the interorganizational structural failure of the United States' only experience with a significant chemical, biological, or radiological incident in its history. Seiple's lessons from Three Mile Island apply as much today as they did over 20 years ago, and they are: (1)crises do happen, (2)uncertainty reigns in crisis response, (3)public health is the ultimate end state, (4)resolution costs in society are high, (5)evacuations are difficult, and (6)planning is everything. These lessons were learned the hard way at Three Mile Island through a poorly structured response.

In his research, Seiple uncovered three fundamental structural shortfalls that crisis response networks can heed today: (1)the Three Mile Island network hub-its emergency operations center-was incapable of rapidly accessing critical information surrounding the crisis, and once information was accessed, it could not identify and gather the appropriate authorities together for analysis and decision making; (2)Public relations was handled through individual organizational methods instead of through one coordinated interorganizational message, and as a result, onsite, federal, state, local, private, media, and speculative sources all contributed differing accounts of the crisis and misinformed the public and each other on several occasions; (3)the crisis lacked a social construct (i.e.: macroculture) through which the response organizations and the larger public could work constructively together to resolve the crisis. The Staff Report to the President's Commission on the Accident at Three Mile Island recommended "the establishment of viable channels for communication and interaction...interface of various units in the development, testing and updating of potential hazards, and appropriate protection action." What Seiple finds distressing in his report is that the organizational structure lessons of Three Mile Island, or its larger cousin of that era, Chernobyl, have not led to more effective response structures beyond the radiological community.

Structuring Communications

Communication is perhaps the single most important factor in shaping and structuring an interorganizational relationship. Information flows are reciprocally interdependent and are good indicators of growth, adaptation, and survival of the interorganizational relationship over time. Similarly, disruptions in information flows due to changed mission, individual organizational changes, or frictions in the medium of information exchange, can damage or kill the interorganizational relationship. In today's interorganizational networks, communication operates according to both traditional theories of effective communication and new mediums of communication that have created new structural components at the interorganizational level. Communication differs from its cultural cousin, language, in that communications is the "how" and language is the "what" mediums through which thinking is conveyed throughout an organized entity in order to achieve a common result.

Organizational theorist Chester Barnard's theories accurately convey the nature and factors of effective interorganizational communications structure. To Barnard, communication must be viewed as authoritative if it is to be acted upon. Barnard states that communication is viewed as authoritative when the communication is understood; when the receiver believes it to be consistent with the purpose of the organization; if it is in line with the receiver's interests; and if the receiver is able to comply with the communication.[320] These principles of effective communication are in line with the unique demands of crisis response networks, because the network communication must be accurate, understandable, consistent with crisis

---

[320]Chester Barnard, *The Functions of the Executive* (Cambridge: Harvard University Press, 1938).

objectives, in line with individual organization interests, and susceptible of accomplishment by the organization to which the task has been assigned.

Barnard also describes the nature of the communication of authority and its corresponding elements:

(1) that the character of authority lies in the assent of those to whom it is sent;

(2) that the system of communication is a constant problem of formal organization;

(3) that there are controlling factors in the character of the communication system as a system of objective authority.

The controlling factors are:

(a) the channels should be definitely known by all parties;

(b) there is a definite formal channel for every member;

(c) the line of communication must be as direct and short as possible;

(d) the complete line of communication should be used to keep all parties informed;

(e) communication filters must be competent because they decide how and where information flows;

(f) interruptions to communication must be handled as a top level organizational priority; and

(g) communication must be authenticated (attached to a specific member) (Barnard, 1938).

The Structure of Effective Interorganizational Communications

The Nature of the Communications
- Communications are tied to the network's authority structure
- Command and control systems must facilitate order giving and receiving
- Shared or collaborative systems must facilitate debate, discourse, and discussion

Factors of the Communications
- Clear channels
- Accessible; open to all members organizations where necessary
- Direct
- Tied to information; information conduit; information hub
- Maintenance; breakdowns do not become failures
- Available where decisions must be made
- Real-time information provided

Means of Communications
- Electronic data
- Voice
- Broadcast messages
- Social exchange
- Tasking mechanism

The network organization's authority system must be established in line with, not opposed to, the nature of communications. It must have the "consent of the governed" organizational members, and so it must communicate its needs in a way that is acceptable, based on agreed upon terms; it must recognize that communication is difficult, breaks down, and is often misunderstood; and it must follow the coordinating factors, keeping in mind such essentials as clarity, timeliness, directness, proper filter maintenance, and authentication. Barnard's theory rests on an acceptable, sound communications system in the interorganizational network, and it emphasizes that keeping aligned with the nature of communications is central to success.

Barnard's observations of communication are especially relevant today, because, while the nature of communication is timeless, its mediums have changed. Low end technologies such as the personal computer and the internet are the most visible signs of the changed face of communications. Part of the reason that interorganizational relationships have been able to bloom is a result of the increased capacity to transmit and receive information from one organization to another, from one organization to its operating environment, and from the environment back to the organization.

Electronic Data Interchange (EDI) has been most instrumental in the transition of information between organizations through its computer-based exchange of standardized business-related content.[321] Once one or more dominant network organizations adopted EDI, then other organizations tended to follow suit.[322] The power and trust placed in "leading" organizations has played a large role in the strategic gains that have been made from alliances based on electronic information sharing.

Going beyond EDI, which is primarily an information sharing network, interorganizational email has exploded the contact between organizations and led to unprecedented numbers of connections at the sub-unit and employee levels.[323] Interorganizational email has been used for three primary functions: (1)broadcasting; (2)tasking; and (3)social exchange.[324] Broadcasting was clearly the most popular use out of the three functions, and this finding suggests that networks use email primarily as a means to provide all organizations with updated information that pertains to the collective purposes for which they gather.

---

[321] Paul Hart and Carol Saunders, "Power and Trust: Critical Factors in the Adoption and Use of Electronic Data Interchange," *Organization Science* 8, no. 1 (January/February 1997): 23–42.

[322] Hart and Sanders.

[323] William Kettinger and Varun Grover, "The Use of Computer-Mediated Communication in an Interorganizational Context," Decision Sciences 28, no. 3 (Summer 1997): 513–555..

[324] Kettinger and Grover, 513–555.

A current policy initiative illustrates an effective implementation of the new electronic information exchange. On May 12, 1998, Vice President Gore announced a new computer network system to track outbreaks of food-borne illnesses.[325] This network, structured completely around technology (and probably impossible just ten years ago), coordinates federal, state, and local agencies together in a "virtual" response to contamination crises. The network uses the internet to broadcast information, assign tasks, and collect feedback among scientists, laboratories, private businesses, and state epidemiologists.[326]

Technology is not the only factor that is changing the structure of interorganizational communications. Key people in interorganizational networks have been witnessed to play important roles as "boundary spanners."[327] These individuals play an important part in building trust within the network. Their roles are particularly relevant in times of risk or uncertainty concerning the motives, capabilities, or dependability of organizations in the network.[328] The boundary spanners act as the "glue" in the communication structure that holds the network together by their creation of sub-networks of interorganizational experts who interact with each other and then share their knowledge with their individual member organizations.

Technology and people often combine with physical factors that can increase or inhibit the effectiveness of communication between organizations. Communications channels in interorganizational relationships; such as a network headquarters, the "look and feel" of a network email system, or the layout of a network's crisis response center; can influence

---

[325]Sandra Sobieraj, "Computer Network Set to Track Food Illnesses," *Philadelphia Inquirer*, 13 May 98, A–15.

[326]Sobieraj, A–15.

[327]Currall and Judge, 151–170.

[328]Steven Currall and Timothy Judge, "Measuring Trust Between Organizational Boundary Role Persons," *Organizational Behavior and Human Decision Processes* 64, no. 2 (November 1995) 151–170.

the success or failure of the network at large. The objectives of an effective environmental design in such channels are:

(1) its ability to convey knowledge;

(2) its ability to facilitate work accomplishment in a setting that minimizes distraction, disorientation, and discomfort; and

(3) its support of operation leaders to communicate most clearly (through layout, aesthetics, psychological, and auxiliary needs).[329]

The key to the physical channel is that it must encourage, versus discourage, organizations, representatives, or boundary spanners to engage in the interorganizational communications structure. Regardless of the channel, the communication network must enhance the ties between organizations, because communications are sometimes the only links between organizations in the network and the organization to the network. If communication structures are frustrating or difficult, they could lead members to discontinue their use, which could stifle the network or even kill it.

As communications increasingly tie more organizations together, thus enabling networks to take various combinations of forms, from dyads, to sets, to networks, and even the same networks using portions of all three forms, a set of evaluation questions can assist any network in identifying its current structural form and perhaps the form it might need to take in the future.

---

[329]Coleman Lee Finkel, "Meeting Facilities That Foster Learning," *Training and Development* 51, no.7 (July 1997).

Questions Pertaining to Network Structure

1. For what kind of crises does the network prepare?
2. Which additional crises exist for which the network should prepare and does not?
3. What are the current crisis management capabilities? How well are plans matched with needs? What is missing?
4. Are there crisis management manuals? Are they up-to-date and user friendly?
5. How is the network alerted to a crisis?
6. What types of communication linkages between organizations are used for crisis management? (phone, internet/email, satellite)
7. How would you describe the organizational structure of the network? Hierarchical, hub and spoke, mutual exchange, different for every crisis?
8. Based on past crises, are lessons widely shared?
9. Does learning explore what went well and what could be improved?
10. Has performance been improved based on past observations?
11. Does the formal network structure impede crisis management efforts in any way?
12. Are communications channels clear and open for all players? Are new technologies used to enhance existing communications channels and add new ones? Are communications technologies used to connect new members to the network?
13. Does a network crisis management team define roles and missions for each crisis?
14. How are crises detected?
15. Is a control mechanism or audit framework used?

The Structure of Wildland Fire Suppression

The wildland fire suppression network is organized to accommodate mobility of people and resources. The structure is designed to allow for exchanges of people and resources across organizations based on the demands of the situation. The network organization is hierarchical, with interorganizational representation at every level. This network structure is also completely integrated, with individual organizations rarely responding to wildfires on their own. The structure is organized to handle its unique fire crises, and it responds to those crises with an integrated approach. The network also must consider political factors that influence its structure.

The wildland fire management network is designed around a concept of "total" mobility, which means that resource allocation begins at the local level and can be expanded all the way through the national level. At the national level, the network's responsibilities are defined for it in the Federal Response Plan under Emergency Support Function #4 (i.e.: firefighting). Requests for assistance are transmitted from the Federal Emergency Management Agency (FEMA) to regional offices, called Geographic Area Coordination Centers (GAACs). The GAACs organize a response to fire incidents until the incidents grow beyond their ability to control. At such a point, the National Interagency Coordination Center (NICC) is summoned to provide national prioritization and support through the total mobility concept.

The structure of "total" mobility is most clearly seen in the movement of its two greatest assets: personnel and resources. Both of these assets are interorganizational in structure. At the local level, local personnel are used until the fire spreads beyond the means of local control. Mobilization of additional personnel are provided at the regional level by the appropriate

GAAC. Once regional personnel are exhausted, the GAAC petitions the NICC for national personnel resources.

Typically, firefighting teams are on assignment for 21–30 days, depending on the types of units being used. Four different types of personnel can be moved in the wildfire system. The first is the Incident Management Team, of which there are eighteen teams available on a national level.[330] The second type of personnel is the specialized "hotshot" and "smokejumper" teams which are used to combat the most difficult types of fires in their most dangerous areas. There are 68 hotshot crews and approximately 350 smokejumpers available for tasking by the NICC across the nation. The third type of personnel are special skills teams, such as the Interagency Buying Teams, which are designed to handle particular pieces of fire management operations (in this case finance). Finally, the fourth type of personnel are Type II crews, or general purpose firefighters, who are available to handle basic fire incidents. These crews are plentiful across the GAACs, and they originate from federal agencies, state forestry agencies, Native American tribes, and even some state prison populations. All Type II crews can be mobilized for national application in fires that occur in any GAAC (with the exception of prison crews). Like other wildland fire resources, personnel are used from the immediate area first, neighboring GAACs second, and across the country as only a last resort. The ever-expanding flow of resources from local through national levels applies for personnel as well as equipment.

As with personnel, local and regional resources are expended before transfers of national level resources occur. In the GAAC structure, all federal agencies and state forestry agencies fall under the control of the

---

[330]For a detailed description of such an organization, see Thomas Ricks's study of the United States Marine Corps titled: *Making the Corps* (New York: Scribner, 1997).

GAAC in their jurisdiction, so transfers inside the region often quell fire incidents. When complex fires reach dangerous levels, resources are mobilized through resource orders placed with the NICC. The system is designed for rapid exchange, and the order of flow can be seen in the diagram below. The NIFC also holds control over some resources as central assets, which are located at Boise or in one or more of the GAACs. These assets must be coordinated through the NIFC from all levels, and they include air tankers, supply caches, smokejumper crews, infrared aircraft, and many more specialized items and teams. As with all of the assets in the ordering system, these assets are detailed in the National Interagency Mobilization Guide, which is available to all agencies and jurisdictions that may need to place orders for such assets. For example, such assets include the centrally controlled "hotshot" crews that perform some of the most difficult fire management practices. There are 65 such crews at the national level, and they can be requested through the resource order system through the NICC. The order forms simply list who needs the assets and who will receive them in order to properly bill for the activity.

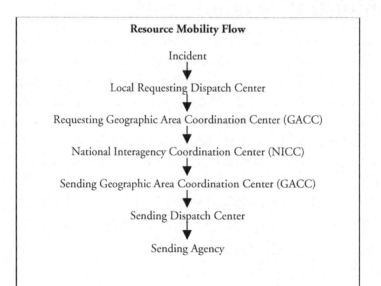

Resource Mobility Flow

Incident
↓
Local Requesting Dispatch Center
↓
Requesting Geographic Area Coordination Center (GACC)
↓
National Interagency Coordination Center (NICC)
↓
Sending Geographic Area Coordination Center (GACC)
↓
Sending Dispatch Center
↓
Sending Agency

Air assets represent another key resource in the total mobility system. The BLM's James Villard runs air resource operations at NIFC, and he keeps updated computerized national rosters for all air tankers and helicopters for use in future fires. According to Villard, tankers are controlled by the NICC but are available to GAACs in the tanker's home area by the home GAAC simply notifying the NICC of their use. Air tankers are agency-owned, so their application to fires is accomplished with little coordination. Helicopters, on the other hand, are provided to the network via three sources: agency-owned; contracted; and "call-when-needed." Villard uses contracted helicopters for most of the NICC's requirements, because agency-owned helicopters are sparse, and "call-when-needed" helicopter pilots are very expensive. As with other fire suppression assets, local helicopters are used by GAACs for initial requirements, and once these are exhausted (or more are required), Villard fills the void with neighboring GAAC resources or the outside contracts.

Administrative Framework

At the administrative level, it is quite clear to member agencies how and what roles they play in the network. With representation at the NIFC board and MAC Group level, all member organizations have input into the structure and workings of wildland fires. If special assets or functions are required of specific members, those members have agreed to them in writing and provide them upon request. One example of such an understanding is in the 1997 Interagency Smokejumper Agreement between the Bureau of Land Management and the U.S. Forest Service for the Forest Service to provide 35 experienced smokejumpers to the Bureau of Land Management for duty in the Alaska Fire Service.[331] This agreement

---

[331] Incident Management Teams are described in detail later in this chapter.

contracted a group of assets from one member organization to another in order to meet an overall NIFC objective of fire suppression in the state of Alaska. Possessing the majority of smokejumpers, the Forest Service and the Bureau of Land Management both recognized that it was the Forest Service's job to provide the asset to the Bureau of Land Management with the expectation of appropriate payment of salaries, expenses, and equipment.

Operational Framework

The operational interagency framework of wildland fire management moves up from the tactical level to the national level under the National Interagency Management System's concept of unification of personnel and resources. Incident Management Teams are prepared for the close-in fight, Area Commands are designed to handle the broader implications that surround complex fires, the Incident Support Organization is designed to act as a clearinghouse for all cross-area coordination and national policy implementation, and finally, the MAC Group stands at the apex of the hierarchical interorganizational structure to provide over-all goals, objectives, and guidance for the system. The interorganizational structure is described in courses offered to all member organizations at the National Advanced Resource Technology Center. The structure provides for the identification of responsibilities, a multi-organizational approach to fire management, and an understanding of the division of labor among the different levels during crisis operations.

The MAC Group resides at the top of the hierarchical structure, and it is designed to take the broadest look at fire management situations in order to properly prioritize resources up to the national level. While the MAC Group concept of representation and prioritization works at all levels, it is at the national level that member organization representation on such weighty issues is most visible. The national MAC Group is composed of members from the U.S. Forest Service, Bureau of Land Management, National Parks Service, Bureau of Indian Affairs, U.S. Fish and Wildlife Service, National Weather Service, Office of Aircraft Services, and occasional representatives from state forestry agencies, Government Services Administration, and the U.S. military. The national group is located at the NIFC in Boise.

The next level down in the interorganizational structure is the Incident Support Organization (ISO). This level carries out the direction and guidance given by the MAC Group and provides two key functions: expanded dispatch and administrative support. Expanded dispatch is concerned with disseminating intelligence, equipment and supplies, aircraft, and personnel for use across areas in complex incidents. Administrative support is provided in areas of procurement, timekeeping, claims, and accounting to ensure that proper charges and reimbursements are awarded affected agencies and effective contacts are made with outside organizations.

The ISO for the national level is the National Interagency Coordination Center (NICC). The NICC is internally organized to support all coordination requirements from the GAACs when the GAACs are overrun in any area of fire suppression. The NICC's staff assistant, Jinny Boyles, states that the NICC is designed to match requirements with resources throughout the entire wildland system.[332] The NICC is divided into air, equipment, personnel, and intelligence sections, and each section is staffed by members from all NIFC member organizations. The sections have complete breakdowns of available people, assets, teams, and special skills associated with their functional areas that can be tasked for movement across jurisdictions in support of hostile fires.

---

[332]National Interagency Fire Center, *National Interagency Mobilization Guide* (National Interagency Coordination Center, 1997), 147.

Both the MAC Group and ISO levels are designed to handle broad decisions that impact across areas and incidents in complex situations. They relieve tactical and area commanders of many responsibilities associated with the logistics and support for operations that cannot be adequately managed from an incident scene. The lower two levels, area command and incident management, are designed to handle the immediate operational and tactical level needs presented by the fire situation. The Area Commander is responsible for a geographic location that is suitably fit to be managed as a whole. There can be more than one such commander for very intense fires.

Under the Area Commanders are Incident Commanders, and it is their job to handle specific portions of a fire management situation. Incident command is managed by Incident Management Teams, which are often composed of interagency personnel. Under the standardization imposed by the National Interagency Incident Management System (NIIMS), every agency and state and local government understands how the pieces of an interagency fire management team fit together. The NIIMS's "Field Operations Guide" describes the components of an ICS fire management force, to include the details of its command, operations, plans, logistics, and finance sections.[333] This guide breaks down each section of the operation to the number and type of personnel required to handle varying types of fires based on size and severity.[334]

---

[333]Jinny Boyles, Bureau of Land Management, interview by author, 6 October 1998, Boise, Idaho, notes with author.

[334]National Incident Management System, *Field Operations Guide* (Stillwater, Oklahoma: Fire Protection Publications, 1983), 2–3.

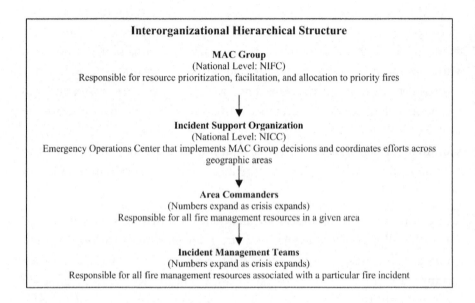

One example of the many skills detailed in the guide is seen in the description of the position, status recorder, which is one small assignment in the scheme of fire management. The guide specifies that the plans section of an ICS should have one status recorder for up to two incidents in one wildland fire scenario (i.e.: same fire with two different hot spots); two recorders if the same scenario increases to five incidents; and three recorders if the number of incidents reaches ten or more.[335] This type of detailed knowledge of personnel and equipment based on the fire characteristics is provided for every single position in the fire

---

[335]Ibid.

management operation. This thoroughness insures that all agencies and governments that must respond in the NIFC system are familiar with the operating procedures and requirements of ICS and, thus, insures that they are all familiar with how and where they fit into a tactical firefight.

The standard Incident Management Team is composed of eight members. They are the incident commander, deputy commander, safety officer, planning section chief, logistics section chief, finance section chief, operations section chief, and air operations branch director. The team can be expanded to include many more specific skills when they are demanded in specific incidents. There are 18 teams at the national level that are available upon request to respond to tactical level incidents.

The wildland fire management structure is designed with the intent that all jurisdictions, agencies, and organizations understand its hierarchy and can implement a fire management situation based on the hierarchical concept. It provides each level with responsibilities commensurate with the scope or breadth of that particular level. Every agency understands how its members fit into such a system, and through representation at the MAC Group level, each organization has representation in the formulation of overall fire management strategy. Typically, an Incident Management Team is comprised of members of the same organizations, but just as typically, the teams can be augmented by members from other organizations or they can be fighting for an area commander from another jurisdiction or agency. The key to the hierarchical system is that all organizations understand that it is not focused on individual organizations fighting autonomously toward a common goal; instead, it is a unique grouping of a network of firefighters and managers that is organized along the lines of a concept that looks different in every situation in which the concept is employed.

The Structure of Emergency Management

The structure of emergency management in Delaware provides for both physical and information-based ways that network organizations can "plug in" to the network during an emergency. The clarity of understanding among the network's organizations is attributed to three characteristics of Delaware emergency management: (1)organization according to the nature of the threats posed in the environment; (2)a central operations center that provides organizations with both physical and informational access to all aspects of the emergency situation; and (3)the clearly defined breakdown of organizational responsibilities into facilitation, support, and incident management.

DEMA's organization is based on the types of threats (i.e.: natural hazard and nuclear, biological, and chemical) it faces in the environment. This organizational form is based on FEMA's recommended model of emergency management and a governor-sponsored set of recommendations to improve Delaware's emergency management. Both sets of recommendations pushed DEMA away from its traditional functional organization (i.e.: plans, operations, administration). The commission report found: poor coordination between functional areas; a lack of responsibility in operations personnel outside of actual emergencies; and a lack of knowledge in operations personnel of emergency plans "even though they are responsible for coordinating the implementation of the plans in emergencies."[336] One example of recent change is visible in DEMA's reorganization of its Radiological

---

[336]Fax between Delaware Secretary of Public Safety and Director of Emergency Management, 12 December 1995.

Emergencies Section to a new section that includes not only radiological emergencies from power plants but other forms of nuclear, biological, and chemical emergencies.

The organization of DEMA around the types of threats it faces in the environment provides for planning, training, and implementation from the same experts at DEMA headquarters. This is a direct contrast to traditional management that provided a planner, trainer, and operator at different stages of an emergency. The new model of organization provides comprehensive coverage of a threat by DEMA subject experts. These experts work at all stages of the emergency with the outside organizations and levels of government involved in a specific area of emergency management. DEMA coordinators are now familiar with their plans and points of contact, so actual emergencies are managed more effectively. It also helps that FEMA is organized in a similar manner, because specific types of crises are now handled by the same personnel at the local, state (at those states that have converted their structures), regional, and national levels.

Boundary Spanners

Many successful networks have individuals that move between and among organizations. These individuals are known as boundary spanners. Boundary spanners provide network links between organizations to help identify and understand the actions of other organizations in the network. At both federal and state levels in Delaware's emergency management network, boundary spanners serve key roles.

From the federal level, FEMA provides a liaison to DEMA from its mid-Atlantic regional headquarters in Philadelphia upon request during a crisis. During Hurricane Bonnie, FEMA State Liaison Officer Nelson Wiles reported for the crisis. According to FEMA's standing operating procedures, Wiles was at DEMA to "serve as a link between the State Operations Staff and the Region."[337] In crises such as Bonnie (where the level of federal support turned out to be minor) the FEMA state liaison officer's job is to offer advice to state officials based on his/her field experience and familiarity with FEMA policies. During an emergency requiring substantial regional and federal support, state liaison officers are the primary interface between FEMA regional headquarters and Delaware, acting as the expediter and coordinator of federal resources until federal field operations can be established in Delaware.[338]

At the state level, DEMA provides liaison officers to its local counties and cities upon request. Acting much in the same capacity as FEMA's liaisons, these DEMA representatives coordinate and expedite state level support for local governments by using their knowledge of DEMA's points of contact, as well as their extensive lists of contacts in other state agencies. During Hurricane Bonnie, Sussex County requested and received such a liaison from DEMA to help in case the hurricane exacted tremendous damages and to coordinate the delivery of many thousands of sandbags from state agencies.[339]

The linking mechanism of boundary spanning liaison officers provides clarity for government coordination in a crisis. With FEMA's representative assisting DEMA and DEMA's representative assisting local governments, the central hub of the network is kept informed of the operations and capabilities of other levels of government. This structural design keeps organizations informed of other network players and provides open lines of communication from which requests for support, critical information, and general awareness can be provided at all levels.

---

[337] Federal Emergency Management Agency Region III, *Operations Section Standing Operating Procedures* (Philadelphia: Federal Emergency Management Agency, 1998), Annex C.

[338] Federal Emergency Management Agency Region III, *Operations Section Standing Operating Procedures* (Philadelphia: Federal Emergency Management Agency, 1998), Annex C.

[339] DEMA staff meeting at 11:45 a.m. on 25 August 1998 to prepare for Hurricane Bonnie.

Operations Center

The structural design of the DEMA operations center provides both a physical and information-based architecture for organizations of the network to join and participate in the operations of a crisis response. The physical feature of an operations center provides the central meeting place around which a crisis is planned and implemented. At DEMA, this central place provides offices for DEMA liaison officers, other state agency representatives, senior decision makers, incident assessment, incident operations, public affairs, and many other functions. The new operations center will go even further, reserving seats at operations monitors before several computer screens that will keep all relevant organizations informed on the status of the crisis and provide detailed information on their area of the crisis.

The Delaware Emergency Operations Center also provides an information structure to organizations of the network. The center provides hurricane, radiological, tidal, and wind software program results from various sources to its local agencies. While most of this information is currently pulled from many areas and faxed or called to local governments or responsible agencies, it will soon be incorporated into the Electronic Information System, available to all organizations in the emergency management network. This system will provide the information structure from which the network will coordinate its overall response, monitor individual programs, and track essential functions such as personnel assignment and logistics during a crisis. It will provide a common network information structure that all organizations will use to perform their roles for the network.

Task Identification

The structure of task identification in Delaware emergency management is fairly straightforward. There are three general types of tasks in the network: facilitation, support, and incident management. The organizations involved in these tasks are provided with a description of how and where their tasks fit into the overall structure of emergency management for a particular situation.

Facilitation is conducted by the central operations centers at three levels. Local government emergency management operations centers handle isolated situations that arise in their particular domain, but they are most often used to handle the local coordination in a statewide emergency operation. DEMA, as has been thoroughly described in this chapter, operates its emergency operations center as the state's coordination hub for emergency response, effectively bringing in local, state, and federal agencies to conduct a response. FEMA operates its Region III (mid-Atlantic states) emergency operations center that provides a structure around which 27 federal agencies converge to plan and resolve wide-scale emergencies. At all of these levels, the structure of emergency response is centralized at an emergency operations center, and these centers allow all organizations to "plug-in" to the overall response where and when they are needed.

Support tasks in Delaware emergency management are structured in two ways: intergovernmental agreements and Emergency Support Functions (ESFs). Intergovernmental agreements help federal agencies and other state governments to understand the type, quantity, and location of assistance in a Delaware emergency. They also provide DEMA with the support function of assisting local Delaware government emergency management agencies with additional state resources. ESFs provide state agencies and local governments with specific support roles for which they have primary or secondary responsibility when the DEOP is employed. Both the intergovernmental agreements and ESFs provide the structure of a collective response which allows organizations to understand how their efforts are being applied in a crisis.

The structure of emergency management in Delaware is one that reflects the nature of its environment and the characteristics of its member organizations. Largely drawing on intergovernmental cooperation and coordination from many levels, this network focus is at the state level, with a command and control styled response. Delaware government is controlled at the state level and provides the executive branch with the authority to structure an institutionalized response network through the DEOP and DEMA's emergency operations center. State organizations recognize their roles in emergency management and plan, train, and implement those roles accordingly. Although private and voluntary organizations play important roles in emergency response, the vast majority of the institutionalized management of the emergency is provided by government organizations. As a result, the state operations center is the recognized focal point to which other public organizations go to perform their individual roles in the network.

The Structure of Public Safety

In comparison with states such as Pennsylvania and New York, Ohio places the lionshare of its responsibility for the public's safety at the municipal and county levels. Lacking the equivalent of Pennsylvania's or New York's state police organizations (that have statewide public safety jurisdictional authority), Ohio limits its policing powers to "state owned and leased property" and protects that property through the Ohio Highway Patrol.[340]

---

[340]Columbus Public Safety Equal Employment Opportunity Officer, Aaron Wheeler, interview by author, 21 July 1998, Columbus, notes with author.

Lacking an overarching state-level organization, the Ohio public safety system has emerged through a framework of local jurisdictions, complete with uneasy alliances between the highway patrol and local jurisdictions, and a system of shared powers between municipal police departments and county sheriff departments. These traditional political arrangements have made the job of structuring networks for public safety very difficult, as turf battles and threats of sovereignty restriction have kept public safety organizations apart.[341] In a system based on jurisdiction, each individual public safety component understood which jurisdiction would handle which emergency based on the location of the public safety incident.

In regard to the provisions for fire and emergency medical services, Ohio operates much like other states. The state provides training and certification for fire and EMS personnel, but it leaves the administration and operation of these functions to the municipal and county levels. For example, the Ohio Division of Emergency Medical Services meets its mission by providing a training environment, research facility, and technical assistance center for individuals in the emergency medical service community.[342] There are currently 88 EMS training facilities throughout the state, and the mission of these facilities is to turn out trained personnel for local EMS units.[343]

The Ohio political system dictates a separated, jurisdictional approach to public safety. It is fragmented between state and localities by the limitations placed on the Ohio Highway Patrol, and it is severed by the conflicting and sometimes competing responsibilities within the localities in areas where county and municipal lines run together. While the political

---

[341] State of Ohio, *Ohio Highway Patrol Online [Internet]*, State of Ohio Webmaster, WWW: http://www.odn.ohio.gov/ohp/duties.html, June 1998.

[342] Columbus Director of Public Safety Tom Rice, interview by author, 20 July 1998, Columbus, notes with author.

[343] State of Ohio, *Ohio Division of Emergency Medical Services Online [Internet]*, State of Ohio Webmaster, WWW: http://www.ohio.gov/odps/division/ems/ems.html#/Mission, June 1998.

structure establishes public safety separation by geographical location, other forces are working to bring public safety to a more collective approach.

Structural Adjustments

The structure of public safety is shifting in part due to new challenges presented in public safety. Four clear challenges have forced structural changes in public safety in recent years: the use of cellular phones in emergency situations; population increases in the Columbus and surrounding areas; the emergent threats posed by Weapons of Mass Destruction; and the advent of information age infrastructure into public safety. The network of public safety, which used to be relatively self-contained to the City of Columbus, is evolving into a regional framework designed to share information, provide mutual assistance, and more effectively and efficiently serve citizen interests.

The advent and rise of the cellular phone created both problems and opportunities in the Columbus public safety system. On the positive side, police and fire officials now have a fleet of mobile emergency observers who can report crimes or fires from cars as de facto public safety observation posts. The problem created with this technology is that cellular phones are not connected to the city's land phone line infrastructure. This infrastructure provides location and other critical information pertaining to emergencies. Cellular phone calls can aide in the timeliness of information, but unless callers are stationary and aware of their surroundings, they cannot give pinpoint locations or caller identification information.

The changes brought on by cellular phones have created a side effect in public safety that has pulled together state, county, and municipal safety systems. The need to geographically pinpoint 9–1–1 phone calls led the U.S. Congress to pass legislation requiring state public safety systems to provide geographical grid coordinates for all 9–1–1 cellular phone calls starting in 2001.[344] Columbus is meeting its requirement by the intro-duction of a shared state-run system that will use Global Prepositioning System (GPS) technology to locate cellular phone emergency calls. The City of Columbus and Franklin County have been designated as the two GPS agents for the Greater Columbus Metropolitan area, and with their shared 800 MHz dispatch operation, the two parties will provide GPS cellular phone linkages for the entire area.

The new state-run system is bringing county, city, and state operations closer together because of the advantages and limitations of the technology being used. The advantages are that GPS will give geographic grid coordinates for the mobile 9–1–1 calls to all jurisdictions, even in the most rural, isolated counties. The limitations of the technology is that it is expensive, large, and difficult to maintain, thus denying small jurisdic-tions from simply purchasing their own systems and operating alone. However, opportunities created by technology have resulted in a statewide framework for one area of public safety with regional sharing of informa-tion that could lead to further shared initiatives in the future. The shape of the public safety structure in Columbus and every other area of the state has changed forever as a result.

Two forms of technology have been introduced into the public safety system that have led the Columbus structure from a tightly controlled, internal municipal arrangement to a larger, more inclusive regional network with strong connections to federal agencies and databases. The first change in technology has been in the area of database management, and it has been a slowly evolving area that has progressed over the last

---

344Ibid.

quarter century with improvements in software and hardware technologies. Beginning in 1967 with the implementation of Law Enforcement Automated Data System (LEADS), the Columbus Police Department has long recognized the advantages of having quick access to driver and vehicle information, detection of wanted persons, stolen vehicles, and criminal backgrounds.[345] The LEADS was the first in a long line of database systems allowing many different jurisdictions to collaborate in order to provide more information for street-level law enforcement. Since the original LEADS installment, information technologies have provided many more reasons for jurisdictions to work together to solve common problems.

The most recent technological development pulling jurisdictions together in the Columbus area is the incorporation of the AVATAR Group's intelliVUE document imaging program. This program was incorporated for the Ohio State Highway Patrol Central Records Unit, and it converts all traffic cash reports, case investigations, background, and polygraph documents to CD-ROM media.[346] The intelliVUE initiative provides a shareable database of criminal information that can be accessed on-line by Columbus and surrounding public safety systems.

Columbus is planning database access systems such as those used in *intelliVUE* in an initiative that goes directly to the heart of interorganizational crisis response coordination: providing public safety through a collaborative structure for crisis resolution improvements *at the scene of the emergency.* Columbus police officers will soon be the direct recipients of an interorganizational database system in which they will have portable, hand-held radios with computers installed for direct document referral capability. Using the latest radio wave technology to deliver the information

---

[345]The details of this requirement were provided in Chapter Two.

[346]State of Ohio, *Ohio Highway Patrol Online [Internet]*, State of Ohio Webmaster, WWW: http://www.odn.ohio.gov/ohp/history.html, June 1998.

from database to radio, an officer will soon be capable of directly accessing criminal history, fingerprints, building layout and design, licenses, hazardous material history, mugshots, and a plethora of additional information as he/she walks from police cruiser to front door in an emergency.[347] Such information is currently provided via the Columbus central dispatcher, but this system is time consuming, requires radio communications to one or more sources, and often does not link with all of the various information database points that need to be connected during a crisis.

The 800MHz shared dispatch system is another huge technological advancement that had the intended side-effect of bringing together previously autonomous public safety organizations. This system provides a common communications structure for every public safety organization in the State of Ohio, as well as federal agencies, to communicate with each other over 28 channels during a crisis.[348] Using a "trunking" communications system, a microprocessor monitors, adjusts, and reuses communications channels to establish talk groups for task forces or special services, broadcast channels for general updates and warnings, and one-on-one lines for private communications.[349]

Technological advancements are continuing to break down organizational and jurisdictional barriers in Columbus. In administration, a new computer network is bringing public safety documents on-line to avoid reams of paperwork for overworked fire and police personnel. A new email system is also being incorporated across the public safety network.

Finally, all public transportation vehicles, to include buses, fire engines, and cruisers will be tracked using GPS technology in an effort to provide

---

[347]The AVATAR Group, *IntelliVUE: Knowledge in Motion*, 24 June 1998.

[348]Columbus Public Safety Communications Division Director, Tom Trufant, interview by author, 21 July 1998, Columbus, notes with author.

[349]Ibid.

even faster emergency response times to crises. Linking the GPS locators with the microprocessors in the 800MHz dispatch system, automatic, instantaneous dispatch could soon be on the horizon. In the case of the fire division, which is one step closer to pure consolidation for crises than is the police division, a virtually instantaneous response beyond the boundaries of jurisdictions will be provided by the nearest available fire engine or EMS team. Columbus is not very far away from a truly collective, interorganizational structure that will prepare for and respond to crises, bringing to bear the closest unit, with the most timely information, and a professional response at the point of a public safety threat.

A Common Crisis Response Feature: Network Hubs

When more than one organization seek to resolve a crisis, the issue of operational coordination arises. Coordination for on-the-ground responses are effectively conducted around a *network hub*, where information and decision makers coalesce to coordinate the interorganizational response. At a strategic level, the hub can be observed at the National Interagency Fire Center where the Multi-agency Coordination (MAC) Group determines network priorities and the National Interagency Coordination Center (NICC) facilitates the allocation of network resources to meet those priorities. At an operational level, such as Delaware's emergency management, the Delaware Emergency Management Agency (DEMA) provides a common gathering point for information flow and decision making among federal contacts, state agency representatives, and other states' supporting liaisons. At a tactical level, the modern 9–1–1 emergency response systems provide a common point through which jurisdictional, neighboring agencies, and federal agencies can gather to support a response.

Other crisis response networks also display the *network hub* feature. In foreign peacekeeping operations, a *Civil-Military Operations Center* provides a collective hub around which military, humanitarian, religious, host nation, and international (e.g.: United Nations) personnel can gather to coordinate their responses. Wherever a crisis unfolds and a corresponding interorganizational response follows, a *network hub* is found. Information, communications technologies, key decision makers, and tangentially affected parties who must support the response all must be plugged into the hub in order to understand the situation, offer organizational expertise, hear the reports and assessments of the ongoing response, and adjust their collective efforts accordingly.

Interorganizational Structure as a Crisis Response Principle

The last hypothesis states that the networks possess interorganizational structures that reflect the nature of the environment and the network's organizations. Such a structure allows for the organizations to understand how they fit into the network and communicate in it. The hypothesis stands, but, upon analysis of the three cases, its meaning has slightly changed in two different ways.

The original intent behind the interorganizational structure was that it would be designed around the type of threat that it faced with consideration of organizational characteristics in its member organizations. Upon reflection, it is apparent that the term "environment" must be interpreted to mean not only the nature of the external threat environment but also the prevailing political, legal, and bureaucratic environments from which the network emerges. Each of the networks display structures designed to meet threats in the environment, but their structures are also influenced by their particular public institutions.

The networks, when working most effectively, also exhibit structural features not originally considered in the hypothesis. Each network displays the ability to expand in breadth and depth in the face of overwhelming crises, and when functioning at their best, the networks plan and practice for such expansions. Network expansion in depth can be seen in the geographic enlargement of a response to compensate for a crisis that grows beyond the original network's ability to control. This type of expansion is seen in the wildfire model of organization that expands from local, to state, to regional, to federal levels in both incident management and resource allocation. The network also maintains detailed skill rosters for every conceivable fire job at regional and federal levels. Expansion can also be seen in the emergency management community's ability to shift its focus from local Delaware governments to DEMA to FEMA Region III for area coverage of a crisis. DEMA maintains control of the crisis (in its state), but its structure expands to include other states' resources in the Emergency Management Assistance Compact or federal resources through contacts with FEMA Region III. Finally, geographic expansion is also present in Columbus's fire departments through their automatic response initiatives with regional partners.

Network expansion in breadth considers the networks' abilities to increase their functional expertise or to gain new functions in the face of particular crises. Whereas depth considers the expansion of a network into greater response capabilities, breadth considers the expansion of a network's capabilities at a particular crisis point. Examples of breadth expansion include DEMA's contracting with businesses for unique specialties in the event of serious disasters, or the Columbus Fire Division's bomb squad burden sharing for the entire region, or the NIFC's detailed skill listings and personnel rosters for every conceivable job at regional and federal levels.

The structure of the wildfire network is a thoroughly integrated system that is disseminated and understood throughout the network. At the operational level, the components of the Incident Command System are described in detail through planning, training, and publications. Operational structural expansion is described through the federal level of operations, with the details of each level and member described. Resource structure works in a separate process, but under a similar concept. Its operations are described and defined in the MAC Group publications, training, and exercises.

The DEMA structure reflects its environment and political structure. The environment influences the network in that the network is physically organized around the types of emergencies to which it responds (i.e.: natural hazards, radiological disasters, etc.). The environment also dictates the organization of responsibilities into facilitation, support, and incident management. The political system of Delaware provides relatively strong powers to the governor and the state executive agencies, thus ensuring a state-centric emergency response system where information and resources flow through a central state coordination body (i.e.: DEMA).

The information architecture is designed around the political apparatus, the Emergency Operations Center. The EOC acts as the information filter for a response, providing links to federal and interstate points of contact, other Delaware state agencies, and local governments. It is every organization's information conduit by providing all emergency software packages and network Bridgeline calls. In the new operations center, all information will be centralized on one shared computer network, thus providing all software, email, and administrative information to all organizations at on-site and remote access terminals. Information is also available through boundary spanners, which are located at DEMA. Boundary spanners from federal authorities locate at DEMA to assist in the response, and DEMA boundary spanners move to local emergency management agencies to assist in the response.

The structure of public safety in Columbus is shaped by political, environmental, and technological forces. Politically, the network must incorporate municipal, township, and county public safety forces under a relatively weak state public safety authority. The result of the local powers and jurisdictional separation is a fragmentation of public safety, instead of consolidation and cooperation.

Both the environment and technological advances have forced the traditionally fragmented system to move to a more consolidated network structure. Cellular phone usage has led to regional geographic tracking of 9–1–1 calls, because the GPS and tower approaches are both too expensive for jurisdictions to purchase on their own. Emergent threats, such as WMD, have forced functions and regions of public safety to plan and train together. Finally, the advantages of being on-line for shared information databases on criminals, housing codes, and insurance records has led to regional and functional alignment on shared 800MHz communications structures. Columbus public safety is moving away from traditional political fragmentation toward a structure geared to regional and functional information sharing and automatic response.

Based on the review of the interorganizational literature and the structural review of the interorganizational crisis response networks, the following principle applies:

Principle Five: Interorganizational Structure

An interorganizational structure exists that reflects the nature of the crisis environment in which the network operates as well as the characteristics of its member organizations. In such a structure the member organizations clearly understand what and how they are to perform their roles for the network, and the network also provides a communications structure through which crisis information can be shared, interorganizational communication can be achieved, and collaboration and decision making and dissemination can occur.

Chapter 8

A Model of Crises
and Organizational Responses

Wildland fire, emergency management, and public safety represent three excellent examples of different approaches to crisis response because the problems faced by each network are so different. Each network works well to resolve some types of crises and poorly to resolve others. Similarities and differences among the networks' responses to certain types of crises show that the character of a network influences the types of crises that it can handle effectively. Also, problems faced in the environment force networks to develop properties that address those challenges. Both observations are supported by the fact that networks show structural adjustments and evolve, to respond to new types of crises.

Some of the crises from the case studies are described below to compare the types of crises that each network handles effectively, as well as the types of crises that each network handles less effectively. The networks' adjustments to respond to new threats are recapped. Once the networks' successes and failures in specific crises are documented, conclusions are drawn that match crisis typologies with interorganizational structures best designed to resolve them.

The Columbus public safety network handles single, definable problems that can be clearly fit into its functional division of labor. Robbery, murder, heart attack, and burning buildings are capably planned, trained for, and responded to on a daily basis by organizations divided by law, fire, and health functions of public safety. The public safety network does not handle crises that are less distinguishable along functional lines. These types of problems include urban decay, preventive health, and weapons of mass destruction (WMD). Columbus public safety methods are centered on emergency response; the system is less focused on mitigation or preventive public safety, such as public/private safety partnerships, community watches, preventive fire and health, or urban renewal. In short, this network is a simple one, because it relies on functional clarity for emergency response, instead of on a completely integrated network that crosses jurisdictions and functions to solve complex problems. This network is evolving across functions and regions as a result of new threats such as WMD and new technologies such as the 800MHz communications system. It is evolving from the simple to the complex.

Delaware's emergency management network handles a variety of threats in its environment that range closer to the types of crises that are considered complex. It is an integrated web of different government levels and organizations all centered on a network hub, the Delaware Emergency Management Agency (DEMA). Through DEMA, and its operation of the Delaware Emergency Operations Center, this network responds to complex emergencies, such as hurricanes or radiological disasters. This network is handling the transition to WMD much more smoothly than is the Columbus public safety system, because the relationships needed to work across functions and jurisdictions has already been established through DEMA's experience at handling crises that require the integration of functions and regions.

The federal wildfire network uses a truly integrated approach to fire management, and it handles one type of problem very well. The NIFC is not designed to handle a variety of disasters or problems with many characteristics, and it does not. Its focus is to plan for and fight wildland fires, and it cannot be easily transitioned to handle other types of emergencies, such as search and rescue operations.

Crisis Variables

The ability of these local, state, and federal networks to respond to crises adequately in some cases and poorly in others can be explained by the different *types* of crises to which the networks must respond. The crises depicted in the case studies possess distinct attributes that, upon analysis, can be broken down according to three crisis variables: intensity, complexity, and familiarity.

Intensity

Intensity refers to the number of problems evident in a particular crisis. A crisis's intensity rating is low when it consists of only one problem. The intensity rating rises as two, three, or more problems are evidenced in the same situation. For example, the vast majority of law enforcement emergencies handled by the Columbus Police Division consist of isolated breeches of the law. A single crime signifies a low intensity crisis. This type of low intensity crisis could be a murder, rape, or robbery.

The level of intensity in a law enforcement situation rises when more than one problem is present in the same emergency. An example of a crisis with a high intensity rating is one in which a bank is robbed. The robbery then leads to the murder of a guard, a hostage situation, and a getaway vehicle racing 90 m.p.h. away from the scene. A real life example of a high intensity crisis is the Lucasville, Ohio Prison Riot previously discussed by Columbus Public Safety Director, Tom Rice. Within the same Lucasville law enforcement situation there was a prison uprising, the death of a prison official, a hostage situation, and the potential for mass casualties. The intensity variable is a description of the number of problems to be resolved in a crisis. In the examples just provided, the intensity rating of the situations rose as more problems were introduced to the crisis. It is also important to understand that intensity measures the number, not the variety of types, of problems encountered.

Complexity

A crisis's complexity rating measures the number of dimensions that a crisis crosses. A situation with a low complexity rating is one that is contained to one crisis dimension. All of the aforementioned law enforcement crises measure low complexity ratings because they arise, and are resolved in, the same dimension of public safety (in these cases, the law enforcement dimension). While both the simple robbery and the murder/robbery/hostage case vary significantly in intensity, they are both resolved in the same resolution public safety dimension: law enforcement.

A high crisis complexity rating is found in one of the examples provided by Columbus Public Safety Assistant Director for Fire Administration, David Sturtz. Sturtz described a complex hypothetical situation where two dimensions of public safety could be involved, in this case both fire and police. Sturtz's case involved a hostage situation that was taking place in a building that housed chemical agents and was on fire. In this situation, the complexity level has risen by the introduction of three dimensions into the problem: the building is on fire, which is a fire division problem; a dangerous hostage situation is taking place in the building, which is a law enforcement problem; and a chemical agent is involved, which is a hazardous materials (HAZMAT) problem. This case is highly complex because of the number of public safety dimensions it crosses. These types of crises require resolution across the multiple dimensions in order to bring the situation to stability. Complexity is concerned with the different types of problems in the same emergency.

Familiarity

The third crisis variable is familiarity. The familiarity rating of a crisis is determined by the frequency of occurrence of the particular crisis in the resolution network. All of the previously mentioned examples in this section are examples of high familiarity ratings for the Columbus Public

Safety Department. The department is used to responding to robbery, fire, HAZMAT, murder, and hostage situations. The different divisions of fire, police, and EMS train for such problems, and they respond to them on a routine basis.

The familiarity rating decreases if the problem is one that the network does not plan, train, exercise, or respond to on a regular basis. Prior to its WMD domestic preparedness training with the U.S. Army in 1998, a terrorist nuclear attack in Columbus would have constituted a low familiarity rating for the Columbus Public Safety Department. Such an attack would have been a nonrecurring event, unique, and unfamiliar in the city's public safety system. Although no public safety official would admit to being unprepared for disaster, there are countless numbers of problems that Columbus (and most other large public safety systems) is not prepared to handle. Also, in light of the lessons of this book, the initial identification and planning of tasks does not constitute true preparedness. The full crisis management objective cycle described in Chapter One— anticipation, preparation, response, and wisdom—must be ingrained through the five key principles (i.e.: common purpose, authority, incentives, macroculture, structure) prior to reaching a high familiarity with a particular type of crisis.

Table 8–1 puts the three variables together to illustrate the many different types of crises that can emerge in a crisis response network based on the many combinations possible between the three variables. An analysis of the typologies of crises that are created out of the variety of mixes explains why each of the case study networks is effective in preparing for, resolving, and recovering from some crises, while these networks are also relatively ineffective in dealing with other crises.

Table 8-1		
Crisis Variable	**Rating: Low**	**Rating: High**
Intensity	one problem	more than one problem
Complexity	one dimensional	multidimensional
Familiarity	nonrecurring event	recurring event

Crisis Typologies

Crisis typologies can be identified by the different combinations possible among the three variables. A categorization of crises, based on their intensity, complexity, and familiarity variables, provides an explanation for the varying levels of effectiveness of the case study networks in dealing with different types of crises. Once crises are typed by their variables, the most effective form of organization can be identified to prepare, resolve, and recover from them. The rest of this section identifies some crisis typologies and ties the most effective organizational structures to them from case study examples.

A crisis that receives a low intensity, low complexity, and high familiarity rating is perhaps the easiest to identify and match with an organizational response structure. These types of crises exhibit one problem in terms of both number and type, and they are also familiar situations to the appropriate response agent. An example of this type of crisis would be any one of the previously mentioned crises: a murder, robbery, rape, fire, or heart failure. It is the lowest rated crisis that all three case studies handle well: the NIFC puts out a single wildland fire that does not spread; the Columbus Police Division responds to a single domestic abuse emergency call; the DEMA's Natural Disaster Section works with local authorities to restore the damage from storm tides to Rehobeth Beach's commercial boardwalk. All of these crises are most appropriately suited for resolution by a single organization (or section or jurisdiction) designed to handle the one problem that this type of crisis presents. Resident in each of the case study networks is one organization or section that handles this type of crisis based on a clear division of labor.

As opposed to a single organization, a full-scale network response to such a low rated crisis would only complicate the situation by bringing more complexity in the human organizational response than is necessary to resolve the situation. When only one number and type of a familiar problem exists, there is nothing a network of organizations can add in resolution that cannot be provided by one qualified organization alone. A good example of an interorganizational failure in a low rated crisis was seen in the attempted rescue of American hostages in Iran by members and units of all four branches of the U.S. military. The mission presented one problem that had been planned and trained for by individual elite units, but political pressures forced multi-service participation in the event. The mission failed miserably because of a lack of communications, interorganizational cultural conflicts, and equipment interoperability among the different units and personnel.

At the other end of the crisis spectrum are those crises that receive ratings high in intensity and complexity and low in familiarity. Such crises are considered to be systems in chaos. They have more than one of the same type of problem; they have multiple types of problems; and they may be unique events in the community that is expected to resolve them. These crises will not be resolved by any one institutionalized organization or network of organizations, for they will have to be resolved (if they can be resolved) at the same level of organization from which they derive their nature.

The only human responses to chaotic crises are chaotic, spontaneous combinations of organizations, networks, and individuals that have never worked together, never planned together, and may not even know each other. An example of such a chaotic crisis might be an unknown, immediate global warming catastrophe in the form of a gaping hole in the ozone; a massive nuclear attack to a metropolitan area; or a violent, virulent, infectious disease that sweeps a nation overnight. No structures are in place to handle such multidimensional, large-scale problems that such crises could create. The only response to such crises would be unexplainable human networks, organizations, and individuals working together in indefinable ways to help overcome the tremendous problems.

In between the two extremes on the crisis typology spectrum are the many types of crises most effectively handled by interorganizational crisis response networks. The case studies themselves reveal differences between networks, proving that some network forms handle some typologies of crises better than others. At the same time, the less effective networks against those typologies are better at resolving other crises with different crisis variable mixes. Table 8–2 describes the types of crises and their corresponding organizational structures. An example of the different types of networks and their different levels of effectiveness can be seen in the differences between the NIFC and the Columbus Public Safety Department in handling a specific typology. The NIFC effectively handles crises that rate high in intensity and familiarity and low in complexity. The typical NIFC crisis under these circumstances is a wildland fire that spreads to multiple jurisdictions. The NIFC network is ideally suited to handle such a crisis because it is a network designed around the principles of total mobility, ever-increasing spans of control, and local-to-federal resourcing "reach back" capability.

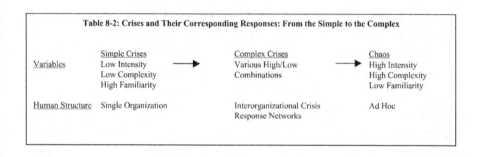

Table 8-2: Crises and Their Corresponding Responses: From the Simple to the Complex

Variables	Simple Crises Low Intensity Low Complexity High Familiarity	→	Complex Crises Various High/Low Combinations	→	Chaos High Intensity High Complexity Low Familiarity
Human Structure	Single Organization		Interorganizational Crisis Response Networks		Ad Hoc

Columbus, on the other hand, handles the same type of crisis quite poorly in some areas of its public safety network. In law enforcement situations that resemble the high intensity and familiarity and low complexity variables, the Columbus Police Division does not have the functional expansion capability to regional and federal levels in the same way that the NIFC does. The Columbus Police Division currently has problems with several surrounding area sheriffs, is not linked into regional databases with other jurisdictions, and does not have automatic response capabilities across other jurisdictions. So, in a crisis where the only increasing variable is the number of problems (within the same public safety dimension), the Columbus public safety network is not most effectively organized to perform this task. The NIFC is well aligned (and Columbus is not well aligned) for this type of crisis because of the types of crises that it must prepare for in its everyday environment.[350]

Another example of a crisis typology shows the Delaware emergency management network's ability to handle a crisis that rates high on

---

[350]The Columbus Fire Division is effective in this type of crisis, so within the same system, the type of dimension being discussed is important. Columbus is capable of handling increasing intensity ratings in one area of public safety but not in another.

complexity and familiarity but low on intensity, whereas Columbus pubic safety and wildfire suppression networks probably could not. Natural hazards, such as those posed by Hurricane Bonnie, exhibit problems across a range of dimensions, and thus require resolution across a range of dimensions. DEMA's planning for Bonnie displayed a level of network organization that matched the dimensions of the problems anticipated in the environment. A look at the number of organizations prepared to handle Bonnie's resolution is included: 27 federal agencies through FEMA Region III; all of the Delaware government departments and agencies; all of the local governments' resources; and several private businesses and voluntary organizations. The broad range of functions and skills were impressive. Bonnie could have caused transport, health, flooding, commercial, housing, education, food, crops, livestock, and many other forms of damage to Delaware society. The varied potential damages were matched by the variety of organizational specialties coordinated by DEMA for the response.

Whereas DEMA exhibits such broad responses to many other crises that rate high on complexity and familiarity and low on intensity, the NIFC and Columbus public safety networks respond much differently to these types of crises. The NIFC is simply not designed to handle crises beyond wildfires, so it would not attempt, nor be asked to, respond to crises that cross more than one dimension. Columbus, on the other hand, can handle crises that cross dimensions in its definition of public safety (i.e.: fire, police, and health) but not beyond. Columbus public safety officials routinely handle such semi-complex crises when fire and police officials work together to solve emergencies that involve both functions. Columbus public safety is not structured to handle problems that range in complexity beyond its very narrow conception of public safety. It is evolving to broaden its conception of public safety in the way that it is approaching WMD training.

Network Types and Characteristics

These examples provide the foundation for the development of a crisis spectrum moving from the simple to the chaotic. Corresponding with the crisis spectrum is the human organizational forms most effective in preparing for, resolving, and recovering from these different types of crises. It is the vast array of crises that fall between simple events (those scoring low on complexity and intensity and high on familiarity) and chaotic events (those scoring high on complexity and intensity and low on familiarity) that demand network responses. As crises exhibit different characteristics in this "middle ground," so do the types of networks most effective at resolving them.

Based on the case study observations, four different types of crisis response networks are evident. The distinctions between network types is a result of the environments in which the networks must operate. Each type of network handles different variations of crises more effectively than the rest.

The functional network is the first type of interorganizational structure on the crisis response spectrum. This type of network is organized according to the functions of the network, such as those witnessed in the Columbus Public Safety Department's fire, police, and EMS divisions (or section in the case of EMS). In such a structure, interorganizational principles exist at the macro level, but they are less dominant than the single organizational characteristics that are defined by the network's clear division of labor. The division of labor allows for less coordination, individual organizational cultures, and network affinity.

As a result of the strong functional aspect of this type of network, it is best suited to most effectively handle the following types of crises: (1)simple crises (i.e.: low complexity and intensity; high familiarity); (2)complex crises (i.e.: high complexity and familiarity; low intensity); and (3)*some* complex/intense crises (i.e.: high complexity, intensity, and familiarity). In simple crises, the single organization out of the network's functional division of labor handles the response. In complex crises, the functions work in collaboration with each other to handle their completely segregated tasks in the crisis (i.e.: Columbus fire and police working collaborating on a hostage situation in a burning building; fire puts out the fire first, then police deal with the hostage situation). In complex/intense crises, the functional organizations can sometimes work together to solve their independent parts (which have multiplied due to the increased intensity rating) in coordination with each other (e.g.: Columbus Public Safety Department handles riots that set businesses on fire in several areas of the city).

The second type of interorganizational response is the "ever expanding capability" network. This form of organization provides the same types of capabilities at increasing levels. Both the NIFC and the Central Ohio fire departments (of which Columbus is an integral member) display this form of organization.[351] The NIFC provides the same set of capabilities (i.e.: wildland fire suppression) at ever expanding levels (i.e.: local, state, regional, federal) in areas of manpower, resources, equipment, and funding. Columbus area fire departments provide the same expansionary capability by their mutual aid, automatic response, and ready-reserve agreements. This network form provides one type of capability in an interchangeable parts construct.

Such a narrowly focused, but ever expanding, network is most effectively suited to handle very high increases in intensity, while complexity remains low and familiarity is high. Ranging from the smallest problem in its area to an intensifyingly large number of similar problems that expand in

---

[351]Although the Columbus Public Safety Department comprises a network form of organization, its fire division is also part of a fire safety organization network.

scope, this network is designed with the capacity to handle monumental numbers of problems *that are of a similar nature.* Both the NIFC and the Columbus Fire Division's regional network handle fire well, but fire is the only crisis that either of them can handle at all. This network offers depth in a response.

The third type of network organization is the "task organization" network. This type of network organizes around the anticipated threats in the environment. Instead of dividing labor by function, this network spreads functions throughout its structure to concentrate on the specifics of individual threats. The DEMA is a good example of such a network. Organized into natural hazards, chemical hazards, radiological emergencies, and training sections, this network works across functions at local levels to coordinate comprehensive responses to specific threats.

This type of network is best suited for increasing complexity and/or decreasing familiarity ratings. In high complexity and familiarity but low intensity scenarios, this network can coordinate the efforts of the different dimensions to resolve the crisis quickly. In low familiarity crises with low intensity and complexity ratings, this network can cope with the unexpected, unique, nonrecurring aspects of the crisis better than other organizational forms because it reaches into all areas of a response across a wide spectrum of functional capabilities. This network offers breadth in a response.

The fourth type of network is the task force network, which is designed to pull all aspects of a response together, to include the specialization of a functional network, the depth of an "ever expanding capability" network, and the breadth of a task organized network. This type of network deals most effectively with the types of crises that approach complete chaos but still need some institutionalized structure in the response. It handles crises that occur when two or more variables are rated high most effectively, and it handles simpler crises, where only one variable is high, less effectively.

The expanded Delaware emergency management network, when federal and external states' support is considered, approaches such a level of interorganizational complexity, but perhaps the closest example is the completely integrated WMD network proposed by the U.S. Army for metropolitan Columbus. This type of network would have strong macro principles while also retaining strong individual organizational principles, which is quite rare. It would require some of the key characteristics of all of the case study examples: the NIFC's network level representation and individual organizational autonomy; the specialized professionalism of law enforcement, fire safety, and health safety in Columbus; and the specific threat preparation and emphasis provided by the DEMA. Such an organizational structure is the most complicated of all humanly possible forms, but it is this type of form that most resembles the threats that face the United States in the near future.

The four different networks are listed in Table 8–3. Each network is categorized according to the crises it most appropriately handles. Along with the earlier mentioned simple crises handled most effectively by one organization, and chaos handled most effectively (if it can be handled at all) by ad hoc human structures, these network forms complete the model of crisis typologies and the human structural responses.

Table 8-3: Matching Crises and Structure			
Network Structure	**Best Crisis Matches**	**Network Characteristics**	**Example**
Functional	Simple crises	Strong individual cultures	Traditional public safety
	Bounded problems		
	Familiar		
Expanded Capability	One problem	Strong macroculture	Wildfire suppression
	Grows in scope	Interchangeable parts	
	Familiar	Depth	
Task Organization	Different problems	Strong outside reciprocity	Emergency management
	Stable in scope	Strong macroculture	
	Familiar or unfamiliar	Breadth	
Task Force	Many problems	Depth and breadth	WMD framework
	Grows in scope	Strong macroculture	
	Familiar or unfamiliar	Strong individual cultures	

Application of the Model

The model can be applied to the environments faced by local, state, and federal communities, as they attempt to bring stability to an uncertain, sometimes violent world. Based on the types of crises faced in the environment, different variations of purposes, authorities, incentives, cultures, and structures are needed to solve them. These networks need to be influenced not only by the types of crises they face but also by the human characteristics that affect their makeup, such as the political and social systems from which they are created and maintained. Hopefully, these systems will facilitate the progress of crisis management to organize in the most effective ways against some of the world's most difficult problems. Human beings cannot remove the devastation of man-made or natural crises, but people can hope to prevent some crises, resolve others, and recover from the rest of them in ways that minimize the devastation and promote stability in the world.

About the Author

Michael Hillyard is the interim Academic Dean and a faculty member at the American Military University. Hillyard is a former U.S. Marine officer with a doctorate in public administration from the University of Southern California. He and his wife, Cara, live in northern Virginia.

Appendix A

Network Evaluation Questions

The questions used in the formulation of this work are generally applicable to crisis response networks. Both general and principle-specific questions are provided in the section below.

Network Questions:

1. What is your overall impression of the organizational network within which you work?
2. How would you characterize the working relationships between organizations in the network?
3. Why do you think that the network works well (or poorly)?
4. What specific elements of the network enable its organizations to work well together?
5. In examples where the network has not met its objectives, why has this occurred?
6. How could the network be improved in its efforts to respond to crises?
7. Is it clear who, or what body of people, is in charge of the network during a crisis? Is a commander or leader in charge or are decisions made by collaboration or otherwise?
8. How do money and resources get provided to the organizations that participate in a crisis? Do the organizations pay for their own involvement, or does a special fund or reimbursement account exist?

Organization-Specific Questions:

1. When you respond to a crisis, is the mission or objective of the crisis response clear?
2. Is it clear what role your organization is supposed to play in the crisis response? Do all people understand this?
3. How does your organization contact and work with the other organizations during a crisis?
4. How does your organization work with the other organizations to prepare for a crisis? Do you train together, attend seminars, or schools? Do you read the same books or manuals? Do you exchange personnel to learn more about each other?
5. Are ways made for your organization to participate in a collective review of the network's effectiveness? After action reports, seminars, etc.?
6. Is a publication available (e.g.: after action report) that I should look at that describes your organization's (or network's) operations?
7. Who else should I talk to about this?

Principle #1: Common Purposes

General questions tailored from Van de Ven and Ferry (1980):

1. Why does this network exist? Is there consensus on the purpose of this network, or are there varying interpretations as to what this network does?
2. Has the purpose of the network shifted over time? Has the environment forced the network to shift?
3. Do all member organizations understand their roles in the network as well as the roles of the other organizations? What happens when new roles emerge? What happens when a dispute occurs over which organization is responsible for a certain task or role? How are disputes over responsibilities resolved?
4. How did the network originate? (Did one or a couple of organizations discover that they needed help so they asked others to participate; or did

legislation or the environment change and thus force organizations to pull together?)

5. Has an organization ever left the network? If so, why?

6. Could any of the organizations of the network accomplish the network's mission on its own?

Principle #2: Authority

General authority questions tailored from Parker Follet, Weber, and Seiple:

1. How are decisions made in the network? (negotiation, collaboration, hierarchical leader, mutual agreement, etc.)

2. What happens when one organization sees things one way and another sees it another? Is resolution made by vote, persuasion, compromise, or dictate from an authority figure, legal agreement, or other means?

3. Where does the network get the information on which it acts (central communications hub, sensors in the environment, field reps)?

4. Do different organizations use different means of gathering and analyzing the information used to put the network in motion (individual sensors, separate communications networks or field agents)? If so, how are network decisions made in the face of conflicting information?

5. Can a disgruntled organization refuse to participate in an event?

6. Is a legal authority behind the network? Legislation, directive, Joint Powers Agreement, etc.?

7. When courses of action are considered in a crisis, what are their origins? Does the situation clearly show what needs to be done? Does a communication center report what is going on and then determine actions? Does a single leader get briefed on all of the actions and then dictate tasks? Are representatives of each organization collected into a decision making body with the authority to speak for their group? Or, are things so clear that actions are laid out based on the situation at hand?

Principle #3: Incentives

General questions:

1. What self-interests are served in your particular organization by being a part of the network?
2. Does your organization receive additional money, equipment, or physical assets for being a member?
3. Does your organization have a "moral obligation" or a "sense of duty" that might attract them to serve the network's cause?
4. Does your organization gain public relations, prestige, or political "points" for being involved in this network?
5. Does your organization get access to valuable information or information technologies by being a member of the network?
6. What are the costs of being a member of the network?
7. Does the organization ever wonder if the costs are high?
8. What would the organization do with the assets tied up in the network if it did not participate?
9. Is there a cost/benefit consideration involved?

Principle #4: Culture

General questions to establish whether culture exists, and if so, what kind, as defined by Schein (1996):

1. Are there visible signs that distinguish the network from its member organizations or other networks?
2. Symbols?
3. Uniforms?
4. Acronyms?
5. Manuals?
6. Orientation books for new network members?
7. Behavioral patterns?
8. Art, artifacts, or visible bumper stickers?

9. Does the network share distinctive values that are different from its member organizations or other networks? Or do the organizations all come to the network with their own values? If so, do the differences between the organizations cause problems in the network? Do people from different organizations have to adjust to each other during a crisis?

10. Core Values?

11. Vocalized Esprit or Pride in Membership?

12. Is Allegiance Tied to the Network?

13. Does a statement or set of statements convey values expected of every member?

14. Are there assumptions that are so basic that they are taken for granted in the organization (an example of this would be the assumption in America is to treat your neighbor as you would like to be treated yourself)?

15. How do you view the relationship of the network in its environment?

16. Does the network dominate, fill a specific need, or respond to the environment?

17. How are resources handled in the organization?

18. Is property individual to members or is it shared by all?

19. Can other members be trusted?

20. How are people of the network viewed?

21. Are there differences between how members of one organization are viewed as opposed to another?

22. Are people in the network generally viewed as go-getters or people who just do their jobs?

23. How are people expected to act in the network?

24. Are they supposed to accomplish the mission, follow regulations, listen to their boss? What is the method through which people take action?

25. How do people relate with one another in the network? Do they cooperate, compete, act as a group or an individual, do they follow rules or just work to get a common job finished?

Principle #5: Structure

1. For what kind of crises does the network prepare?
2. Which additional crises exist for which the network should prepare and does not?
3. What are the current crisis management capabilities? How well are plans matched with needs? What is missing?
4. Are there crisis management manuals? Are they up-to-date and user friendly?
5. How is the network alerted to a crisis?
6. What types of communication linkages between organizations are used for crisis management? (phone, internet/email, satellite)
7. How would you describe the organizational structure of the network? Hierarchical, hub and spoke, mutual exchange, different for every crisis?
8. Based on past crises, are lessons widely shared?
9. Does learning explore what went well and what could be improved?
10. Has performance been improved based on past observations?
11. Does the formal network structure impede crisis management efforts in any way?
12. Are communications channels clear and open for all players?
13. Does a network crisis management team define roles and missions for each crisis?
14. How are crises detected?
15. Is a control mechanism or audit framework used to evaluate or test the network's ability to respond?

Appendix B

Comments on the Original Inquiry

This work began with five hypothesized interorganizational network principles and throughout the investigatory process evolved into five crisis response principles. The original hypotheses and their corresponding principles are provided in the section below.

Hypothesis One: Member organizations of a crisis response network have common, shared purposes. A commonly understood purpose is defined as: (1)a clear, coherent understanding of the overall objectives of the crisis response; and (2)the understanding of each member organization's responsibilities to support the collective effort.

> *Principle One: Common Purposes*
>
> Crisis response networks have shared collective purposes and divisions of labor among member organizations. Network effectiveness is decreased in two circumstances: (1)when common purposes are unclear or disagreed upon; or (2)when divisions of labor are unclear or competitive among member organizations. Therefore, when organizations can agree on common purposes for coming together and identify which organization will do what for the whole, the foundation for a successful network has been established.

Hypothesis Two: The network has a singular source of authority from which collective action by the network and individual divisions of labor for member organizations emerges. The source of authority could be a computer model, a collaborative assessment of the situation, a negotiated political arrangement between organizations, or an authoritative tasking by a network leader, but there is a common source by which the network derives its actions.

Principle Two: Authority

Crisis response networks possess administrative and operational authority. Administrative authority legitimizes a network through its provision of a societal, political, and legal foundation. Operational authority is the decision making responsibility at the point of crisis resolution. Operational authority is effective when it functions on two levels: incident management and resource allocation. Incident management concerns the authority to make decisions "on the ground" with the resources at hand. Resource allocation concerns the bigger picture: allocating limited resources based on a broad understanding of the situation and overall network priorities.

Hypothesis Three: Incentives attract member organizations to participate in the network. These incentives could be monetary (through a unified budget or pay-to-play model), information, moral, access to opportunities, or physical resources. The incentives do not have to be the same for every member organization, but each organization must be meeting some self-interest incentive in the network.

Principle Three: Incentives

Incentives attract member organizations to participate in a network, and they contribute to the strength, character, and structure of the network. These incentives are varied in type, and organizations in the same network may be attracted to different types of incentives. Incentives also vary in flow based on the direction, amount, and variability of resource distribution among a network's organizations.

Hypothesis Four: A network "macroculture" exists and distinguishes the network as an organization separate from the identities of its members or other networks. Characteristics of a interorganizational culture might include some form of common education and training; shared ethos (i.e.: esprit, symbols, folklore, tradition); common lexicon; a shared sense of duty; and technical interoperability (e.g.: communications, information technologies).

Principle Four: Macroculture

A network possesses a macroculture that distinguishes it from the identities of its members or other networks. The strength of a network is attributable to two variables: (1) the characteristics of the crises it faces in the environment; and (2) the relative dominance of the network in the roles and missions of its member organizations. If the crises predominately dictate responses handled by single organizations, then the network macroculture will be relatively low in comparison with single organizational cultures of member organizations. If the crises in the environment demand integrated network responses, then the network macroculture will be relatively strong in comparison with single organizational cultures of member organizations. If the network comprises the predominance of its member organizations' responsibilities, then the macroculture will be relatively strong. If the network comprises only a portion of member organizations' responsibilities, then macroculture will be relatively weak.

Hypothesis Five: An interorganizational structure exists that reflects the nature of the crisis environment in which the network operates as well as the characteristics of its member organizations. In such a structure the member organizations clearly understand what and how they are to perform their roles for the network, and the network also provides a communications structure through which member organizations can communicate with each other.

> *Principle Five: Interorganizational Structure*
>
> An interorganizational structure exists that reflects the nature of the crisis environment in which the network operates as well as the characteristics of its member organizations. In such a structure the member organizations clearly understand what and how they are to perform their roles for the network, and the network also provides a communications structure through which crisis information can be shared, interorganizational communication can be achieved, and collaboration and decision making and dissemination can occur.

Research Method

The method used in this study was adapted from a method suggested in *The Discovery of Grounded Theory* by Glaser and Strauss (1967). An adaptation of Glaser and Strauss's method was successfully implemented and defended by Lee Mortenson in his 1991 University of Southern California doctoral dissertation: *Management of Interorganizational Policy Conflict: A Study of Mission and Policy Conflict Between Agencies.*

Glaser and Strauss developed the "constant comparison method." This method focuses on the use of inductive qualitative research to produce general implications in the development of grounded, formal theory.[352] The method's use of qualitative research is based on data collection many different times in a content or subject area. The method suggests that qualitative data can be analyzed in four stages: (1)comparing incidents applicable to each category; (2)integrating categories and their properties; (3)delimiting the theory; and (4)writing the theory.[353]

This study followed Mortenson's (1991) application of the method by its collection of data against a set questions used in interviews (which are provided later in this chapter).[354] The questions were developed to provide knowledge of the hypotheses. In this study's selection of three cases studies from a related environment (i.e.: crisis response), Glaser and Strauss's comparison and integration between related incidents led to the proposal of a grounded general model. The development of such a model supports Glaser and Strauss's belief that qualitative research can have general implications that can be used as a "springboard" to the development of formal theory (Glaser and Strauss, 1967:271).

Evaluation of the five fundamental hypotheses in the three case studies was based on interview and document review findings. The case study questionnaire provided the template under which information from each of the three approaches was gathered. Each set of questions was drawn from the theories and evidence that surrounded the hypotheses.

---

[352]Barney Glaser and Anselm Strauss, *The Discovery of Grounded Theory* (New York: Aldine Publishing Company, 1967), 271.

[353]Ibid., 105.

[354]Unlike Mortenson's dissertation, this study also used document reviews to answer questions surrounding the hypotheses.

Case Study Presentations

The information gathered in the interviews and document reviews was used to formulate the case study presentations. The information focused on the five hypotheses to determine if and how those principles play roles in the success and/or failure of the network. The information was also used to determine whether other principles exist or if case-specific reasons explain why the network functions effectively. The presentation of each case consists of a description of how the network operates with regard to the hypothesized principles, an analysis to determine the validity of each hypothesis in the specific case study, and a summary of the important principles that underlie that particular case study network.

Specifically, the cases presented information from two sources: interviews and document reviews. From interviews, the researcher determined what key people in the network think, feel, or perceive to be true. For example, the researcher tested *common purposes* by asking key stakeholders in the network to define the purpose of the network and each of the member organization responsibilities in the network. The researcher probed further with some interviews to determine why the network exists, how it was started, and what happens when (or if) organizations leave the network.

From document reviews, the researcher identified actions that naturally led to the principle being tested. For example, in testing network macro-culture, the author found network education classes to be important contributors to culture. These classes were designed to initiate new members into an accepted way of doing business or informing them of the code of conduct or procedures. In performing those indoctrination functions, these classes support Schein's observations of culture.

While questions were primarily answered by interviews and document reviews, the physical location of the interviewer in the crisis response environments provided some direct observation of network characteristics. As a result, some questions were answered by direct observation. For example, the researcher witnessed the Delaware Emergency Management Agency (DEMA) implement the Delaware Emergency Operations Plan (DEOP) in response to Hurricane Bonnie. The researcher also observed the National Interagency Coordination Center (NICC) transfer fire support assets to California fires. In such situations, the researcher was able to answer some questions surrounding the hypotheses on his own.

Case Study Analysis and Integration of the Analysis

Under the "constant comparative method," the final step of the study was to analyze the cases as a whole and integrate their commonalties into a conclusive set of general statements. These statements provide the foundation for the general model proposed in the last chapter of the book. The model completes Glaser and Strauss's method by its production of an integrative "springboard" that emerged from a cross-case study analysis to propose a general model of organizational crisis response.

Bibliography

Advisory Commission on State Emergency Communications. *TDD/TDY Accessibility: Checklist for PSAP's in Texas.* Austin: Advisory Commission on State Emergency Communications, 1998.

Alberts, David and Thomas Czerwinski. *Complexity, Global Politics and National Security.* Washington: National Defense University, 1997.

Anthes, Gary. "Red Alert." *Computerworld* 31 (no. 27 1997): 83.

The AVATAR Group. *IntelliVUE: Knowledge in Motion.* Company sales document, 24 June 1998.

Barnard, Chester. *The Functions of the Executive.* Cambridge: Harvard University Press, 1938.

Baughn, Chris, John Stevens, Johannes Denekamp, and Richard Osborn. "Protecting Intellectual Capital in International Alliances." *Journal of World Business* 32 (Summer 1997): 103–117.

Boyles, Jinny, member U.S. Bureau of Land Management. Interview by author, 6 October 1998, Boise, Idaho. Notes with author.

Bridegan, Gaylord, Dan Chilcutt, B.H. Basehart, and Marvin Dickerson. "Contained Response: Environmental Emergency Planning." *Risk Management* 44 (no. 5 1997): 40–42.

Chapman, Christy. "Before Disaster Strikes." *Internal Auditor* 53 (no. 6 1996): 22–28.

Chavis, Melody Ermachild. *Altars in the Street: A Neighborhood Fights to Survive.* New York: Bell Tower, 1997.

Chisholm, Rupert. "On the Meaning of Networks." *Group and Organization Management* 21 (June 1997): 217.

Clausewitz, Carl von. *On War*. Trans. Michael Howard and Peter Paret. Princeton: Princeton University Press, 1976.

Cook, Karen. "Exchange and Power in Networks of Interorganizational Relations." In *Organizational Analysis: Critique and Innovation*. Beverly Hills: Sage, 1977.

Cretien, Michael, president of The AVATAR Group. Interview by author, 24 June 1998, Columbus, Ohio. Notes with author.

Currall, Steven and Timothy Judge. "Measuring Trust Between Organizational Boundary Role Persons." *Organizational Behavior and Human Decision Processes* 64 (November 1995): 151–170.

Delaware Emergency Management Agency. *How to Prepare for a Hurricane*. New Castle, Delaware: Delaware Emergency Management Agency, 1998.

Eller, John. "9–1–1 Has Become a Real 'Life-Saver.'" *9–1–1 Magazine* (May/June 1998): 72.

Estes, Kenneth. *The Marine Officer's Guide*. Annapolis: Naval Institute Press, 1985.

Falone, Emily, director of radiological programs at the Delaware Emergency Management Agency. Interview by author, 24 August 1998, New Castle, Delaware. Notes with author.

Federal Emergency Management Agency, Region III. *Operations Section Standing Operating Procedures*. Philadelphia: Federal Emergency Management Agency, 1998.

Finkel, Coleman Lee. "Meeting Facilities That Foster Learning." *Training and Development* 51 (July 1997).

Frey, Tom, member of the U.S. Forest Service. Interview by author, 14 July 1998, Washington, D.C. Notes with author.

_____. Interview by author, 5 October 1998, Boise, Idaho. Notes with author.

Foster, Bud, natural hazards section head for the Delaware Emergency Management Agency. Interview with author, 26 August 1998, New Castle, Delaware. Notes with author.

Friedrich, Carl. *The Philosophy of Law in Historical Perspective*. Chicago: The University of Chicago Press, 1963.

Glaser, Barney and Anselm Strauss. *The Discovery of Grounded Theory*. New York: Aldine Publishing Company, 1967.

Guyton, Deborah, director of Network Integrity, E9–1–1 Solutions, Business Community Planning. Presentation at the 17th Annual Conference of the National Emergency Number Association, 23 June 1998, Cincinnati, Ohio. Notes with author.

Hall, Richard. *Organizations, Structure, and Process*. Englewood Cliffs, New Jersey: Prentice-Hall, 1972.

Hannon, John, Ing-Chung Haung, and Bih-Shiaw Jaw. "International Human Resource Strategy and its Determinants: The Case of Subsidiaries in Taiwan." *Journal of International Business Studies* 26 (Fall 1995): 531–554.

Hart, Paul and Carol Saunders. "Power and Trust: Critical Factors in the Adoption and Use of Electronic Data Interchange. *Organization Science* 8 (January/February 1997): 23–42.

Hartsell, Robert, assistant director for support services for the Columbus Public Safety Department. Interview by author, 21 July 1998, Columbus, Ohio. Notes with author.

Hazen, Mary Ann. "A Radical Humanist Perspective of Interorganizational Relations." *Human Relations* 47 (April 1994): 393–415.

Howard, Michael. *Clausewitz.* Oxford: Oxford University Press, 1983.

Ingram, Paul and Crist Inman. "Institutions, Intergroup Competition, and the Evolution of Hotel Populations around Niagara Falls." *Administrative Sciences Quarterly* 41 (1996): 629–658.

Intellinetics Online [Internet]. Intellinetics, Inc., WWW: http://www.intellinetics.com, July 1998.

Jaffe, Dennis and Cynthia Scott. "How to Link Personal Values with Team Values." *Training and Development* 52 (March 1998): 24–30.

Kettinger, William and Varun Grover. "The Use of Computer-Mediated Communication in an Interorganizational Context." *Decision Sciences* 28 (Summer 1997): 513–555.

Kiel, L. Douglas. *Managing Chaos and Complexity in Government.* San Francisco: Jossey-Bass, 1994.

Litwak, Eugene and Lydia Hylton. "Interorganizational Analysis: A Hypothesis on Coordinating Agencies." *Administrative Sciences Quarterly* 6 (1997): 395–420.

Maclean, Norman. *Young Men and Fire.* Chicago: The University of Chicago Press, 1992.

Mitroff, Ian, L. Harrington, and Eric Gai. "Thinking about the Unthinkable." *Across the Board* 33 (no. 8 1996): 44–48.

Mulhern, Sean, director of the Delaware Emergency Management Agency. Interview by author, 24 August 1998, New Castle, Delaware. Notes with author.

Munro, D.P. *The Emergency Management Assistance Compact Guidebook and Standard Operations Procedures.* Washington, D.C.: Southern Governors Association, 1997.

National Interagency Fire Center. *Lifeline to the Fireline: National Interagency Fire Center.* Boise: National Interagency Fire Center, 1994.

_____. *Joint Fire Science Program Online [Internet].* National Interagency Fire Center Webmaster, WWW: http://www.nifc.gov/joint_fire_sci/ JointFire.html#Introduction, July 1998.

_____. *National Interagency Fire Center Online [Internet].* National Interagency Fire Center Webmaster, WWW: http://www.nifc.doi.gov/ NifcInfo.html, June 1998.

_____. *National Interagency Mobilization Guide.* Boise: National Interagency Coordination Center, 1997.

_____. *Interagency Call-When-Needed Helicopters.* Washington, D.C.: U.S. Government Printing Office, 1989.

_____. *Wildland Firefighter Safety Awareness Study—Identifying the Organizational Culture, Leadership, Human Factors, and Other Issues Impacting Firefighter Safety.* Open-file report, National Interagency Fire Center, 1996.

National Wildfire Coordinating Group. *Interagency Incident Business Management Handbook: NWCG Handbook 2* (Boise: Incident Business Practices Working Team, 1996)

_____. *The National Interagency Incident Management System: Teamwork in Emergency Management* (Boise: National Interagency Fire Center, 1984).

_____. *National Fire Equipment System—Catalog Part 1: Fire Supplies and Equipment.* Boise: U.S. Government Printing Office, 1998.

_____. *National Fire Equipment System—Catalog Part 2: Publications.* Boise: U.S. Government Printing Office, 1998.

National Incident Management System. *Field Operations Guide.* Stillwater, Oklahoma: Fire Protection Publications, 1983.

Orlikowski, Wanda and JoAnne Yates. "Genre Repertoire: The Structure of Communicative Practices in Organizations." *Administrative Sciences Quarterly* 39 (no. 4 1997): 541–574.

Parker Follett, Mary. "The Giving of Orders." In *Classic Readings in Organizational Behavior.* Belmont: Wadsworth, 1996.

Pearson, Christine, Sarah Misra, Judith Clair, and Ian Mitroff. "Managing the Unthinkable." *Organizational Dynamics* 26 (Autumn 1997): 51–64.

Peterson, Paul E. *The Price of Federalism.* Washington, D.C.: The Brookings Institution, 1995).

Police Officers for Equal Rights, et al. v. City of Columbus, et al., C–2–78–394 (6th Circuit, 1989).

President's Commission on the Accident at Three Mile Island. *Report of the Emergency Preparedness and Response Task Force.* Washington, D.C. October 1979.

Reintzell, John F. "When Training Saves Lives." *Training and Development* 51 (January 1997): 41–44.

Rice, Tom, director of public safety for Columbus, Ohio. Interview by author, 20 July 1998, Columbus, Ohio. Notes with author.

Saunders, E. Gayle. *Safety Herald.* Columbus: Columbus Public Safety Department, 1998.

Schank, Roger. "Virtual Learning: A Revolutionary Approach to Building a Highly Skilled Workforce." *Training and Development* 51 (November 1997): 88–89.

Schein, Edgar. "Coming to a New Awareness of Organizational Culture." In *The Great Writings in Management and Organizational Behavior*. New York: McGregor-Hill, 1987.

Seiple, Chris. *The Consequences are the Crisis—The Consequences of WMD Terrorism, Crisis Management Theory and the Lessons of Three Mile Island.* Unpublished paper. December 19, 1999.

Seiple, Chris. The U.S. Military/NGO *Relationship in Humanitarian Interventions*. Carlisle: U.S. Army War College, 1996.

Sheffield, Jim and Brent Gallupe. "Using Group Support Systems to Improve the New Zealand Economy—Part II: Follow-up Results." *Journal of Management Information Systems* 11 (Winter 1994/95): 135–153.

Spencer, Carol, communications operations administrator for the Delaware Emergency Management Agency. Interview by author, 26 August 1998, New Castle, Delaware. Notes with author.

State of Delaware, Department of Public Safety. *Radiological Emergency Plan*. New Castle, Delaware: Delaware Emergency Management Agency, 1998.

_____. *Delaware Emergency Management Agency Online [Internet]*. Department of Public Safety Webmaster, WWW: http://www.state.de.us/govern/agencies/pubsafe/dema/indxdema.htm, August 1998.

_____. *Delaware Emergency Management Agency Online [Internet]*, Chemical Hazards Section. Department of Public Safety Webmaster, WWW:http://www.state.de.us/govern/agencies/pubsafe/dema/chemhaz.htm, August 1998.

_____. *Delaware Emergency Management Agency Online [Internet]*, Natural Hazards Section. Department of Public Safety Webmaster, WWW:http://www.state.de.us/govern/agencies/pubsafe/dema/nathaz.htm, August 1998.

_____. *Delaware Emergency Management Agency Online [Internet], Radiological Programs Section.* Department of Public Safety Webmaster, WWW: http://www.state.de.us/govern/ agencies/pubsafe/dema/rep.htm, August 1998.

State of Delaware, Office of the Governor. *Delaware Emergency Operations Plan.* New Castle, Delaware: Delaware Emergency Management Agency, 1998.

State of Massachusetts, Massachusetts Emergency Management Agency. Massachusetts Emergency Management Agency Online [Internet]. State of Massachusetts Webmaster, WWW: http://www.magnet.state. ma.us/mema/deptdes.html.

State of Ohio, Ohio Division of Emergency Medical Services. *Ohio Division of Emergency Medical Services Online [Internet].* State of Ohio Webmaster, WWW: http//www.ohio.gov/odps/ division/ems.html#/mission, June 1998.

State of Ohio, Ohio Highway Patrol. *Ohio Highway Patrol Online [Internet].* State of Ohio Webmaster, WWW: http//www.odn.ohio.gov/ ohp/duties.html, June 1998.

Steinfeld, Carol. "Challenge Courses Can Build Strong Teams." *Training and Development* 51 (no. 4 1998): 12–16.

Sturtz, David, assistant director of public safety for fire administration in the Columbus Public Safety Department. Interview by author, 21 July 1998, Columbus, Ohio. Notes with author.

Terrell, Kenneth. "Help, 911! Where Am I?" *U.S. News and World Report* 124 (22 June 1998): 73.

Thayer, Michael, senior manager of the Warner Group management consultants. Presentation at the 17th Annual Conference of the National Emergency Number Association National Convention, 23 June 1998, Cincinnati, Ohio. Notes with author.

Thomas, Robert, president of 9–1–1 mapping systems. Interview by author, 22 June 1998, Erlanger, Kentucky. Notes with author.

Toffler, Alvin. "A New Science of Instability Throws Light on Politics." In *Laws of Nature and Human Conduct*. Brussels: Task Force of Research and Information and Study on Science, 1985.

Trufant, Tom, communications division director for Columbus Public Safety Department. Interview by author, 21 July 1998, Columbus, Ohio. Notes with author.

Unattributed. "A Start-Up Guide to Distance Learning." *Training and Development* 51 (December 1997): 39–47.

Ullius, Diane. "Art: Acronyms Reinforce Training." *Training and Development* 51 (February 1997): 9.

United States Army, Chemical and Biological Defense Command. NBC *Domestic Preparedness Training Course Outlines: Incident Command.* Washington, D.C.: United States Army, 1998.

_____. *NBC Domestic Preparedness Training Course Outlines: Senior Officials Workshop*. Washington, D.C.: United States Army, 1998.

_____. *Training History to Include Nunn-Lugar-Domenici Legislation.* Washington, D.C.: United States Army, 1998.

United States Marine Corps, Office of the Commandant of the Marine Corps. *Commandant's Planning Guidance*, by General Charles Krulak. Washington, D.C.: United States Marine Corps, 1995.

Van de Ven, Andrew and Diane Ferry. *Measuring and Assessing Organizations*. New York: John Wiley and Sons, 1980.

Varadarajan, Rajan and Margaret Cunningham. "Strategic Alliances: A Synthesis of Conceptual Foundations." *Journal of the Academy of Marketing Science* 23 (Fall 1995): 282–296.

Villard, James, member U.S. Bureau of Land Management. Interview with author, 6 October 1998, Boise, Idaho. Notes with author.

Waldrop, W. Mitchell. *Complexity: The Emerging Science at the Edge of Chaos.* New York: Bantam Books, 1992.

Warren, Keith, Cynthia Franklin, and Calvin Streeter. "New Directions in Systems Theory: Chaos and Complexity. *Social Work: Journal of the National Association of Social Workers* 43 (July 1998): 362.

Warren, Roland, Stephen Rose, and Ann Bergunder. *The Structure of Urban Reform.* Toronto: D.C. Health, 1974.

Weber, Max. "The Theory of Social and Economic Organization." In *The Great Writings in Management and Organizational Behavior.* New York: McGraw-Hill, 1987.

Wheeler, Aaron, equal employment opportunity officer for the Columbus Public Safety Department. Interview by author, 21 July 1998, Columbus, Ohio. Notes with author.

_____. *Closure to the "Worm" Newsletter Investigation,* memorandum to Columbus Director of Public Safety, 15 May 1998.

Wiles, Nelson, state liaison officer for the Federal Emergency Management Agency. Interview by author, 26 August 1998, New Castle, Delaware. Notes with author.

Wilson, James Q. *Bureaucracy: What Government Agencies Do and Why They Do It.* New York: Basic Books, 1989.

Wingate, Dallas, major in the Delaware National Guard. Interview by author, 26 August 1998, New Castle, Delaware. Notes with author.